Praise for Mike Hutton's previous books:

The Vice Captain
'Fascinating details of Soho from a completely different angle. It made me nostalgic to visit the watering holes of my youth... I can thoroughly recommend this book on London's naughty square mile. It's beautifully written.' (George Melly)

'So easy to read – so hard to put down.' (Colin Dexter)

The Story of Soho: The Windmill Years 1932-64
'Hutton has an engaging style and the story races along.' (Theatre Magazine)

'This is a lively memoir, uncovering tales of villains and tarts and the birth of the sex industry...fascinating stories, well told.' (Books Monthly)

Life in 1940s London
'Well researched and well paced, this scrupulous account is occasionally hilarious, often touching and all the better for the author's recollections.' (Brian Sewell)

'Hutton transports you through a period of difficulty and triumph. His personal recollections bring the city to life.' (BBC History Magazine)

Life in 1950s London
'A fascinating read.'
(Books Monthly)

1919
'It is a captivating book....exploring virtually every facet of British life in 1919.' The author was invited to host a 'Meet the author day' at the British War Museum in 2019.

Full Circle
'A brilliant book and fascinating read. The author has a wonderful insight into the world of showbiz. I loved it.' (Bernie Keith, BBC Radio Northampton)

Children of the 1940s
'I loved this whole book – so many memories came back to me. With the author's dramatic description of the Blitz, I suddenly realised there was something symphonic about the whole thing. Above spitfires appeared hunting down invading bombers. There were flashes of searing light whilst incendiaries fluttered down like candy floss. The stories told are wonderful.' (Mitch Murray CBE, leading composer and songwriter)

Mike Hutton is a writer of social history and a novelist. He has a keen interest in early twentieth century British art. He lives with his wife in the heart of England.

Crime Scene London

Crime Scene London

Murder, Violence and Sexual Scandal on the Streets

Mike Hutton

First published in Great Britain in 2025 by
Pen & Sword True Crime
An imprint of Pen & Sword Books Limited
Yorkshire – Philadelphia

Copyright © Mike Hutton 2025

ISBN 978 1 39903 947 5

The right of Mike Hutton to be identified as
Author of this Work has been asserted by him in accordance
with the Copyright, Designs and Patents Act 1988.

A CIP catalogue record for this book is
available from the British Library.

All rights reserved. No part of this book may be reproduced,
transmitted, downloaded, decompiled or reverse engineered in
any form or by any means, electronic or mechanical including
photocopying, recording or by any information storage and retrieval
system, without permission from the Publisher in writing. No part of
this book may be used or reproduced in any manner for the purpose
of training artificial intelligence technologies or systems.

Typeset by Mac Style
Printed in the UK by CPI Group (UK) Ltd, Croydon, CR0 4YY.

The Publisher's authorised representative in the EU for product
safety is Authorised Rep Compliance Ltd., Ground Floor,
71 Lower Baggot Street, Dublin D02 P593, Ireland.
www.arccompliance.com

For a complete list of Pen & Sword titles please contact

PEN & SWORD BOOKS LIMITED
47 Church Street, Barnsley, South Yorkshire, S70 2AS, England
E-mail: enquiries@pen-and-sword.co.uk
Website: www.pen-and-sword.co.uk
or
PEN AND SWORD BOOKS
1950 Lawrence Road, Havertown, PA 19083, USA
E-mail: uspen-and-sword@casematepublishers.com
Website: www.penandswordbooks.com

This book is dedicated to my secretary Joan Beretta.
For over seventeen years it has been with the help of her
enthusiasm, interest and knowledge that has allowed me to
complete so many books. A much deserved thank you.

Contents

Acknowledgements ix
Introduction x

Chapter 1 A Breeding Ground for Crime 1
Chapter 2 A One-way Ticket to Tyburn 9
Chapter 3 Murder Most Foul 14
Chapter 4 Lady Killers 25
Chapter 5 Let the Punishment Fit the Crime 36
Chapter 6 Banged Up 42
Chapter 7 Freak Shows 49
Chapter 8 Abolition 56
Chapter 9 Mother's Ruin 62
Chapter 10 Letting Off Steam 66
Chapter 11 More Tea, Vicar 77
Chapter 12 Bawd Games 86
Chapter 13 Gay's the Word 94
Chapter 14 Your Money or Your Life 103
Chapter 15 A Bit on the Side 111
Chapter 16 Turning a Pretty Penny or Two 118
Chapter 17 Bertie 124

Chapter 18	The Long Weekend	132
Chapter 19	Dodging the Bombs	141
Chapter 20	Traitors	150
Chapter 21	Sex and the City	159
Chapter 22	Where There's Muck There's Money	167
Chapter 23	The Godfathers	172
Chapter 24	Swinging into the Sixties	181
Chapter 25	Changes and Reflections	190
Bibliography		198
Index		199

Acknowledgements

The author would like to thank the following for their input and information that helped make this book possible:

Staff at the Westminster City Archives
Staff at the Museum of London
Staff at the Jewish Museum, London
Staff at the Museum of Soho
Maurice Poole
Tony Shrimplin
James Morton
Rocky Knight
Susan Scott, Archivist at the Savoy Hotel

Photographic Acknowledgements
The author is grateful for the following permissions to reproduce photographs featured in this book:

The Mary Evans Picture Library
Soho Books
The Museum of Soho
Mirror Pics
Joan Beretta
Images from the author's own archive

Introduction

With the confidence of youth I confronted the huge figure as he sauntered towards me alone and with tobacco stained teeth in Hatton Garden. This was the man who had swindled the company I was working for out of hundreds of pounds just weeks before. He was accompanied by a tough looking character with long sideboards and slicked down greasy hair.

I worked for a leading supplier of leather goods in Essex Road, Islington. I was in temporary charge of the showroom offering a wide range of high quality products, all beautifully displayed. A huge figure wearing a Prince of Wales check suit was ushered in. He informed me he had opened a company selling leather and gift items in Clerkenwell Road. He picked a few items seemingly at random and insisted on paying in cash. He gave me a couple of references that were taken up by our finance department. Within days he was back placing a larger order, informing me that he could see his outfit becoming an important customer for us. He still paid in cash, telling me to keep the change as he was in a rush. I said I would credit the balance to his account. He shrugged and smiling, ambled off. Although outwardly friendly he did convey an air of menace.

Within a week he was back placing a sizeable order, amounting to close on a thousand pounds. I checked out the premises in Clerkenwell Road. It was a scene of great activity, a pool of attractive typists and a well laid out warehouse. Having made our bulk delivery I drove down the following day to find a totally empty building. No typists, no sign of any activity. They had cleared off, leaving me with egg on my face and a very angry boss. Subsequently I found out that this was a swindle known as 'the long game' in which the Kray twins were leading operators. They drew in unsuspecting suppliers and then overnight vanished, later selling off the goods at cut prices, but obviously showing a healthy profit.

The huge figure looked down on me, his face wreathed in a kindly smile. This was unnerving. More so than if he had been aggressive. His sidekick was smirking, showing a set of uneven tobacco-stained teeth. Drawing a finger across his throat he told me ever so sweetly that if I fancied keeping my looks I should 'piss off'. I had caused him as much alarm as if a piece of fluff had landed on his lapel. I could hear them laughing. My bravado evaporated and rather ashamed I skulked away. Over twenty years later, watching late night television, this familiar figure appeared on screen. He was being interviewed inside a South African prison having been charged with murder.

Islington, before it became gentrified, was a hot-bed of crime, albeit generally of a lesser nature. I was approached in the Carved Red Lion pub within days of becoming engaged, by a man offering me a ring made supposedly from jewels stolen from the notorious lady docker. Even as a young man I was not that green. The pub was always filled with small time crooks and a common phrase I heard repeatedly was 'put me in the swindle'. One guy was a brilliant snooker player and he would draw in the unsuspecting by letting them win the first couple of frames before taking a sizeable bet and clearing the table in short order.

So it was that London had changed little since the Romans first arrived on the southern banks of the Thames with their camp followers. Murder, robbery, violence and small time crooks joined with bawds and their brothels, setting out a pattern that was followed enthusiastically for centuries to come.

Chapter 1

A Breeding Ground for Crime

Bankside was an unappetising marshy stretch of land bordering the River Thames. From its inception as a staging post it had become known for its riotous inns and bawdy brothels. By the early 12th century it had the distinction of becoming London's first official red light district. King Henry II granted rights to the bishop of Winchester to extend and exploit the numerous disreputable inns and stews on Bankside in Southwark.

The area acted as a convergence of the roads from Sussex, Kent and Surrey, providing a constant stream of potential customers. Standing outside the city limits the brothels or stews were easily identified, being painted white and showing a distinctive sign often in the form of a cardinal's hat. The ladies who worked in these squalid buildings were known fondly as 'Winchester geese'. It was reckoned there were around twenty of these establishments, variously known by such names as the 'Half Moon', the 'Boar's Head' or the 'Elephant'. All had their regular visitors frequently shipped over from the more fashionable north shore by Thames ferrymen, giving them a very lucrative extra source of income.

By the beginning of the 16th century general lawlessness and the spread of syphilis caused King Henry VIII to order the closing down of Southwark's brothels in 1546. Surely ironic with his medical record. After the King died the following year the order was rescinded only for the bordellos to be closed again by Queen Mary Tudor. With Elizabeth's accession to the throne in 1558 the brothel owners rejoiced as they were allowed once more to open their doors. Occasionally a few of the street girls were hauled off to Bridewell prison, but generally the area was left very much to their own devices.

Bankside was the departure point for many a devout pilgrim on their way to Canterbury. It is quite possible that the delights on offer at the

'Sugar Loaf' or 'the Queen's Head' might have led them astray. If not tempted by the ladies perhaps a visit to the local bear garden was in order. Whatever, the following morning with the pious bearing of a pilgrim they set off to receive absolution.

It was abject poverty that bound the London rookeries and provided a perfect background for every conceivable crime. Perhaps the most notorious of these was St. Giles in the Fields, in an area now dominated by the wealth of New Oxford Street. Before it was swept away in a swathe of slum clearance taking place in central London, it was a maze of filthy courtyards, narrow alleys and rotting rooming houses. It was a place where the sun never penetrated; sewage ran through the streets to a constant background stench that worsened in the heat of the summer.

The fortunes of St. Giles in the Fields like so many areas of London changed over the years. Created by the building of a small chapel and leprosy hospital in the 12th century by Queen Matilda, it took its name from St. Giles the patron saint of cripples (disabled) and outcasts. A new church was built on the site of the hospital in 1623. During the 17th century the parish enjoyed a brief spell of relative prosperity but it was short lived. Soon the area was attracting large numbers of foreigners fleeing from pogroms and injustice. With St. Giles becoming overwhelmed with newcomers the wealthier residents fled.

The parish became known as 'the holy land' or 'little Ireland' as a large Irish population was swelled by the potato famine of the 1840s. The Irish obtained a reputation for fighting, often fuelled by drink. The area was wretched and previously had been used as a background for William Hogarth's famous works of 'Beer Street' and 'Gin Lane'. Only the unwary would enter the rookery and it became a virtual no-go area. Despite this a series of escape routes were set up in cellars, often interlinked allowing wanted men to slip away.

Prostitutes worked the theatres around Drury Lane, luring their unsuspecting clients into what was a thieves' kitchen. Once undressed a gang member would rob the unfortunate punter, often taking most of his clothes, with expensive shoes particularly prized. By the mid 19th century the parish had sunk even lower. Some residents were starving and children roamed the streets in winter without shoes. It was a case of survival of the fittest and all this taking place in central London just a few streets from people with extreme wealth. Violent gangs roamed the streets. Tramps, pickpockets, whores, all seeking the means for their next meal. Charles Dickens carried out research in the area and reported on 'scenes of the most repulsive nature, of bodies bloated not of excess but of disease and hunger, with faces ravaged by drink'.

The partial slum clearance of 1847 had only made matters worse. Whilst the New Oxford Street was being built, those displaced flocked into the remaining already overcrowded slums, now a living hell. They were not alone.

A close neighbour of St. Giles in the Fields was an area known as 'Seven Dials'. Lying to the east of Covent Garden it occupied marshy ground originally owned by the hospital of St. Giles, but by the turn of the 17th century the freehold had been acquired by Thomas Neale, one of an early breed of property developers. The area was known originally as 'Cock and Pye Fields'. His idea was to develop the site to appeal to the respectable trading classes. Seven Dials took its name from a column that was the meeting point for seven converging streets. The column contained multiple sundials. Initially his plan appeared to attract the type of residents he was seeking, including lawyers and prosperous businessmen. Soon they were joined by craftsmen like wigmakers and woodcarvers. Other builders started to develop the streets further back from the column. This brought a new set of traders with the area becoming known for small printers of political pamphlets. Caged birds and domestic animals drew in a new raft of customers. The sale of cats, rabbits and dogs created a market-like atmosphere which was the first indication of the area's decline.

The early 18th century London witnessed something of a population explosion. These were largely working class people avoiding depravation in their own country and lured by the possibilities London offered. Instead these poor people were herded into filthy overcrowded accommodation they rented from unscrupulous landlords. Large families were crammed into single dark unventilated rooms.

Many young girls, mostly Jewish or Irish, were met at the docks by men claiming to be relatives or old friends of the family. Within days they were put to work selling their bodies. The Irish arriving mostly came from rural backgrounds and they found it difficult to settle for this foul urban life. These men worked mainly as labourers helping to build London's roads and the new areas being developed as London's insatiable need for expansion continued.

Many of the houses in Seven Dials had pocket sized gardens and these added to the hostile environment directed at the Irish. To the mix of open sewers, muddy streets and fetid air, pigs were added. In Ireland having a pig being fed up to be slaughtered added a certain kudos. Other residents objected to these animals grubbing around in the filth which caused great dissent, continual fights and brawls. Some of the animals were even brought into the houses leading to a general dislike of the Irish as being dirty, violent and drunken. Those throwing rocks were hardly ones to criticise, at least most of the Irish worked hard for their money by their own physical labour.

With a window tax being levied, houses were left open to the elements or boarded up, adding to the misery. How was it possible to escape this nightmare? Surrounded by pimps, prostitutes, coiners and violent gangs, life must have been unbearable. Access to water was difficult and that gathered from the Thames was contaminated. Illnesses swept through the rookeries and people in their thirties looked years older. Many of the alleys in Seven Dials were dead-ends, leaving someone new to the area with the problem of being confronted by 'footpads'. Charles Dickens based the terrifying rookery described in 'Bleak House' on Seven Dials. As the area continued to decline a decision was made to clear much of the area to make way for what is now Shaftesbury Avenue and Charing Cross Road.

Clustered not far away was another cess-pit of crime and lawlessness. A Thames-side slum called 'Alsatia'. It was situated in an area previously occupied by the Whitefriars Monastery south of Fleet Street. Even when the monastery was open the area had obtained a reputation for crime and violence. It also offered the right of sanctuary for the needy. This was extended to include debtors and wanted criminals. The authorities were loathe to enter and so the area became increasingly popular with rogues and criminals of every description. The name Alsatia was derived from Alsace, the disputed region on the French/German border, which for a time was itself outside normal legal jurisdiction, despite the right to sanctuary being revoked in 1697.

Today Covent Garden is a tourist attraction. It offers a huge range of restaurants and expensive shops laid out in what was a fruit and vegetable market until 1974. Culture is provided by the Opera House where tickets for the opera or ballet can challenge even the deepest pockets. It is a unique area where over the years trade, the arts and pleasures of the flesh collided or existed alongside each other. Although strictly speaking not a rookery, the alleys and courtyards surrounding it played host to pickpockets, footpads and whores aplenty. The market dates back to the mid 17th century with stalls set up in the Piazza. The noise created by these traders was enough for the Earl of Bedford to decamp from his mansion in The Strand and turn the area into a source of profit for him. He obtained a licence from the King to hold a market every day bar Sundays and Christmas Day. With crowds being drawn into the area, by the mid 18th century the rebuilding and development of the area had taken place.

By 1732 a theatre had been built on the site that now hosts the Royal Opera House. Established as the most luxurious theatre in London it drew in a new and wealthy clientele for a host of more exotic erotic pleasures which were also on offer. The traditional sounding Rose Tavern was described as 'that black school of Sodom'. Nearby the Shakespeare's Head ran a whores' club that met each Sunday. It was run by Jack Harris who had hit on the idea of publishing a pamphlet advertising the services on offer of the girls working in Covent Garden and the squalid alleys running off Drury Lane. A number of taverns, whilst not brothels, offered an early form of striptease for a rowdy group of drinkers. These inns were riotous and dangerous for those perhaps entering the area for the first time. The most notorious of all taverns was Derry's Cider Cellar in Maiden Lane close to Rules, London's oldest surviving restaurant.

Girls as young as twelve were paraded as bait around the fashionable theatres. The unwary were led into a maze of alleys and courtyards to be confronted by the girl's gang masters. With the girl fading into the darkness the man who had been fool enough to be tempted was relieved of his wallet. That is if he was lucky, often he was roughed up by the thug posing as the girl's outraged father. For those not wanting to be seen entering a brothel there was a more convivial alternative. Bagnios were ostensibly just upmarket bath houses, very luxurious and expensive. Here a chap could request some female company who could be sent out for rather like a Chinese take-away. If particularly well known and pretty she would be brought on a sedan chair. All very refined with food and good wine also on the menu at a price. These establishments created the sense of a gentlemen's club with expensive furnishings and a general feeling of decorum. For those risking entering one of the overtly homosexual molly houses, one could also arrange for a good-looking young man to be sent for. All tastes in Covent Garden were catered for, with flagellation being amongst the favourites, but discretion was assured and a sedan available to take you safely back to your lodgings.

Sohoe is an Anglo French hunting call 'Sophie the hare is found'. Lying to the west of the infamous rookeries Soho was once a hunting ground much favoured by Henry VIII. Today it is a unique part of central London. It covers a square mile and is hemmed in by the growling traffic of Regent Street, Trafalgar Square and the Charing Cross Road. There is no public transport in the area other than down the Victorian addition of Shaftesbury Avenue. To the south lay what is today Chinatown and Leicester Square.

After the Great Fire of London there was obviously a severe shortage of housing. Leases were acquired by developers on what had been ancient hunting fields. The area had only a few isolated dwellings and these were soon consumed in a tide of speculative building. Most of the houses were of a poor quality and as such were not of interest to the wealthy. Instead it led to an influx of not just Londoners but foreign traders fleeing persecution and injustice.

It was the French Huguenots who established Soho's reputation for skilled craftsmanship. These early arrivals specialised in millinery and tapestry making, to be followed by makers of musical instruments. Greeks arrived in the area escaping the brutality of the Ottomans. Jews set up as tailors and jewellers. The reputation that Soho has for good food was heralded by groups of Italians who set up small restaurants whilst also selling street food. The smell of fresh bread came from German bakers. By the 18th century the area already had a cosmopolitan atmosphere, setting it quite apart from its London neighbours.

This heady mix was also attracting criminals and prostitution, but a reputation for tolerance in Soho was already being established. Talented artists, writers and musicians were being drawn to the area. Antonio Canal (Canaletto) was reputed to have had a studio in Beak Street, a section of Soho known then as 'Devil's Acre'. Despite boasting the spacious Golden Square and Soho Square the speculative building continued. Gradually the gentry took flight and Golden Square was given over to cheap lodgings often controlled by pimps. The earliest reference to prostitutes dates to 1641 and a lady called Anna Clarke, but along with its reputation for fine food was added sex tourism. People living in the 18th century were far less prudish than their outwardly moral Victorian cousins. Young girls were traded for huge prices, sometimes sold on by their own parents. Flagellation was in much demand, administered in such foul sounding places as the Coal Hole.

The famous continued to be attracted to Soho, drawing a wide ranging cast including at various times William Hazlitt, Karl Marx, Wolfgang Mozart, John Hunter and Jessie Matthews. By the 1920s a more sinister reputation for Soho became embedded with the emergence of the Sabini gang. They ran a protection racket enforced with extreme violence. Even during this turbulent period and the violence on the streets, during the 1950s it was still possible to visit restaurants without threat. The violence tended to be directed at other criminals or gangs as one faction sought more control. In fact visiting Soho during these times added a certain frisson. Emerging from the safety of a fashionable restaurant on a warm summer's night it was possible to think you were in Paris or Rome. As the taxi drew up to take you to the safety of your hotel you were aware of groups of men wearing trilby hats smoking strange smelling cigarettes. There would be a babble of foreign languages. Ladies of the night stood in doorways inviting passers-by if they were looking for a good time and there were plenty of takers.

Whilst Italians added to the mix of nationalities making Soho such a cosmopolitan part of London, many more settled in Saffron Hill, an area known as 'Little Italy' situated between Mount Pleasant, Holborn and to the west of Farringdon Road. Its environment was similar to other London slums consisting of a maze of narrow alleys and filthy courtyards.

Those arriving during the 19th century found themselves forced by circumstances into a form of 'padrone'. This enabled the owners of property in the area to let out rooms in exchange for a percentage of the tenants' earnings. Most of those living in the area were tradesmen but also included a formidable criminal element. Traditionally the trade practices included tilers who were responsible for undertaking work in both St. Paul's and Westminster Abbey. Further work was undertaken at Brompton Oratory and the Bank of England as the Italians' skill was unrivalled in Britain. Many of those from Saffron Hill found employment in the hotel trade. It was impossible not to find Italian waiters in London's swankiest hotels. Many of those still living in Saffron Hill also concentrated on selling food not normally available in London. They sold their wares from handcarts, particularly becoming famous for ice creams. Whilst often very tasty the hygiene in their kitchens and small factories was non-existent, often filthy and infested with mouse droppings. Outbreaks of food poisoning were increasingly reported.

Small cafes were opened in Clerkenwell as was London's first delicatessen. Barrows loaded with cheeses were hawked around the West End and Italian knife-grinders became a regular sight on the streets. Increasingly the knives were becoming part of a criminal fraternity's armoury as the Sabini family extended their savage influence to the lucrative West End, and the reputation that Italians were the prime players in organised crime in London was cemented.

On a lower level fights often broke out to secure the best pitch for the sale of produce. Barrows were overturned and threats made. Rather like the Irish the Italians' reputation suffered and they were viewed with suspicion by many. The thinly disguised animosity to all foreigners remained deeply rooted.

So the scene was set. Much of the crime committed over the decades in London can in part be attributed to the quite dreadful conditions many were forced to live in. But crime there was and it continues today and although much of the ancient capital has disappeared under slum clearance and wartime bombing, many of the Georgian and Victorian streets remain. It is to their ghosts and shadows that we now seek out London's often frightful, often shocking, past. Its scandals and all human weaknesses revealed.

Chapter 2

A One-way Ticket to Tyburn

As drivers sit fuming in the endless traffic jams around Marble Arch, relatively few will realise that they are just metres away from London's main execution site from 1571 until the gallows were dismantled in 1783. The earliest execution is recorded as having taken place as far back as the 12th century. Tyburn was thought to be a suitable place for executions because it was still an outlying suburb in the 16th century and therefore large crowds were able to attend without causing disruption to the city centre. After 1783 Newgate became the main execution site in the capital. It is from Newgate that our journey begins as it did for thousands of condemned prisoners, but for them there was no return.

It was quite possibly a great relief as the prisoner had his shackles removed for his final journey. To be able to breathe fresh air again having been incarcerated in shocking, filthy, crowded conditions and subject to the brutality of the jailors. Outside the prison gates a horse drawn cart was waiting. There were often several of these as executions of twenty or more were conducted at the same time. A macabre feature often being the prisoner sitting on the coffin which his body would occupy later that day. He would be just one of an estimated fifty thousand to have been put to death at Tyburn. Today the journey from Newgate (now the site of the Old Bailey) to Marble Arch would take under half an hour even allowing for the traffic. Back all those years ago the final journey could take up to three hours.

Executions were normally undertaken on a Monday. For well over a century until 1744, on the stroke of midnight on Sunday the bellman of the Holy Sepulchre in Newgate Street would make his way by a series of tunnels to the condemned cells. They could hear him coming as he rang his hand-bell. This really was a case of for whom the bell tolls. Then in a mournful voice he cheered them up no end by reciting:

'All you that are in the condemned hole do lie
Prepare for tomorrow you shall die
Watch all and pray, the hour is drawing near
That you before Almighty God will appear
Examine well yourselves, in time repent
That you not to eternal flames be sent
And when St. Sephulcher's bells tomorrow tolls
The Lord above have mercy on your souls'

Execution day had something of a pre-football match atmosphere. All was excitement and anticipation as crowds lined the route, hanging out of upstairs windows in order to get a better view. Moving along Newgate Street the carts rattled over the bridge on Snow Hill that crossed the River Fleet. The Holborn Viaduct that was constructed in the 1860s today bridges the old valley of the Fleet. By now the procession had reached the first of numerous inns lining the route. Many condemned men drank so much that by the time they reached Tyburn they were totally drunk. If a particular prisoner showed bravado he was likely to receive many a flagon of ale or perhaps a pint of wine. Those cringing were often showered with mud from the road or worse. The crowd demanded a good showing from the prisoner on his final journey.

Whilst the prisoners and even the constables walking at the side of the carts joined in the drinking binge, one group of men were forbidden a single tipple on pain of frightful retribution. The phrase 'on the wagon', denoting someone who has given up drinking, refers to the cart drivers whose job it would be to whip the horse, forcing it to bolt at the scene of the execution allowing the condemned man to dangle and hang. As the procession continued its journey along Holborn the crowds were getting bigger and more rowdy as the alcoholic intake continued to increase. Cheering, jeering, swearing, this was London in full voice. Chancery Lane allowed the legal profession to add their voice to what easily became an almost riotous atmosphere. How many shoppers hunting for bargains in Oxford Street today would believe that centuries before this thoroughfare with its smart department stores formed the final stretch of a journey for a date with the hangman. Past where Selfridges stands today, and the scene is set for an outrageous spectacular example of street theatre.

By the beginning of the 18th century concerns were being voiced about the executions being held regularly at Tyburn. No longer a leafy outpost, the vast crowds attending were causing traffic congestion and wealthy house owners were abandoning the area.

There had been regular executions at Tyburn since 1671 when the original Triple Tree was set up. The gallows consisted of three uprights extending to about eighteen feet. These were joined at the top by beams forming a triangular gallows large enough for three large carts to be backed in. This enabled up to twenty four prisoners to be hanged at the same time. The gallows remained in place until 1759 when they were demolished. For a time until 1783 the smaller mobile gallows were used, a kind of pop-up service until the main London execution site was shifted to Newgate.

Contemporary accounts of execution day at Tyburn paint a vivid picture. The event veered from a sense of entertainment and theatre to the crowd becoming frightening and out of control. People paid large sums to get a good vantage point on a raised platform, rather like a small grandstand. The Sheriff of the City of London invited guests to a house overlooking Tyburn. They stood on a balcony taking refreshments as if in a box at the theatre. Below them crowds pushed and shoved to get a better view. A foreign visitor was surprised by the leisurely pace of events. It was as if the whole procedure was being drawn out adding to the tension. Hawkers moved amongst the crowd selling food and drinks. There were souvenir sellers, but also pickpockets who worked in pairs. The one to cause a distraction whilst the accomplice went to work. If caught it would not be long before they too would be mounting the gallows, but the temptation was too great for the most daring.

The wealthy condemned were allowed to arrive in their own coach which was flanked by constables. Like the lesser mortals the convicted prisoner would have his or her hands tied in front of them. For those brave enough it was time for a speech, trying to be heard above the shouting of the crowd.

All now was set. The condemned now donned a white linen shirt to protect their clothes and a cap. The group were then transferred to three larger carts that were backed into place. They stood now with their backs to the horses. The carts were surrounded by burly constables as the rowdy crowd pressed forward. A rope was now passed round their necks and the end tied to the gibbet. All around the noise was increasing. Cheering mixed with jeering and chants. A chaplain joined the prisoners on the cart and invited them to pray. Now relatives were allowed through the throng to say their farewells. Again there appeared to be no rush and it was another ten to twenty minutes before they were moved on.

Then the horses were suddenly whipped causing the cart to lurch forward, leaving the condemned dangling. The drop was very short, ensuring a slow awful death as they fought against the constriction of the rope. They fought for breath and cast about frantically with their legs dancing the 'Tyburn jig'. Sometimes the relatives were allowed to pull on the prisoners' legs to shorten the ordeal. This usually required a tip to be paid to the hangman.

After about ten minutes when there were no further signs of life the corpses were cut down, but the spectacle was still not over. The clothes of the executed, by tradition, belonged to the hangman. Those wearing their best outfits could sometimes have their ordeal shortened by the hangman pulling on their feet. Now the surgeons and their assistants arrived and unseemly fights often broke out in an attempt to secure the body. Relatives sometimes sought to out-bid the medics, to avoid the ignominy of having their loved one dissected in front of a crowd of students and other onlookers. Sales of the bodies was a very important source of income for the executioner.

In 1740 the body of sixteen year old William Duell was taken to a local surgeon for dissection. He had been convicted of the rape and murder of Sarah Griffin. As he was placed on the slab at the Surgeons' Hall it was noticed that he was still showing signs of life. He was duly revived and returned to Newgate jail. Eventually the authorities decided his survival was the will of God and his sentence was commuted instead to one of transportation.

Years earlier on Christmas Eve in 1705 John Smith was still showing signs of life having been left hanging for a full fifteen minutes. The crowd became restless shouting out: 'reprieve reprieve'. Worried that a full scale riot seemed likely, Smith was cut down and eventually revived. He described that he suffered shocking pain on being cut down, whereas previously he had lost any sense of suffering.

Another amazing reprieve was granted to three condemned men in 1717. On their way to Tyburn the procession was halted when a writ was served on the hangman. Over the years several executioners appear to have got into debt and found themselves in prison. Arriving at Tyburn without their hangman the authorities asked for volunteers to take on the job, offering a substantial sum by way of encouragement. This enraged the crowd and after one volunteer was beaten up there were no further takers. Eventually the men were reprieved.

Perhaps the most bizarre of many witnessed at a Tyburn execution concerned a drunken hangman. There is evidence that executioners found the job increasingly stressful. The constant putting to death of all manner of prisoners, including the young and particularly women, took a toll on their nerves and an increase of their alcoholic intake to deaden the senses. There is a record of a hangman being so drunk that he grabbed the attending chaplain and placed the noose round his neck rather than one of the condemned. Horrified, it took three burly constables to set him free as the crowd yelled their delight. As the frightened cleric stumbled away the hangman resumed his duties and the execution continued.

June in 1759 saw the last major execution at Tyburn. That doubtful honour was awarded to Catherine Knowland, one of a rare breed of female highway robbers. Taking a final bow the hangman would certainly have benefitted from the small lengths of rope he would have sold to eager memento seekers. This custom led to the phrase still used today: 'money for old rope'.

Chapter 3

Murder Most Foul

Currently on average there is a murder committed approximately every three days in London. Many of these involve knives and are drug related. Whatever the causes, this body count awards London the unenviable title of 'murder capital of Europe'. The major causes for murder have remained the same over the centuries. Heading the list are greed and financial gain. In personal relationships jealousy often spills over into violence, as does a deep-seated resentment that manifests itself in the need for revenge. Add in the spasmodic outbreak of gang warfare and you might be persuaded that it is unsafe to venture out at all.

The fact that so many people come to London to seek their fortune, or at least improve their circumstances, adds to the temptations. In addition to the excitement of one of the most vibrant cities in the world is an undercurrent of greed, some would say represented by the towering office blocks in the city. Ostentatious wealth existing cheek by jowl with areas of deprivation and poverty. This mixture somehow creates a certain swagger where financial success is celebrated. There is a perception that Londoners are generally garrulous, bolshie and cocky. For centuries the influx of newcomers has been met with resistance from the native population, and yet within a couple of generations the new arrivals have been integrated and have taken on many of the characteristics of Londoners that on first arriving they had found so difficult to relate to.

Over the centuries it has never been any different. A heaving mass of expectation creating a heady brew that frequently led people astray. Perhaps it is the foggy backstreets and alleys of Victorian London that we most associate with murder. The unsolved mystery of Jack the Ripper is the most obvious, but 'Penny Dreadfuls' printed weekly carried increasingly lurid descriptions of all manner of crimes, illustrated before photography took over by detailed pen and ink line drawings. For those reading these flimsy broadsheets danger was waiting around every corner. Although many Victorian murders have become almost part of our folk history, it was a century earlier when murders were so prevalent in London that it led to the passing of a new draconian act with punishments so horrendous in an attempt to dissuade potential killers.

The Murder Act of 1751 was passed into law the following year. It stated 'whereas the horrid crime of murder has of late been more frequently perpetrated than formerly ... it has thereby become necessary that some further terror and peculiar mark of infamy be added to the punishment of death now by law inflicted as such as shall be guilty of the said heinous offence'.

The law stipulated that there was to be no appeal once the sentence had been passed. The execution was to take place two days after sentencing, unless it fell on a Sunday when another day of life was granted. The traditional last meal of choice was withdrawn and the prisoner was only to be fed on bread and water. No murderer was to be allowed a Christian burial and in many cases the right of access to a cleric was also withheld. In a time when religion was still central to life, the denial of a chance to rise again from a consecrated grave on the day of judgment was reckoned to be a further disgrace.

Further humiliation could be heaped upon the convicted man as he contemplated his final hours. Many were left hanging from a gibbet after execution, normally at busy crossroads for all to see and act as a warning to others.

Spared the gibbet, the only other alternative for the convicted murderer was an appointment at Surgeons' Hall for dissection. Today many leave their body in order to further medical research, but in the 18th century it was viewed as a disgrace to the prisoner's surviving family. A work by William Hogarth vividly portrays the grisly scene of a dissection being carried out by the president of the College of Physicians. Dozens of onlookers gaze down whilst an incision is made. One bored by events reads a book whilst others avert their eyes. A macabre detail sees a dog biting at entrails. It has the feel of being more like a circus rather than a serious medical examination. Presumably this again was meant to act as a deterrent. Of course dissection did lead to a better understanding of anatomy, with the Hunter brothers among the most eminent physicians of the 18th century.

It is sad to note that the first person to be executed following the passing of the Act was a one-armed seventeen year old. Thomas Wilford was born in Fulham to desperately poor parents. They placed him into the workhouse, presumably realising that his eventual earning potential would be restricted due to him only having one arm. Growing up in the workhouse would have been incredibly tough but Thomas did earn a few coppers by running errands.

Sarah Williams, who had grown up in St. Giles in the Fields, found herself consigned to the same workhouse and soon set up a friendship with the impressionable young boy. Sarah was a part time prostitute, but presumably not a very successful one, although she managed to attract the vulnerable lad who proposed marriage to her. They were awarded forty shillings by the church wardens to start a new life together. Was the money the incentive for Sarah? Whatever, Thomas no doubt felt some elation to have landed an attractive wife and some money to spend.

They headed back to St. Giles where they took lodgings among the narrow teeming alleys. It took only a few days for Sarah to return to her old ways, no doubt thinking that a little extra money would help them both. Perhaps poor Thomas was too naive to understand how his new bride was going to help their joint finances. When four days after their wedding she stayed out until past midnight. Where had she been, he demanded? Only to the park, she replied, presumably to conduct her business. Thomas was consumed by jealousy. Sadly the young man really did love his wayward girl. A massive row turned violent. Seizing a knife he threw Sarah to the ground in an uncontrollable rage. He hacked at her neck until her head was almost severed.

Staggering outside onto the landing he met a neighbour from the adjoining room. At once he told the woman he had murdered his wife. With him probably covered in blood, the woman went straight away to inform the landlord. In St. Giles there was honour amongst thieves but this did not extend to murder. Wilford made no attempt to escape as the watch was called for. In fact he repeated to anyone prepared to listen that he had killed his wife despite his love for her.

He was carted off to Newgate where he continued to express his guilt. The trial at the Old Bailey was a forgone conclusion with the youngster pleading guilty. Sentenced to death on a Friday allowed an extra day for him to contemplate his wretched life, before he was led to the scaffold the following Monday. He was hanged in chains as the new Act took its toll, one that ran until it was amended in 1837. There were further revisions over the years but the Act was not finally abolished until 1973.

Murdered and murderers have, of course, never been confined to the poor, but the contrast between Thomas Wilford and the 4th Earl Ferrers underlines the fact. Laurence Shirley is the only peer to have been executed for murder. A vast land owner in the East Midlands, he had estates stretching from Derbyshire to Northamptonshire. His major residence was at Staunton Harold Hall in Leicestershire.

Despite him being born to wealth and status he acquired a reputation for drunken and unruly behaviour. He was also something of a womaniser, having four children born out of wedlock with his long time lover, Margaret Clifford. Like most aristocrats he was anxious to produce a son and heir. In 1752 at the age of thirty two he made what appeared to be a good match when he married the sixteen year old daughter of Sir William Meredith, a Cheshire landowner. The marriage was not a success from the start, fuelled by Ferrers's excessive drinking. He treated the young girl appallingly, at one stage beating her unconscious in a drunken rage. Within six years matters had declined to such an extent that, very unusually, Mary obtained a separation by Act of Parliament. This must have required very telling evidence of his horrendous behaviour towards her. As part of the settlement Mary was awarded income from rents collected from his estates. A steward, John Johnson, was appointed a trustee and he had control of the rental money. Being to the manor born Ferrers resented having to deal with Johnson. There is also a hint of jealousy and even a suspicion that Mary was having an affair with the steward. Matters came to a head when the Earl discovered that Johnson had given Mary fifty pounds without his permission.

Ferrers visited Johnson and invited him to come up for a meeting at the Hall. It appears that the noble Earl sent his mistress and daughters together with all the male servants away for the day. The two men got down to business in the Earl's study. Soon a heated argument developed and the steward was shot. Some accounts tell of him being made to kneel before the gun was fired. The shot was not fatal and there was talk of the man being left in agony before he died hours later. It seems more likely that a Doctor Kirkland was called from nearby Ashby de la Zouch. In his version of events Ferrers continued to scream and abuse Johnson before falling asleep in a drunken stupor, allowing the doctor to take the injured steward back to his own house where he died the following morning. Furious and dismayed by Ferrers's action, the doctor accompanied by a local workman went up to the hall and arrested the Earl who was nursing a monumental hangover. At the inquest a verdict of death by wilful murder was recorded and the noble Earl was remanded in Leicester prison. A peer could not be tried at Leicester Assizes and so Ferrers was transferred to the Tower of London under the custody of Black Rod.

Ferrers's trial took place in the grand setting of Westminster Hall in April 1760. The hearing was conducted before the Lord High Steward Lord Henley. Having killed a steward he was now relying on the support of other aristocrats. The prosecution was led by Lord Pratt the Attorney-General and the Solicitor-General Sir Charles Yorke.

As was customary Ferrers conducted his own defence. He decided not to try and justify his action, rather depending on a plea of insanity. Sober for once, he made a convincing case with evidence of his frequent irrational rages. A servant told of how Ferrers had assaulted his wife, whom the Earl had accused of mistreating his horse. He then went on to attack the servant with a sword. Ferrers did not help his case by insisting that surely a man of his standing had every right to reprimand a negligent servant, arrogantly assuming that he was above the law.

The evidence of Doctor Kirkland was particularly damming. Despite Ferrers presenting his case to the best of his ability, he failed to convince his fellow peers that he was insane. It is likely that his reputation for drunken and offensive behaviour was well known within aristocratic circles. Surely he had let his class down badly and as such prompted little sympathy. He was found guilty and sentenced to die by hanging and afterwards to suffer the indignity of being dissected following the Murder Act of 1752. Although most hangings took place two days after sentencing, the execution was delayed in order to make arrangements for the huge crowds expected. Ferrers, ever the snob, was appalled that he was to be treated like a common criminal. He petitioned the King, requesting that he should be beheaded like a true gentlemen. How strange this seems to us now with neither prospect having much appeal. The King refused the doubtful honour of being decapitated, which was reserved by those peers found guilty of treason.

Waiting in the Round Tower for his trip to Tyburn, the noble Lord lived high on the hog. Not for him a bread and water diet, rather fine food and wine. Perhaps rather cruelly he was denied visits from Margaret Clifford, his long term mistress. He did however leave her and his four illegitimate daughters sizeable sums. The King signed the death warrant on May 2nd and the execution was set for May 5th.

It was show time in London. The hanging of a nobleman was pure box office. Prices to view the proceedings soared. He was spared having to stand on a cart whilst the horse was whipped away. Instead a new scaffold was erected with a trap door, presumably designed to speed death. Arranged with almost military precision, black cushions were laid out for the prisoner and his chaplain to offer final prayers. The crowd expected a show and Ferrers was not about to disappoint. Dressed in his finest suit of satin he must have cut an imposing figure. He rode in his own Landau and six flanked by a troop of cavalry. Due to the huge crowds it took over three hours to reach Tyburn. There he gave five guineas to the chaplain and thought he had also given the same amount to the hangman, but in his confusion gave it to a bystander. A brief fight developed until the hangman had collected his dues. As he mounted the scaffold the crowd erupted, cheers mingling with howls of derision.

William Hickey witnessed the execution. He reported 'he met his death with fortitude though many persons said there was a wildness in his eyes and countenance that strongly indicated a deranged mind'. No wonder, with his hands tied behind his back Ferrers refused to give the sign he was ready to the hangman. This was done by the sheriff on the dropping of a handkerchief. Never trust new technology until it is properly tested. The new trap door, far from speeding death, left His Grace dangling for a full four minutes giving his own rendition of the Tyburn jig, according to Robert Walpole who was part of the vast crowd. The body was put on display for three days but was spared from being dissected. Instead it was laid to rest in St. Pancras church. Years later when the interest had died down his coffin was taken back to Staunton Harold Hall and interred in the family vault. Ferrers did enjoy some final privileges denied poor young Thomas Wilford, but the end result of their violence was the same.

Most murders are usually rather squalid affairs and the perpetrators rather sad people. However, amongst the thousands of murders carried out in London over the centuries some fascinate and it is a handful of these that must serve our purpose. Of course there are many that go undetected and some that remain clouded in mystery. These taunt and tantalise us, none more so than in the case of poet and playwright Christopher Marlowe.

Marlowe was born in Canterbury in 1564. Although the son of a cobbler of modest means the boy was educated at King's School. Obviously a bright pupil he won a scholarship to Corpus Christi College in Cambridge. Here it is probable that he met people of power and influence. His passage through university was not a smooth one and it seems he left for a period when it is thought he was recruited by the government to carry out espionage work. Here again there is confusion in that he was refused a degree based on rumours that he had Catholic leanings.

Perhaps one of the few known facts about Marlowe is that he was quick tempered and liable to fits of rage. In 1589 he spent time in Newgate jail accused of murder, no less. Subsequently he was acquitted but it is obvious his nature led him to make enemies. Amongs all this turmoil he was already making his mark as a dramatist with his first work Tamburlaine the Great. Rumours of homosexuality and heresy swirled around him as he continued to publish new works. His creative years were confined to just six, during which time he completed The Jew of Malta, The Magical History of Doctor Faustus, The Queen of Carthage, Edward the Second and The Massacre at Paris. In between all these he squeezed in a series of highly regarded poems.

We move on now to Deptford where we do know that Marlowe was supposedly killed on May 30th 1593, or was he? Even the meeting place is disputed. Was it just a common tavern or in fact a house owned by Dame

Eleanor Bull. A rather tenuous connection links her to Queen Elizabeth. Eleanor's sister was the daughter of Blanche Parry who had been the nanny of the infant Elizabeth. The plot thickens. Was Marlowe really killed in a drunken brawl or was he assassinated? Another theory relates him being spirited away to the continent to stop him spilling the beans about people in very high places. Deptford was a leading port in those days so it would have been easy to move him onto a waiting ship unnoticed.

What was the reason for all this cloak and dagger stuff? The early version of events stated that Marlowe was killed by Ingram Frizer, variously described as a friend or a business agent for Marlowe's patron Thomas Walsingham, a cousin of the recently deceased spy-catcher Sir Francis Walsingham. Thomas was also involved in the murky world of espionage. It was alleged that a fight broke out between Marlowe and Frizer over an unpaid bill. Frizer drew a knife and in a tussle that followed Marlowe was stabbed above an eye and the blade entered the brain resulting in instant death. Marlowe was buried with undue haste in an unmarked grave at the parish church in Deptford. Frizer was charged with his murder and sent to prison. Within a month he was awarded a Queen's pardon and released to continue his service with Thomas Walsingham.

Other known facts about Marlowe point to him being a controversial character. In 1593 he had been deported from the Netherlands for attempting to pass off counterfeit gold coins. His own charge of murder was the result of a street brawl. He appears to have courted controversy, openly championing atheism (very dangerous in Elizabethan England), accused also of Catholic heresy. He was arrested ten days before his death with a charge of heresy, which if found guilty he would have suffered death by being burnt at the stake. Strangely (as with everything about this case) he was released on bail so the mists continue to swirl. Was he really killed in a brawl? Was he killed because he knew too much about those in high places? Did he really take himself abroad and the truth covered up? Many theories but no definitive answers. One final twist was that Marlowe was born in the same year as William Shakespeare, begging the question – was the Bard's output all his own work? We all love mysteries, but Christopher Marlowe's is like an onion and each peel reveals new doubts and sore eyes.

Possibly the best known serial killer in London is the shady figure of Jack the Ripper roaming the streets of Whitechapel. What is largely unknown today is that there was another serial killer at large during roughly the same period. These killings were even more gruesome than those committed in the East End, and like the Ripper the culprit was never found.

Some fifteen years before the first Ripper victim was discovered in 1888, part of a woman's torso was discovered in the River Thames at Battersea. Further sections of the same corpse were subsequently discovered along the river with the head found at Limehouse. A verdict of wilful murder by person unknown was recorded. It was noted that the body had not been hacked but dismembered by someone with a degree of medical knowledge. The following year in June 1874 another dismembered body was found in the Thames at Putney. Here there was just a torso but no limbs or head. The national newspapers began linking the killings and curious onlookers began peering anxiously into the river, ghoulishly hoping to spot other bodies or for clues which might have been missed by the police. Whilst an open verdict was recorded it was again noted that some medical knowledge had been exercised in the dismembering. Was there a demented doctor on the loose?

These killings were largely forgotten until October 1884 when another dismembered body of a woman was discovered. This time the victim was not thrown in the Thames, but found in separate locations around Tottenham Court Road in the heart of the West End. An arm was discovered in Bedford Square decorated with a tattoo, which suggested in those days that the woman was a prostitute. Within five days there was another gruesome discovery. A policeman pounding the beat in fashionable Fitzroy Square happened upon a parcel wrapped in brown paper. Imagine his consternation discovering a human torso inside. In Victorian London fashionable streets were constantly patrolled by police, which only allowed a fifteen minute opportunity for the body to be left. Either the culprit was very daring or lucky, or possibly both. At the inquest after other sections of the body had been discovered, medical evidence suggested that the body had been dismembered 'by someone skilled but certainly not for the purpose of anatomy'. Once again no culprit was found and life moved on.

Now we return to the Thames in 1887, a year before the Ripper started his killing spree. Once more a woman's torso was pulled from the Thames. In the following weeks further parts of the body were discovered. The body was reconstructed in the local morgue except for the head and upper chest that remained missing. It is doubtful at this stage that the police had linked this murder to earlier killings, but again the reference to some medical expertise on the part of the killer was noted. A second body was discovered in the Thames in 1888 at the height of the hysteria surrounding the Whitechapel atrocities. The initial discovery was at Pimlico with the torso turning up on the site that would become the home of New Scotland Yard. The skill of dismembering was again noted, with suspicion of the killer extending from doctors to butchers and nagsmen.

On June 4th another part of a female body was pulled out of the Thames from under the Albert Bridge at Chelsea. Over the following weeks various body parts were fished out of the river. From Battersea to Limehouse each day revealed another horror. Despite the head never being discovered this time the victim was established as being a prostitute who had worked the streets of Chelsea.

It was possible the earlier Thames killings and the later river murders were connected, with the time gap explained by the killer possibly having spent the intervening years either in prison or even a mental hospital. The Thames and Tottenham Court Road killings all bear a similar trademark, but as with the Ripper we are left wondering. Another mystery unlikely ever to be solved.

Victorian murders represent a high tide of violent killings in our perception, but of course the killings carried on unabated into the 20th century. Many of these will be featured later but a number of controversial cases led to increasing demands for the death penalty to be abolished. The wrongful execution of Timothy Evans was highlighted by the journalist Ludovic Kennedy, whilst the execution of the nineteen year old Derek Bentley caused huge public disquiet in 1953. Two years later Ruth Ellis became the last woman in Britain to be hanged, causing a massive public outcry. Surely executions, particularly of a woman, were barbaric in a modern society, but the politicians were not convinced and so the executions continued, albeit at a reduced rate.

The last execution at Wandsworth jail was of a young Polish refugee, Henryk Niemasz, on September 8th 1961. Two months earlier Edwin Bush, a twenty one year old of mixed race, was the last prisoner to be hanged at Pentonville jail. It was the solving of this murder that pointed the way towards technology becoming increasingly important in the detection of crime.

Edwin Bush like so many young offenders came from a very troubled family background. Due to his Indian roots he became very interested in daggers and swords from the sub-continent. In March 1961 he went on a tour of antique and bric-a-brac shops around Charing Cross Road. Several remembered him enquiring and examining the few items they had in stock. He returned to a shop in Cecil Court where initially he had spoken to the owner. Returning later an assistant, Elsie Batten, was looking after the shop. He had explained his father was Indian and he was interested in a dagger he had seen earlier. According to Bush, Elsie Batten thought he was a time waster and subjected him to an extremely offensive racial slur, prompting him to viciously attack her. He left her with dreadful wounds and a dagger embedded in her neck. She was found shortly afterwards and a murder hunt was started with the help of a new method of identification imported from the United States.

The antique shop owner from Cecil Court built up a picture of Bush using 'identikit'. Other shop owners in the area were also asked to build up a picture using the same method. The results were distributed to all the police forces in the country. It did not take long for Bush to be picked up in Soho by an alert constable. Bush made little attempt to defend himself and the jury was not convinced that a racial slur was sufficient mitigation and he was duly sentenced to death. In London at least the long history of murder and civic retribution came to an end. The last execution in Britain took place in 1964, although it took a further thirty four years until capital punishment was finally abolished.

Before we leave this murky world of murder, what of the ladies? Were their motives and methods so different from their male counterparts? Were they more calculating or driven by the same incentives of greed and jealousy?

Chapter 4

Lady Killers

It was in 1928 that women over twenty one finally got the vote, having been partially enfranchised ten years earlier. It was the ending of the Great War that also witnessed the decline in the influence of the church, which in earlier years had been all encompassing. As the march towards sex equality also increased, so did the attitude towards women involved in murders, culminating in the execution of Ruth Ellis, which was instrumental in the eventual abolition of capital punishment. The connection with religion is relevant and underlined by a shocking case, albeit that it took place almost three hundred years ago.

The River Thames appears to have acted as a dumping ground for bodies over the centuries. A severed head was plucked from the murky waters, seemingly very soon after it had been thrown in. Before it started to decompose it was put on display in the hope that someone would be able to identify it. Very soon constables came calling on Catherine Hayes who lived on Tyburn Road (the site of modern day Oxford Street). A woman in her thirties, she identified the head as being that of her husband, who she claimed she thought was on a business trip to Portugal. Feigning real grief her story soon unravelled as it transpired that she had already tried to get her hands on his fortune of some fifteen hundred pounds, which had been delayed pending enquiries.

Sensing she was in trouble she changed her story, insisting he was an atheist and as such deserved to die like a dog. To be an atheist in early 18th century England was considered to be a heinous crime. Good try, Catherine, but her story continued to fall apart. She had two lodgers, Thomas Wood and Thomas Billings, both of whom claimed to be her lovers. Another stain on her character. The plan was to get Catherine's husband drunk and kill him in return for a slice of her inheritance. This they did, beating him to death, disposing of the body and casting the head into the Thames in the hope that the tide would eventually hide it for all time. No such luck! This is where the story gets darker still.

It appears that our Catherine was far from a meek and mild subservient wife. Despite her now insisting that her husband beat and abused her, the evidence against her was damning. She had been outspoken and quarrelsome towards her husband. In addition, she had taken lovers including supposedly her stepson, so adding incest to the list of offences she had committed. Worst, of course, was that she had killed John Hayes, 'her lord and master'. The charge now under the law was one of heightened murder or petty treason. The sentence for any woman found guilty of this offence was to be burnt at the stake. There was no right of appeal and Catherine was sent off to Newgate to consider her fate.

Thomas Wood was perhaps lucky as he died of jail fever before he was taken to the scaffold. Thomas Billings kept his appointment at Tyburn with the hangman, but worse was awaiting Catherine. It was customary for the hangman to strangle his victim with a rope before the body was burnt. Lighting the fire away from her body, the flames leapt towards him before he could complete the garrotting, forcing him back and leaving her to an excruciating death. Contemporary reports suggest it took minutes before her screams were finally silenced. This is a case where women were treated far more harshly than men. She was hardly a poster girl for 'women's lib' but her punishment in 1725 was surely barbaric at a time where cruelty formed a background to many lives.

What triggers a seemingly normal mother into a sadistic killer? Elizabeth Brownrigg was born into a poor but respectable family in 1720. By the time she was in her mid forties she had given birth to sixteen children, of whom only three had survived infancy. Her marriage to her husband James was apparently a happy one and the family thrived as his business expanded. There is no evidence that Elizabeth was ever cruel to her own children in their house off Fetter Lane.

As Elizabeth was working as a midwife she was entitled to take on apprentices. After a one month trial when both parties could decide if they liked each other enough, a deal could be signed. Seemingly during this trial period Elizabeth and her family treated the young girls really well, but this all changed when the 'liking' period was completed. The first warning signs came in 1765. Elizabeth had taken on two young girls from the Whitefriars Foundling Hospital. Mary Mitchell arrived first to be followed shortly afterwards by Mary Jones. Having initially been treated well, they were soon to be subjected to the vilest abuse and savage beatings for any perceived minor failings. These humiliations were watched and supported by the family, with James also adding further to the girls' punishments. Eventually Mary Jones managed to escape, returning to the Foundling Hospital. Here she was examined by the resident doctor. She was covered in bruises and sores, which resulted in a letter being sent to the Brownriggs, threatening to institute prosecution proceedings. Eventually they were informed that on this occasion no further action would be taken, allowing the abuse to continue and accelerate.

Mary Mitchell spent a full year suffering horrendous abuse before she too made a break for it. Spotted by one of the Brownriggs' sons she was forced back to endure even worse treatment. She was joined in the house by a fourteen year old Mary Clifford. After her trial period Elizabeth went into overdrive. The child's stepmother called at the house in 1767 but was refused entry. She then visited the Brownriggs' next door neighbour and asked if the owner, a Mr. Deacon and his servants, would keep a look out as she was worried about the young girl. She had every right to be. As well as regularly being beaten with a horse whip, milk cans and broom handles, the child was fed mainly on just bread and water, being forced to sleep in a filthy coal hole.

Early in August a servant for the next door neighbours saw an emaciated young girl in the yard covered in bruises and sores. The matter was reported to the overseer at St. Dunstan's. Joined by the overseer from Whitefriars who knew Mary, they demanded to see her. After a heated argument they gained access and were horrified by what they found. Apparently in a fit of uncontrolled rage Elizabeth had attempted to cut the girl's tongue out. Her face was swollen to almost twice its normal size. She was unable to speak and her whole body was covered in scabs and infected wounds. Several days later Mary died in hospital and the two Brownriggs were charged with wilful murder, although together with one of their sons they managed to escape.

Advertisements with illustrations of the couple were circulated across London. They were eventually tracked down to lodgings in Wandsworth. They were brought to trial at the Old Bailey. The evidence was of cruelty that at times took on an almost maniacal level of hatred. Other members of the family either looked on or joined in, dealing out dreadful beatings to the young girls for seemingly no reason. Evidence was given of Mary being tied up to a hook in the kitchen and beaten until the blood ran down her shoulders. Confirmation of the treatment of the girls was given by a young man apprenticed to James Brownrigg. There was only one verdict possible for the couple. Or was there? Whilst Elizabeth was obviously the instigator of the crimes, both her husband and son had supported her and also abused the girls themselves, and despite being found guilty they were only sentenced to six months in prison and fined one shilling. No such luck for Elizabeth. The case had received wide publicity and a huge crowd gathered at Tyburn to witness her death, calling down eternal damnation upon her.

Questions as with so many murders remain. Being a midwife requires care and kindness and there were no complaints made about the service she gave. She was also a loving wife and there is a report of their final tender parting in the prison yard at Newgate. Why then this crazy demented desire to inflict harm on helpless young girls? But mystery is what tantalises and engages us, and none more so than a case that occurred a century after Elizabeth Brownrigg danced her final jig at Tyburn.

There is nothing worse than a nagging toothache, particularly if no available pain killers seem to have any effect. Dentistry in 1880s London obviously was a far cry from modern day care. Poor Edwin Bartlett, rather than having extractions had his teeth sawed down to gum level to make way for a new set of dentures. Within months the roots became infected causing increasing pain and discomfort, and so the scene was set for one of the most bizarre and murky cases of murder recorded in Britain.

Some years earlier Edwin had married a nineteen year old girl called Adelaide. By any standards their marriage was weird. An understanding was established that there was to be no sexual intimacy and to start with the marriage was not consummated. Enter stage left George Dyson, a Wesleyan minister who formed a close relationship with the couple. So close that Edwin encouraged the pair to kiss and cuddle in front of him. He even stated quite openly that if he were to die he would want George and Adelaide to marry and his will was amended accordingly.

Edwin's health was giving cause for concern. Plagued by his rotting teeth, but suffering also from severe gastric problems. Despite this Adelaide appeared surprised and distressed to be woken in the early hours of New Year's Day 1886 by her maid to come quickly. Edwin was dead. Doctor Alfred Leach was called for. He had been making regular visits to the house in Pimlico and he was later to testify that Adelaide had always been tireless in the care she had given her husband. As the death was unexpected a post mortem was ordered. This revealed that Edwin had consumed about four ounces of chloroform. Strangely there were no signs of burns either in the throat or stomach. Chloroform is caustic and would normally damage any soft tissue it comes into contact with.

The police made a thorough search of the Bartletts' house but no trace of chloroform was found. Despite this and with public interest sparked Adelaide was charged with wilful murder, with the Reverend George Dyson charged as an accessory. His charge was dropped later and Adelaide appeared at the Old Bailey in April 1886. A contemporary photograph pictures a young woman who despite her clothes could fit quite well into today's society. An intense face that stares at us from across the years but which gives little away. A perfect face for the enigma that was Adelaide Bartlett. She was unable to give evidence on her own behalf (until the passing of the 1898 Evidence Act), but slowly the key facts were presented to the jury. They learnt of the strange relationship Adelaide had with the cleric. It was Dyson who bought the chloroform which Adelaide insisted was only used to rub on Edwin's infected gums. She also claimed that she used it to calm her husband as he had suddenly started making unwanted sexual advances to her. The case against her seemed fairly compelling as she was unable to explain how Edwin had been poisoned. After a full week of testimony the jury recorded a verdict of not guilty. They insisted that the prosecution had not provided any evidence, proof or explanation of how she had poisoned her husband. After the trial the surgeon Sir James Paget asked: "Now that she has been acquitted for murder and can't be tried again, she should tell us in the interest of science how she did it?"

There are several theories to consider. Did Edwin swallow the poison himself to relieve the incessant pain from his inflamed gums? If so why no burns to his throat? Perhaps that night he reached out for what he thought was just a painkiller, taking the chloroform by mistake. Again why were there no burns to his mouth or throat?

A believable and intriguing theory does point the finger of guilt directly at Adelaide. The vapours from chloroform could have been used to anesthetise Edwin. Then with him unconscious a length of tube was possibly used to pour the poison down his throat without causing burns. Of course we will never know, but fascinatingly the mystery deepened. Somehow Adelaide managed to disappear from the country without trace, as did George Dyson. The theory is that they went to America where they split up, but there is no definitive evidence of this either. Presumably they changed their names and evidence of their whereabouts never surfaced. Had that young woman really got away with murder? Today forensic science would easily have solved the case, but for us the mystery remains.

The rather grand surroundings of St. James church, Piccadilly witnessed the marriage of Maria and Frederick Manning. There they vowed to honour each other in sickness and health till death did them part. They did at least keep the last part as they did die together, unfortunately on a scaffold in front of a crowd estimated to be close on fifty thousand.

Maria de Roux was born in Switzerland in 1821. She always longed for the good life and she was able to witness it when she secured the post of lady's maid to Lady Blantyre, a daughter of the Duchess of Sutherland. She was now able to visit some of the grandest houses in the land, punctuated with trips abroad. It was on a return journey from Boulogne that she met Patrick O'Connor. He was obviously attracted to her and she sensed an opportunity. Chatting away on deck she established that here was a man of some means, and although much older than her he might eventually provide a route for her to enjoy the good life. Matters became a touch more complicated on her return to England when she met Frederick Manning, another man who also claimed to be wealthy. Perhaps it was her sexy French accent that bewitched these two ardent admirers, as photographs of her show a rather plain looking woman. Both men proposed to her but she reckoned that O'Connor was too old and anyway he drank too much. So Frederick it was who won her hand. They moved into a stylish home in Miniver Place in Bermondsey. With the rent not paid and with no sign of the promised legacy that Frederick had promised, Maria was forced to realise that she had backed the wrong horse, although O'Connor continued to call on them, obviously still entranced by Maria.

With the money they did have they moved to Taunton where they worked in a pub. They were arrested for theft but released, so then they returned to London where they opened a beer shop in Hackney Road. Visits from Patrick O'Connor increased again and it is possible that he was by now having an affair with Maria. This was confirmed when they ran away together. Frederick tracked them down and persuaded Maria to return to him. It was at this stage that Maria informed her husband that O'Connor had made a will leaving all his money to her. Poor Patrick's fate was sealed.

Assuming for a moment we can convince ourselves that Adelaide Bartlett was clever enough to get away with murder, the same cannot be said of the Mannings. Their over-riding desire for money clouded their senses. With O'Connor continuing to make regular visits, the plan was to kill O'Connor, dispose of the body and for Maria to claim her inheritance. They were deluded. As if any lawyer would believe that their client had just disappeared and hand over the money. Maria had gone and purchased some quicklime which they assumed would take away any traces of the body, but their plans were disrupted anyway. Arriving on time for a pre-arranged supper, O'Connor turned up with a colleague from work. Thrown off guard the couple acted strangely, he remembered later. Another supper date was arranged and this time Patrick did arrive alone. Prior to the serving of the meal he went to the kitchen sink to wash his hands. Turning, he was met by Maria brandishing a pistol. She fired, hitting him in the head but not killing him. Lying helpless on the ground, Frederick Manning now took a jemmy and beat him until he died.

Now came the messy job of cleaning up. Blood was splattered up the walls and on the work surfaces. Flagstones were removed and a grave dug. Quicklime was applied to the body and he was laid to rest under the kitchen floor. They waited a few days finalising their plans when they were visited by other colleagues of O'Connor who were worried that he had not turned up for work. Before leaving they registered an unpleasant smell and again were suspicious of the Mannings' nervous behaviour. Maria had already made a visit to O'Connor's lodgings, gaining access from the landlord. She then proceeded to carry off anything of value, again raising suspicion. Now the couple parted, with Frederick travelling to Jersey whilst Maria boarded a train for Edinburgh. Meantime Patrick's friends had alerted the police to their suspicions.

By now a manhunt had been set in place. The cab driver who had taken Maria to Kings Cross station alerted the police. The Met contacted their counterparts in Scotland only to learn that Maria had already been arrested for trying to sell some of O'Connor's stock holdings to a local stockbroker. Frederick was arrested in Jersey and the two were committed to Horsemonger Lane Gaol to await trial. It took the jury less than an hour to reach their verdict of guilty. Maria was not about to go quietly. She screamed at the judge that she had been treated like a wild animal as sentence was passed.

November 13th was indeed unlucky for the Mannings. A gallows had been set up on the flat roof of the jail acting as a perfect stage setting for the vast crowds assembled. The Times reported: 'At quarter past eight Manning and his wife entered the chapel. The sacrament was administered to them, then the governor appeared and said that time pressed. Calcraft also came forward and the wretched pair were conducted to different parts of the chapel to be pinioned.' The article goes on to describe that Maria almost fainted as preparations continued, but fortified by some brandy she regained her composure. She requested that a black silk handkerchief be tied so she might be blindfolded. A black lace veil was added. With her husband by her side the small procession made its way towards the gallows whilst the prison bell sounded. They were not the last couple to be involved with murder and suffer the ultimate sentence that the law could hand down, but this time there was a public outcry.

When passion, infatuation and jealousy become intermingled the outcome is seldom a happy one. In the case of Edith Thompson the result was disastrous for all concerned. She was an attractive twenty eight year old married to Percy, who worked as a shipping clerk in the city where she also was employed as a book-keeper. They had a modest but comfortable lifestyle centred on their house in Ilford.

Trouble started when their young lodger Frederick Bywaters joined them on a summer holiday. Frederick was eight years younger than Edith, and worked as a ship's steward. A good looking young man who had become besotted with Edith. Perhaps she was flattered and finding Percy unable to give her the excitement she appeared to crave. Whatever, on return from the holiday Percy took exception to the attention the young man was paying his wife and duly ejected Frederick from the house. It appears that Edith continued to meet her young lover regularly. Frederick had apparently witnessed a number of violent rows between the married couple, and with the impetuosity of youth decided to confront Percy.

On October 4th 1922 the Thompsons were returning from an evening at The Criterion Theatre in London. They needed to enter a dark alley to get to their house. It was here that Bywaters leapt out of the dark, attacking Percy with a knife. Pushing Edith aside, the two men grappled with Percy being thrown to the ground where he was fatally stabbed. Edith cried out: 'Don't, oh don't!' But it was too late, Percy was dead. Edith was hysterical when interviewed by police and she made her first mistake by claiming her husband had been killed by a stranger. Fanny Lester, who also lodged at the Thompsons' house, told the police about the rows between the couple prompted by her closeness to young Frederick. Bywaters was arrested. A search of his cabin on the S.S. Morea moored at Tilbury revealed a bundle of over sixty love letters from Edith. Bywaters was charged with murder as was Edith shortly afterwards. What had started for her as a passionate love affair had turned into a nightmare. Bywaters continually told police that Edith had nothing to do with the killing, but evidence that came out at the trial suggested that she had intended to kill her husband.

In her letters to her young lover Edith boasted of trying to poison Percy and putting crushed up pieces of light bulbs in his porridge. Following the post mortem on Percy's body, this claim was dismissed by the pathologist Sir Bernard Spilsbury. It would appear that Edith was something of a fantasist, fuelled by her reading of fanciful romantic novels. Edith had also sent newspaper cuttings describing murder cases involving poison. None of these revelations were going to help her case, nor either the fact that she had undergone an abortion. She was advised by her lawyer not to take the stand but she ignored him and offered what seemed lame excuses for her behaviour. Whilst the judge's summing up was fair, he said: 'You will not convict her unless you are satisfied that he and she agreed to do it and by arrangement between them he was doing it.' The judge made much of Edith's adultery as being a further stain on her character. It was obvious that Bywaters was going to be found guilty but it took the jury over two hours for them to return the same verdict on Edith.

Both the lovers lodged appeals that were heard by the Lord Chief Justice and two other senior judges. Both were dismissed, but it was Edith's character that drew the greatest criticism. She was an adulteress, abortionist and a woman who incited the murder of her husband. This emphasis on her sexual morals that supposedly offended public opinion was surely a sham, with the high society involved in bewildering examples of bed-hopping and not just with the opposite sex either.

Edith was sent off to Holloway Prison whilst across town Frederick settled into the condemned cell at Pentonville. Public opinion was changing. At first the press had been very critical of Edith, but with the final appeal to the Home Secretary being turned down, there was a massive swing both in the papers and with the public. A petition for Edith to be reprieved attracted about a million signatures, but to no avail. At 9.00am on January 9th 1922 the couple were executed at their respective prisons. Edith's hanging was quite awful, botched like so many of those centuries before at Tyburn. During her last few days Edith and her warders obviously expected her to receive a reprieve. Her mood changed alarmingly from supreme optimism to frightened hysteria. On the day of the execution she was sedated and carried to the scaffold. The hangman John Ellis never recovered from the trauma and committed suicide some years later. The prison staff also found the whole spectacle extremely harrowing. Unusually at a hanging there was a great deal of blood and it is possible that Edith was pregnant. If so, she could have arranged a stay of execution and possibly a reprieve as public opinion continued to increase.

The case of Edith Thompson accelerated a move amongst the public for the abolition of capital punishment, although it was to take another forty years to be passed into law. Other cases like Timothy Evans, Derek Bentley and of course Ruth Ellis finally encouraged the politicians to act. It was 1964 that witnessed the last execution in Britain, completing centuries of legalised killing.

Chapter 5

Let the Punishment Fit the Crime

For centuries retribution has been the response to crime in Great Britain. It seems astonishing to believe that it was only in 1948 that the birching of prisoners was banned by law. In a country seemingly endlessly embroiled in wars and bloody disputes, witnessing cruelty and violence was part of everyday life. This was particularly true of a turbulent London.

Unruly crowds flocked to watch executions passed down by the authorities. Seemingly ever more gruesome methods were inflicted by way of warning to the general population. Hanging or garotting were surely bad enough, but not with drawing and quartering added to the menu together with burning at the stake. It was surely impossible to imagine a worse death. Wrong, there was one. An important lesson for young men, particularly those living in the 16th century. Don't infuriate your boss, particularly when he happens to be a bishop.

In fairness the Bishop of Rochester had every right to be furious. We will never know why Richard Roose, a sixteen year old cook responsible for feeding the Bishop's household, decided to poison their food. A grudge perhaps, but whatever the reason the result was that two members of staff died and over a dozen were taken ill. Men of the cloth all those years ago were not known for their mercy but the Bishop invoked a bizarre and macabre sense of justice by sending his cook off to Smithfield to be boiled alive. A fire was lit under the cauldron as a large crowd watched the young man undergo an excruciating death that took a full two hours before he was finally silent. Ten years later Margaret Davy was to suffer the same fate.

By the beginning of the 18th century the aristocracy and the land-owning squirearchy were feeling under threat from what they reckoned to be a sullen and potentially riotous working population. This resulted in the passing of the Waltham Black Act of 1723, which subsequently became known as 'The Bloody Code'. This led to an extension of the crimes liable to capital punishment in excess of two hundred. Many were for minor offences such as cutting down a tree or being found at night with a blacked out face. Now being hanged for a sheep rather than a lamb had a real resonance. For landowners poaching was the ultimate sin.

Being a woman did not allow you to evade the reach of the law. By 1800 over one thousand five hundred women had been condemned to death, although most were reprieved, leaving about three hundred and fifty mounting the gallows steps. Of these about thirty were burnt at the stake, the rest hanged. Most were committed for crimes against property, although murder was on the mind of almost two hundred of these ladies. By the mid-18th century over one thousand people were being sentenced to death, although increasingly many were being reprieved to suffer in other ways.

Ridicule as well as retribution was a powerful weapon in an attempt to reduce crime. To be placed in the stocks or worse still the pillory was to face total humiliation and possibly serious injury. Our usual understanding is to link the two but they were very different, albeit a horrible experience for all who were sentenced. The stocks were reckoned to be a lesser form of corporal punishment. The offender had their feet placed through two holes whilst being attached to a wooden board. The stocks were usually placed at busy crossroads or in a prominent square in order to attract the largest crowds. The stocks were normally reserved for minor offences where the captive was subjected to verbal abuse as well as being pelted with rotten vegetables or animal excrement, but rarely missiles that would cause serious injury. This was not true of the pillory as generally the culprit on view would have seriously offended public opinion and deserved punishment.

The pillory consisted of a wooden post and frame fixed onto a platform that stood several feet off the ground. There were holes just big enough for the head and hands to be held securely. Being forced to bend forward with just the head and hands showing was extremely uncomfortable as the captive was normally required to stay for several hours. The raised platform created a feeling of theatre and a large placard detailed the sins of the person restrained. Those in the pillory normally attracted real public anger or disgust, bringing out the worst of those attending. Added to rotten vegetables were mud, dead animals and human excrement. Those causing the greatest anger also became like a human coconut shy with pebbles and stones being hurled. Men had hair and beards shaved off whilst the most reviled women had their heads completely shaved. It was a woman known as Mother Clap who seemingly enraged a crowd to shocking violence. She was accused of keeping a number of male brothels known commonly as 'molly houses'. She endured a seemingly endless barrage of missiles, the result of which she died several days later.

In the boardrooms of central London earnest advertising executives endlessly discuss branding. For them it is about bringing their products to the public's notice. Earlier in our history branding had an altogether more sinister connotation. Here was yet another way for the authorities to heap further pain and humiliation on the criminal class. This medieval practice continued in various forms until the 19th century. Here was a punishment that literally marked a person for life and was often administered for what we would term minor offences. Those claiming benefit of clergy were only branded on the thumb but more serious offenders could be branded on the cheek. Astonishingly the punishment was often carried out in court. Amid the screams the brander would call 'A fair mark, my lord' and justice was done and seen to be done.

Each letter made indicated the offence. 'V' for vagrant, 'T' for thief. The practice was finally abolished in the early 19th century, but continued being used in the army for years to come. The marking was usually restricted to deserters who were branded under their armpit. It is difficult to judge whether all these terrible punishments really did reduce crime, but it certainly did not encourage it.

Having been convicted and sentenced to a term in prison, there was now a new form of torture to endure. Sir William Cubitt was outraged by the amount of indolence he observed with prisoners lounging about with nothing to occupy them. Despite the dreadful conditions they had to endure he wanted to see them set to work. Enter the treadmill or treadwheel, sometimes referred to as the never ending staircase. This involved steps that were set into two large wheels which drove a shaft that could be used for a variety of purposes, including pumping water or milling corn. This really was to be hard labour as prisoners were worked to exhaustion.

From 1865 the Prison Act decreed that all male prisoners aged sixteen and over had to serve at least three months doing hard labour. By the end of the 19th century there were about forty treadmills in use in English prisons. As ever London was to the fore, anxious to set the tone for the rest of the country, with the first treadmill being introduced at Brixton prison in 1824. The notoriously harsh conditions at Coldbath Fields prison required inmates to complete a six hour shift reducing them to a state of collapse. A trend for self harm was established as inmates sought excuses to avoid being put on the treadmill.

The treadmill most popular in British prisons consisted of a long wooden cylinder with metal framing. There were wooden steps on the outside of the cylinder, each about eight inches in height. Facing a wall as the prisoner put his feet on the step, it depressed the wheel and he was forced to move onto the step above, creating the never ending staircase. To think today people willingly go to gyms to work on a modern day version in an attempt to get fit. Back to our prison version, there were individual cubicles separated by wooden partitions, so for six hours not speaking and only seeing the wall in front of them they completed this soul breaking task. Finally in 1902 the use of the treadmill was abolished as Britain felt its way gradually to a more humane society.

Ever since Elizabethan times people have been banished or deported from our shores. Others have decided to leave of their own volition to avoid arrest or disgrace, but it took the arrival of the industrial revolution for the government to institute a system of transportation to the colonies. The Transportation Act of 1717 pointed the way with a system of transporting convicts who might otherwise clog up our prisons. Whilst industry brought great wealth to the city it also witnessed a massive crime wave. With conditions in the slums so dire many were forced to rely on crime in order to feed themselves. Initially several thousand prisoners were packed off to America, but this source of disposing of our criminal class was cut off by the arrival of the American revolution against the British. Something had to be done and the solution was prompted by Captain

Cook's discovery of Botany Bay in Australia, known then as simply New South Wales. In May 1787 the first convoy set sail to the furthest known part of the world. To an uncharted territory and an unknown future. It was so frightening for some that they chose death rather than transportation. Nonetheless, Prime Minister Pitt was convinced that transportation would eventually cleanse Britain of its criminal class.

Old hulks lined the River Thames in preparation for the dreadful journey which was to take over six months. On board one of those first to sail was nine year old John Hudson and an eighty-two year old woman who had been charged with larceny. This odd couple were joined by over seven hundred prisoners and two hundred crew. Conditions were dire with the prisoners living cheek by jowl. Food was sparse and illness claimed several lives. The journey for women was horrendous as they were used and abused by the crew, even being sold to other shipmates.

The eleven 'hell ships' made their way slowly to a frightening unknown future. Although many of the prisoners were initially told 'You will be transported across the seas for the term of your natural life', in effect most saw their terms reduced to seven or fourteen years, although few would ever have enough money to return. Gradually settlements were set up and many subsequent arrivals were set to work on government projects or farms. The government advertised for volunteers to join the convicts to develop the land without much success, so this was left to the prisoners who had completed their sentences. The number of prisoners being deported to Australia increased dramatically after the ending of the Napoleonic war and more ships being made available. By 1833 over thirty ships made the journey, taking over seven thousand prisoners. The following year Tasmania witnessed the opening of the first prison camp for youngsters aged between nine and eighteen, and segregated from adults. By the mid 19th century transportation was slowing. It was the Australian gold rush that led to thousands of voluntary immigrants arriving. By 1868 the last transportation boat of prisoners had arrived in Western Australia. Between 1788 and 1868 over one hundred and sixty thousand prisoners had been transported to Australia including twenty four thousand women. The scheme did nothing to reduce the amount of crime in Britain but it did give these new Australian subjects a chance to forge an exciting new life in an expanding country. Who was it that eventually had the last laugh? Meanwhile the prisons in London continued to fill. Its citizens continued to break the law with undimmed enthusiasm.

Chapter 6

Banged Up

To be 'in clink' has become an almost generic term for being in prison. How strange this name has lived long after closing its gates over two hundred years ago. Other well known phrases like 'as black as Newgate's knocker' transport us back to the murky world of filthy fetid gaols scattered around London. The need to control a potentially rebellious population continued. There is some dispute regarding which was the oldest prison in the capital. A single lock up cell can be attributed to the clink back in the 9th century, but the Tower of London should perhaps claim the title. In 1101 Ranulf Flambard, the Bishop of Durham, became the first recorded prisoner for selling benefices.

The building of the Tower of London was a statement by King William of his power over the local population. It was built on the site of a previous fortress that was destroyed by a great fire in 1077. The project took twenty years to complete. The White Tower soared some ninety feet skywards and was built with stone imported from Normandy, underlining the French power and influence. Today after a thousand years it remains one of London's biggest tourist attractions. Virtually every child living in the London area has been taken on a guided trip to the Tower, sparking for many an on-going interest in history and trying to imagine what it was like to be incarcerated, or worse being led out for execution.

Today the Tower seems sanitised but in previous centuries to be sent there would have been truly frightening. It certainly did not appear to inhibit the Bishop of Durham too much for as well as being the first prisoner he was also the first to escape. He managed to get his guards hopelessly drunk before climbing out of a window and reaching the ground safely with the use of a rope. So began a constant stream of prisoners charged with every shade of offence. Hitler's deputy Rudolf Hess was held in the tower for four days, having flown into Scotland on an ill conceived peace mission. Treason looms large in the Tower's history. with eleven German spies being shot there in the Second World War.

Suspicion of foreigners or those of different faiths was underlined as early as the thirteenth century, when some six hundred Jews were detained for clipping gold coins. Of these almost half were executed. Within fifty years there was a robbery at Westminster Abbey with suspicion pointed at members of the clergy, several of whom were held in the Tower, although it was Miles Pudlicote, the Keeper of the Royal Palace, who paid the ultimate price. Later Tower Hill was designated as the official site for beheadings, with Sir Simon de Burley setting a precedent for many to come.

Time now for a little torture to be added to the fear of those sent to the Tower. The dreadful inducement of the rack led to many choosing death rather than incremental pain as the rack was tightened ever further. In 1471 Henry VI was murdered in the Wakefield Tower whilst praying. So was set in train a succession of royals to meet their death in the ancient Tower. The bodies thought to be the young sons of King Edward and Elizabeth Woodville were discovered in 1674. The skeletons of twelve year old Edward and Richard, his nine year old brother, were found in a wooden box by workmen under a staircase leading to the chapel in the White Tower. On the instructions of King Charles II the bones were interred in Westminster Abbey. There they remained until 1933 when scientific examination was carried out in an attempt to settle the mystery of the murdered princes. Their findings that these were those of the remains of the princes is still disputed by some. Today who would like to see a re-examination using the latest DNA techniques. Until this happens the mystery remains. London only gives up its secrets grudgingly.

Famously it was during the reign of Henry VIII that witnessed an increase in torture being used to extract confessions. It is difficult for us today to get into the minds of our ancestors who imposed such horrific punishments, and yet must have lived in fear that it may be their turn next. Anne Boleyn, who had besotted the King for a time, became the most famous victim of Henry's wrath. Accused of having an adulterous affair with her own brother (a convenient pretext), she joined a growing list of famous individuals put to death at the Tower. She was joined later by Thomas Cromwell, formerly the King's most powerful minister. Infidelity was also the excuse for beheading Henry VIII's fifth wife, Catherine Howard. Henry's decision to break away from Rome continued to have grave and long standing implications. Religion had spawned a toxic culture. Many rightly lived in fear that to be close to the centre of power was dangerous.

Whilst the Tower was in essence just a prison, the blood-letting of England's aristocracy continued into the reign of the boy King Edward VI, and whilst later the virgin Queen Elizabeth brought a sense of stability for the country, the executioner continued to be kept busy. In among all the blood-letting a couple of famous names did survive their ordeal in the Tower and were released. In 1592 Sir Walter Raleigh spent a few uncomfortable days in the Tower for seducing one of the Queen's ladies in waiting. Over a century later the diarist Samuel Pepys was sent briefly to the Tower, accused by the 'Popish Plotter' Titus Oates of passing naval secrets to the French. He was eventually released to continue his career. The botched execution of King Charles I and the arrival of Oliver Cromwell heralded another bloody lurch in British history.

Having served as a prison for over eight hundred years the Tower of London was about to enter a less dramatic phase of its existence, but not before it had a few more shocks to deliver. On 31st January 1941 a German plane took off from Schiphol airport in Holland. On board was another colourful character soon to be added to the long list associated forever with the Tower.

Josef Jakobs was born in Luxembourg in the last years of the nineteenth century. As a young man he saw service in the German infantry where subsequently he rose to the rank of Lieutenant. Drafted into the Wehrmacht in 1940, he was again promoted, until it was discovered that he had served a term in jail in Switzerland for selling counterfeit gold. Reduced to the ranks, he was obliged to join the Meteorological Service before serving in the Abwehr, the intelligence arm of the German army. In many ways he fitted the role of a potential spy, a chancer, someone prepared to take risks to achieve his goal. So it was that Josef descended upon an unsuspecting British public. Unfortunately for him his parachuting skills rather let him down with a bump, resulting in a broken ankle. He had landed in Ramsey in Huntingdonshire (now part of Cambridgeshire). Stumbling across uneven fields, his lack of mobility was obviously causing problems. Why he fired a shot from his pistol is unclear, but it drew attention to himself and after two farm labourers reported into the local home guard he was promptly caught and taken to the local police station. Vitally he was still wearing his flying jacket, together with five hundred pounds in currency plus forged papers. Worse still he was also in possession of a radio transmitter. Supposedly he was to make contact with a German singer and actress living in Birmingham. He claimed her acting ability had stretched to a believable brummie accent. Named as Clara Bauerle, she was never located at the time, although later it was claimed she had died in Berlin in 1942.

Jakobs must have realised that he was in big trouble, but after a visit to hospital and his ankle was set he was transported to London. Here he underwent a court martial before a military tribunal held at the Duke of York's headquarters in fashionable Chelsea. It appears a double agent had tipped off MI5 about Jakobs' plan. The hearing lasted barely two days before Jakobs was found guilty and sentenced to death. It was at the rifle range that witnessed the last execution to take place at the Tower of London on August 15th 1941. At last the blood-letting was over, but the Tower had one more bizarre event to record before becoming mainly a tourist attraction. In 1952 Ronnie and Reggie Kray (more of them later) became the last prisoners to be detained in the Tower for refusing to enlist for National Service. They only spent a few days banged up in the Tower, but it does underline that truth is often stranger than fiction.

Where the Old Bailey stands today had been the site of a prison since the twelfth century. A more substantial prison had subsequently been erected in 1423 with money left by the Lord Mayor of London, Richard Whittington. The building became known as 'The Whit'. From the start the prison gained a reputation for violence and disorder. The jailers supplemented their earnings by allowing favours for those who could pay. Meanwhile it was reported that those detained for their religious beliefs 'raved amidst their shackles'.

It was in the sixteenth century that the legend of 'the black dog' emerged. This ghostly figure prompted many interpretations, the most common being that it was a phantom created by the wickedness of the jailers. The filthy rotting prison was swept away by the ravages of the Great Fire of London in 1666. Here was an opportunity to build a new modern jail. The building work took six years but in 1672 the rather grand exterior hid from public view what lay inside. By 1719 it was described as 'a place of calamity….a habitation of misery…a bottomless pit of violence'.

Newgate stood five storeys in height and divided to take prisoners of varying categories. A welcoming jailer made sure the new inmates were 'fettered and ironed' before they were despatched to their appropriate cell or dungeon. On the left of the entrance was the Keeper's House, below which was the 'hold' where the condemned awaited their trip to Tyburn. For the rest they were cast into crowded cells where it was difficult to tell if it was day or night. The smell was overwhelming, with an open sewer running through the middle causing a stench 'that entered every corner'. Hooks and chains were fastened to the floor to restrain the 'stubborn and unruly'. The stench from the prison was so bad that it affected the whole neighbourhood. It was unwise to walk close to the prison as chamber pots were emptied into the street below, whilst prisoners urinated out of windows. Prisoners who could pay their jailers were allowed to drink themselves insensible and for a time unaware of their dire surroundings. Gin was made from a still in Newgate. A deadly brew known as 'kill – grief or cock-my –gap'.

Whilst Newgate was considered to be our equivalent of a maximum security unit, escape was not impossible. The most notorious of all the escapees was Jack Sheppard. He was born in Spitalfields in 1702 before being sent to the Bishopsgate workhouse. His first spell in prison was in 1724 when he was locked up in the St. Giles Roundhouse. Within a few hours he was free. Had up weeks later for theft, he was sent to the new prison in Clerkenwell. Despite being pinioned he cut through his chains and then bored his way to freedom. Others escaped from Newgate through the sewers, with a couple drowning having been overcome with the stench.

Sheppard may have been a great escapologist, but a rather average robber and thief as he was arrested regularly. Having escaped the death cell already he was again sent to Newgate where he was double-fettered to the floor. He was now something of a celebrity and people paid to come and see him. A file was found on him and he was transferred to 'the stone castle' on the fifth floor. Astonishingly, despite regular visits from his jailers, he managed to escape. Using a nail, he released his irons and unlocked four locked and bolted doors. Finding himself on the roof, he slid down the outer wall with the help of a blanket which he spiked to the wall. In the following days he carried out a series of robberies, making enough to buy a fine suit of clothes and even a carriage for him to be driven past the prison that he had just escaped from, thus in a very theatrical way 'cocking a snook' at authority. Inevitably he was arrested again. Now his fame was such that he allowed the painter James Thornhill time to paint his portrait whilst still in prison. Captured in chalk and pencil, he gazes towards a small barred window of his cell. A small figure with cropped hair, he looks rather wistful, as well he might be for his days were numbered. Although hardly a conventional hero, he never hurt anyone in his constant thieving and robberies. Nonetheless, his escapes from Newgate and other prisons were marvelled by many at the time. There were wild rumours that Sheppard would attempt to escape somewhere along Oxford Street on his way to Tyburn. He was sure the crowd would help him once he leapt from the cart. It was true he had managed to conceal a small penknife, but it was spotted as he tried surreptitiously to loosen his chains. Instead he had to settle for a final drink at a tavern where the John Lewis store in Oxford Street stands today. The cart continued its way through the thronged crowds. Sheppard refused to make the traditional final address, asking instead people should buy the pamphlet describing his life and incredible escapes. There was chaos at the execution as the crowd tried to touch him even after he had stopped convulsing. Many thought touching a condemned body had healing powers. There were fights as various factions tried to claim the corpse but it is said that he was finally buried at St. Martins in the Fields, some claiming he was laid to rest clutching two tarnished silver spoons.

The drama surrounding Newgate continued with the burning down of the prison during the Gordon riots (more of which later). Rebuilt within three years the new prison was initially an improvement on what had stood before. With executions no longer taking place at Tyburn from 1783, hangings were now to be conducted in the grounds of the new prison. The dire conditions at Newgate did not take long to reappear. It was described as having 'a haunted and brooding air'. The influence of Elizabeth Fry did prompt some improvement in conditions in 1817. Within a few years the Inspector of Prisons was reporting on the misery and squalor witnessed. In 1859 Newgate was redesigned with a number of individual cells being introduced. For a time it became something of a tourist attraction with it being open to the public for three hours on Wednesdays and Thursdays. Sightseers could see casts of notorious criminals and the chains used to restrain them, some even asking to be locked in the condemned cell for a few minutes.

It was time to move on. The last execution took place in 1902 just shortly before demolition started. Newgate had gone, leaving behind its ghosts, tales, poems and songs dedicated to its inglorious history. Gradually, falteringly a more humane penal system was starting to evolve.

At the age of twelve the novelist Charles Dickens witnessed his father being sent off to jail for a debt of forty pounds he had incurred and was unable to pay back. This event had a profound effect on him and his writing. Marshalsea prison was situated in Southwark, not far from London Bridge. It had been a prison for centuries, but in Victorian London it mainly housed debtors. Many were left languishing until friends or family could pay the debt and obtain release. Essentially if the debt was not paid the prisoner had to remain, and whilst conditions were not as bad as in Newgate, many died whilst there through lack of food or due to the unbearable heat during a hot summer.

Marshalsea and Victorian prisons were a recurring theme for Dickens, particularly in 'Pickwick Papers' and 'Little Dorrit'. He also mentions being drawn by the 'looming gatehouse of the dark prison' that was Newgate. Today London still locks up its criminals, many in overcrowded prisons built during the reign of Queen Victoria. Even being locked up in a new-ish establishment like Belmarsh must be tough, but it is a far cry from the clink in the twelfth century, or worse the barbarity of eighteenth century Newgate. Until fairly recently cruelty appeared deeply embedded in London life. To visit a mental hospital (lunatic asylum), to point and taunt for an afternoon's entertainment seems astonishing to us now, but were these people really cruel or just curious?

Chapter 7

Freak Shows

It is often said that you have to be slightly mad to live in London. In doing so you become a bit player, an extra in what is essentially a gigantic film set. People everywhere, some striving just to survive, others confident of advancement, many seeking to make their fortune and a few reaching that elusive star of fame. All this effort takes its toll. It is reckoned that mental illness stalks the city more so than anywhere else in the country, as it has always done.

In 1247 the Priory of St. Mary of Bethlehem was opened, later to become known as the Bethlem Royal Hospital. It was to help 'those who were inflicted with insanity' and was the first mental hospital in all of Britain. Thus started the association of madness with London. Sir Thomas More questioned whether or not the whole city was not a madhouse.

By the beginning of the fifteenth century a small number of patients were supervised by a master, his wife and a few servants, but the number of inmates grew steadily with the hospital now being referred to as 'Bedlam'. It was a refuge for those who had 'fallen out of their wit'. Some refuge for the inmates who were often kept in chains and regularly whipped to purge their madness. A few were allowed to leave 'the madman's pound' to wander the streets. They were obliged to wear a badge indicating their status (shades of 1930s Germany). These lost souls were known as 'God's minstrels'. Their antics drew pity and scorn in equal measure, with little understanding in the public of mental illness.

In the sixteenth century Bedlam was situated alongside Bishopsgate. A contemporary account describes walking through a gate into a courtyard with a number of stone buildings, a church and a garden. Whilst there remained under fifty patients they were living in very crowded conditions. The noise they made was frightening to passers-by. Amidst the rattling of chains some were screeching, others swearing and crying. There were roars of frustration and defiance which helped mask the pathetic jabbering of those who had given up all hope. A century later Bedlam remained the only hospital for lunatics.

Most inmates were recorded as being either vagrants or servants, but there was a sprinkling of those described as 'gentlemen'. Certainly Lady Eleanor Davies was unusual because of her noble background, and also at the time the hospital housed very few women. Lady Eleanor consistently proclaimed she was a prophet and in deference to her background and probably because her relatives were paying for her stay, she lived in the Steward's house. Despite enjoying this greater comfort she described Bedlam as a living hell, being abused by her captives when they were drunk.

Bedlam became a source of gossip and public discussion, leading it to be featured in a number of plays performed at the beginning of the seventeenth century. Thomas Dekker's drama 'The Honest Whore' was the first to feature imagined scenes from within Bedlam. The 'Duchess of Malfi' and John Fletcher's 'The Pilgrim' were also centred on problems with mental health.

The old madhouse had been steadily falling into disrepair. Civic pride was bruised and it was decided in 1673 that a new modern hospital should be built in Moorfields. The contrast was staggering when two years later an extraordinary building likened to the Tuileries in Paris was opened. Designed by Robert Hooke, it was described as the only palace in London. John Evelyn said the building was very beautiful but its exterior hid the starkness and squalor of the interior. The entry gate contained memorable sculptures of two semi-naked bald figures, the one representing 'raving madness' and the other 'melancholy madness'.

The link between London and live theatre was extended with the introduction of spectators paying a small entrance fee to come and observe the behaviour of the inmates. Now as well as public executions it was possible to abuse and shout insults at these lunatics. There was little understanding of mental illness, and surrounded every day by cruelty the public had become immune and few saw the harm in gawping at these poor demented souls. It was not just the ordinary citizen who was drawn to this new attraction. William Hogarth in one of a series of paintings recording 'A Rake's Progress' captures fashionable ladies witnessing the mayhem that was Bedlam. One holds a fan presumably trying to lessen the stink they were encountering. Bedlam has become a generic term for turmoil and chaos and this is what Hogarth successfully created in his epic painting. Some felt that living conditions in large parts of London were so bad that the madness of Moorfields had spread like an infectious disease across the city.

Once again despite its grandiose facade, Bedlam was now filthy and a blot on the greatest capital in the world. It was time for change. Visits to gawp at the inmates were banned in 1770 and a more enlightened approach was gradually introduced. Bedlam was now an eyesore for a part of London that was becoming more fashionable and in 1815 the hospital was moved south of the river to Southwark. Here its third incarnation was created, not as grand as its predecessor, but fitting comfortably into an area that had traditionally been home to a number of prisons. The hospital featured a grand dome and a portico dominated by soaring columns. The original sculptures from the Moorfields building were preserved and had a prominent place in the entrance hall. Although the treatment of patients was not as barbaric as previously, much still revolved around restraint. It took two critical inquiries that eventually led to a more lenient regime in the mid-nineteenth century. Keeping inmates busy and giving them jobs to do was thought to help, whilst new drugs were also starting to be administered. Having their own water supply protected staff and inmates from cholera, which was sweeping through London.

By now there was a virtual epidemic of mental illness being recorded in London, which led to the building of other mental hospitals. These asylums were normally built outside and yet within easy reach of the capital. They were vast gloomy buildings, but at least away from the noise and chaos. Although surrounded by high walls to avoid escape, they did have extensive grounds and trusted patients were allowed to wander and hopefully be calmed by the singing of birds and the well tended gardens. Conditions were still grim compared to those of today, but the medical profession was now showing a real interest in mental health and what could be done to improve it. That search continues as the stress of modern life creates another generation in need of help.

London and violence have long been locked in an uncomfortable embrace, which continues today. The shout 'a ring, a ring' would quickly see a crowd gather whilst two men stripped to the waist to settle some perceived insult. Bets would be placed as the men set to until a bloodied but triumphant winner emerged. With the pillory and public executions being attended by vast braying crowds, the need to witness pain and suffering seems weird and strange to us. What was it that so attracted citizens of every class? Perhaps like children who are abused becoming abusers themselves. Whatever the cause, pain and humiliation suffered was multiplied by the baiting of animals. Regularly witnessing violence in everyday life appeared to increase the need or at least give passive agreement to the most horrendous cruelty.

For centuries holidays or holy-days offered Londoners the excuse to indulge in 'violent delights'. A love for jousting and archery drew large crowds. An early form of all-in football descended into mass brawls. Moving on there were cock-fights to enjoy where hefty bets were placed on the outcome. Great care was given to those events drawing the greatest crowds, the preamble adding to the anticipation. Each bird was weighed to avoid a mismatch. Height was also important, together with their wings and tails being clipped. The cocks did not require much goading as the birds soon threw themselves at each other as the crowd screamed their support, and as wagers were won and lost, fights would break out.

Queen Elizabeth I was said to enjoy the spectacle and it is certain that members of her court were enthusiastic followers. There was an upmarket venue in London known as 'The Royal Cockpit'. It was situated in central London between Birdcage Walk and Queen Street. This was built in the eighteenth century and the price of entry ensured an upper class clientele. Here huge sums were wagered and whilst cheered on enthusiastically there was seldom any trouble as bets were cashed in.

Whilst criticised by an increasing number who found the spectacle demeaning and cruel, there were even crueller events taking place across London. Bankside had been the traditional home for bear-baiting. There was a pause when it was banned by Cromwell (as were most forms of entertainment). For a period hare-coursing was the only form of sport involving dogs allowed. The arrival of the Restoration again saw the return of the Bankside Bear Garden. The bears were given pet names but their treatment and torment is truly barbaric to modern eyes. Normally the chained bear was set upon by bulldogs or mastiffs, but a report from the seventeenth century pictures an event painful for us to comprehend. The visitor to Bankside tells us that a chained blind bear was set upon by six men armed with horse whips. The bear is defenceless, although he does strike out, knocking a tormentor to the ground if he comes too close. He manages to catch a whip and breaks it to a background of the crowd baying for blood.

Visiting foreigners were appalled by the violence and barbarous cruelty of Londoners. Fights between children were watched and encouraged by their parents as a ring is formed.

Still it was animals that bore the brunt of this strange desire to watch helpless creatures tortured to death. Even on the hunting field horses were frequently ridden to near exhaustion despite being generally highly prized, spruced and well cared for. This could not be said of a giant mount owned by the Earl of Rochester. In 1675 a savage horse he owned had seemingly killed a number of other horses he owned together with some cattle. It had to go. Standing a giant nineteen hands, he sold it to the Marquess of Dorchester but there was no improvement in its behaviour, injuring his groom and eventually sold onto a brewer. Set to work hauling beer barrels, it started attacking people in the street. It really was a rogue, possibly due to the treatment it had received. Rather than put it down it was sold on to be baited. Such a huge and wild beast would surely draw in the crowds.

Expectations were high. The Ambassador for Morocco and a host of the nobility were invited to attend at the Hope Theatre, which had been converted to host baiting events. Savage dogs normally took little time to take down a horse no matter how fierce. Not this time. The initial dogs sent in were either killed or maimed. Others followed with the same result. It was decided to remove the horse, a rare winner indeed. The crowd threatened to riot, demanding the baiting to continue. Eventually it took a sword to complete a sordid finale.

By the turn of the eighteenth century baiting had migrated to Hockley in the Hole in Clerkenwell. This was the centre for the breeding of bull terriers and therefore a natural centre for baiting, although the call for its abolition was growing. There appears to have been much pride attached to local dogs. To prove this a match was arranged where two dogs from Newgate market were put against a single fierce animal representing the pride of Clerkenwell. Such contests drew large raucous crowds urging their favourites on as they ripped into each other. For a time Hockley in the Hole was also the centre for bull-baiting before moving to Spitalfields, caused by the continued development of the Fleet. The bulls being baited were driven to rage by having fireworks attached to their backs. There was also bull-baiting held regularly in Bethnal Green and at the Adam and Eve Inn in Tottenham Court Road. It was here a horse bought at great expense from Arabia was worried to death by dogs. The enclosure was packed with people prepared to pay half a guinea to gain entry. Today most of us (but probably not all) struggle to understand how reasonable people could find such brutality entertaining, but attitudes were changing.

The artist William Hogarth again came to the fore campaigning against the cruelty inflicted on animals, 'the very sight of which renders the streets of our metropolis so distressing to every feeling mind'. His paintings were influential in framing public opinion and were so popular because they were reproduced as prints which were widely available. His 'Four stages of cruelty' monitored the gradual downfall of Tom Nero. In the first work Tom, a charity boy from St. Giles, is pictured torturing a dog, whilst a friend pleads with him to stop. Tom's decline eventually leads to the gallows. All Hogarth's works carried a strong moral tone which contributed much needed changes across society.

Hockley in the Hole was not quite done with yet. New attractions included women pitted against men. The ladies tore at their opponents, ripping at their faces with long nails to the taunts and cheers of the crowd. Women also fought against each other boxing or wrestling, often only half dressed, adding to the attraction.

The politician Richard Martin was at the forefront of heightening public awareness of animal rights. In 1822 the Act to prevent the cruel and improper treatment of cattle was introduced to Parliament and passed into law. It was Martin who first brought a costermonger to trial for abusing a donkey. The animal was fetched into court to show the extent of the injuries inflicted, resulting in William Burns being the first person to be convicted of cruelty to animals. Finally in 1835 Parliament passed an Act prohibiting the baiting of animals, although this only caused it to go underground, even continuing in isolated events today.

Chapter 8

Abolition

In the eighteenth century slavery was added to the cocktail of violence and humiliation that dominated London life. Slavery had been present in Britain since Roman times and it was the Greek philosopher Aristotle who described them as 'only a living tool' to be worked and abused as their master saw fit. In Anglo-Saxon Britain a slave woman found to be stealing could be savagely whipped or even burnt to death. In this case eighty other slave women were instructed to bring one log each to form the pyre. Anglo-Saxon law required savage punishment, with men stealing from their master being stoned to death, with again eighty slaves required to bring one stone each to be hurled at the captive.

Seemingly the further we go back in time the worse the punishment, but the treatment of black slaves from the West Indies registered a new low and still inflames opinions. John Hawkins is reckoned to be the first English exponent of the Atlantic slave trade. Initially it is thought that Queen Elizabeth I did not approve of the dealing and selling of human beings, but her attitude changed when she realised the potential for making huge profits from the trade. Enter John Hawkins, the son of a wealthy family of shipbuilders. His portrait shows a rather mean faced man with shifty cold eyes. He was born in the naval port town of Plymouth in 1532. His cousin Francis Drake was brought up in the same house and the two men were destined to be seafarers. By the age of twenty Hawkins had killed a local man and had to rely on his father to obtain a Royal Pardon.

In his late twenties he moved to London where he shrewdly married Katherine Gonson, the daughter of a leading Royal Navy administrator. Hawkins had already sailed to Brazil. He made voyages to the Canary Islands and it was here that he learnt of a developing Atlantic slave trade. Natives were captured off the coast of Guinea and were sold to the Spanish

Caribbean colonies. He set sail in 1562 with three ships on the perilous journey to the African coast, eventually arriving in Sierra Leone. He was reported to have captured about three hundred poor wretches and it is likely this was achieved with the help of local people. He journeyed on to the Caribbean and successfully sold the slaves on. The syndicate he had formed to finance the trip would have been delighted with the profit made. His escapade did not go unnoticed and he was awarded his own coat of arms, which in future was to be displayed on his enslaved men. He had created a fine business in the prospect of selling slaves and returning to England with his ships loaded with rare goods to be sold on.

The Queen's principles soon evaporated when she realised the profits to be made. Hawkins's second trip was backed by investors from her court. Then as now greed and profit created a heady mix that few resisted. The investors included Robert Dudley, Earl of Leicester, and Henry Cecil, the first Baron Burghley. Hawkins was allowed to charter one of the Queen's ships proudly bearing the Royal Standard. It accompanied the other ships that set sail from Plymouth in October 1564. Despite various problems they encountered it was estimated that the trip showed a sixty percent profit for the investors. On the Queen's instructions it was now left to others to take on the mantle as she banned Hawkins from taking to sea. Sir John Lovell's trip departing in 1566 hit trouble despite him capturing three slave ships through piracy. Travelling to the Spanish West Indies, he failed to sell his slaves on and was forced to abandon them onshore. Lovell had failed and was open to much criticism, particularly from Hawkins.

John Hawkins was a persuasive man and he obtained permission from the Queen to make a third trip. He set sail again from Plymouth in October 1567. He recruited the King of Sierra Leone to forcibly capture around five hundred men. Having sailed across the Atlantic, he sold two batches of the poor slaves, but at Rio de la Hacha the Spanish governor refused him permission to trade, resulting in a battle between the English privateers and Spanish naval ships. He was constantly harassed and ultimately defeated, eventually returning with only one ship and a severely depleted crew.

By now a few black slaves had arrived in London and so started a series of myths that was to poison the minds of the local population. A doubt about all foreigners deepened into fear. Black equated to darkness and visible difference. They were heathens. Did they have a soul? Surely they were dangerous and sexually frightening. The blackness of their skin surely made them somehow less than human. Although tiny in number, they prompted unease as well as curiosity. A letter from the Queen was sent to local authorities stating that there were already too many black moors in the country and so was set in trail the centuries long prejudice.

Tea parties were now all the rage in fashionable London salons dominated by the adding of a couple of teaspoons of sugar. Perhaps the irony eluded those ladies who were now becoming more vocal in the abolitionist cause. Helping to stop slavery was all well and good but it was also important to be at the cutting edge of the latest fad in town.

It is William Wilberforce who most people today associate with the abolition of slavery and rightly so, but his connection with Thomas Clarkson was vital. Clarkson was born in 1760 in Wisbech in Cambridgeshire, just months after Wilberforce. It was as if their paths were destined to merge. Clarkson was the son of a cleric and from an early age showed great academic promise. Moving from the local grammar school where his father was headmaster at the age of fifteen, he went on to St. Paul's School in London where he excelled. In 1780 he went up to Cambridge where his academic reputation soared. Slavery had already caught his attention and writing in Latin his essay on the subject won him the Cambridge competition prize. Having already achieved a BA degree, he became the first student to win the MA competition as well. At the time of writing his essay Clarkson knew very little about slavery, but his interest was sparked. The legend goes that he got off the horse he was riding down to London and sitting on the roadside, decided that someone had to mount opposition to this evil trade. From this moment he devoted most of his life to abolition. It became an all encompassing obsession.

On arrival in London he published his original essay translated into English. It received wide coverage and hit a nerve with many like minded people, including James Ramsay and Granville Sharp. They had also written pamphlets urging abolition. Having formed the Committee for

Abolition of the African slave trade, Clarkson took it upon himself to find out more first hand. He travelled to Bristol and Liverpool where he was not welcomed, indeed threatened by some of those benefitting from their involvement. Some things never change and then as now for many money was their god. People were just pawns in their game of chance. Back in London Clarkson and his committee arranged for the MP William Wilberforce to take the campaign to Parliament. Resulting from this there was a meeting of the Privy Council to take evidence. With Clarkson continuing to gather evidence, it was William Wilberforce who was making the case for abolition in Parliament. The cooperation between the two men was to prove vital in the eventual success of the campaign.

William Wilberforce was born in Hull in 1760. He also went up to Cambridge and it was whilst there that he meet the future Prime Minister William Pitt the Younger. He came from a prosperous family, and with influential connections he was elected as member for Kingston on Hull at the age of twenty one. As a young man he was considered to be something of a rake living a dissolute life. It appears he experienced a dramatic change and by 1790 had become an evangelical Christian. His interests initially centred on social reform and the improvement in conditions in factories and mills. He was noted to possess great charm and eloquence, but it took his meeting with Thomas Clarkson to fire his desire to make a lasting contribution to the abolition of the slave trade. His considerable wealth helped him gain the ear of those close to the centre of power, whilst always being influenced by his Christian faith.

Working closely with Clarkson now, he absorbed all the dreadful evidence presented to him and dedicated the rest of his life to the cause. By 1799 he had made preparations to present his Abolition Bill to the House of Commons. His speech was much praised and the Star reported that merchants from Liverpool hung their heads in sorrow, for in the paper's words 'for the African occupation of bolts and chains were no more'. Actually they had no need to worry, at least in the short term, as delaying tactics were now employed. More evidence was required. Those with a vested interest were not about to give up their lucrative trade without a fight. By January 1790 it was judged that the whole question of abolition was taking up too much Parliamentry time and further discussion was kicked into the long grass. Despite his constant work, by 1791 the mood against abolition had hardened. When the House divided the Bill it was defeated by seventy-five votes. The following year Wilberforce tried again. This time it was passed but only by inserting a 'gradual' move towards abolition. Further delays as again more evidence was demanded. Gradual abolition equated to no abolition and the traders, merchants and bankers continued to rake in the money, giving little or no thought to the welfare of the indentured slaves.

The outbreak of the war with France saw the interest of the public decline further. Wilberforce continued to make impassioned speeches but now they were falling on deaf ears. As the century drew to a close Wilberforce wrote a book on theology and found time to marry Barbara Ann Spooner. Despite his marriage, the early years of a new century saw many of his former admirers withdrawing their support. He doggedly continued presenting his Bill to the House of Commons, seeing it defeated both in 1804 and the following year. Perhaps the tide was turning with the recruitment of a number of young joining the committee. Parliament may have been blocking him but the public mood was shifting again in favour of abolition. After fifteen years of prevarication and delay finally the dam was breached on February 23 1807 when Parliament voted overwhelmingly in favour of abolition of the slave trade. Normally applause is forbidden in the House of Commons. This was not normal. The Morning Chronicle reported that three hearty cheers echoed through the chamber.

Whilst the Abolition Act received Royal Assent, slavery continued. In British colonies he continued to campaign, make speeches and publish pamphlets. He led the Anti-Slave Society to demand the emancipation of all slaves in British colonies. It was in 1833 that the Emancipation Bill received its final reading. Three years previously Thomas Clarkson had taken over as Chair of the Committee due to Wilberforce's declining health, and so the two men who contributed most to the abolition of the trade and the emancipation of slaves joined a triumphant circle celebrating their unending work in the search for justice of the most abused and tormented members of society.

To obtain abolition and the emancipation of slaves huge concessions were made in the form of reparation. Astonishingly this was not awarded to the slaves but the slave owners. In 1833 West Indian plantation owners lodged compensation claims for their loss of income due to abolition. The equivalent of three hundred million was paid out to banks, merchants and families, many of whom are still benefitting today. Doctor Nick Draper of University College London has made a detailed study of the distribution of these funds. Just one example gives a flavour of how these investors in human misery were rewarded. John Austin apparently owned four hundred and fifteen slaves for which he received twenty thousand, five hundred and eleven pounds, which equates to close on seventeen million pounds today. This injustice is obvious, as is the way that London's involvement in slavery has been partially air-brushed.

Latterly statues have been torn down and demands for compensation made. The whole subject is charged with emotion today. Apologies are demanded but is it really possible to apologise for something that happened centuries ago? Opinions vary but what is certain is slavery leaves a dark stain on London, made worse by seemingly turning a blind eye.

Chapter 9

Mother's Ruin

As far back as records go London has had a reputation for drunkenness. The desire to drink can be seen each night as offices close and the bars and pubs buzz with activity. Of course most are just socialising after a hard day, but there are those who deliberately go out to get drunk. Elsewhere in Europe youngsters are normally gradually introduced to alcohol by their parents and it is unusual to see marauding drunks on the streets of Paris or Rome. Here getting pissed is almost worn like a badge of honour. Getting legless has also extended to the laddish behaviour of young women. They are following in a tradition firmly embedded by many of their ancestors.

In the early eighteenth century beer was thought to have health giving properties and it was safer than drinking water. Wine was also used as a medicine, although it was too expensive for the poor. Samuel Pepys certainly enjoyed the odd pint of wine with his luncheon, whilst brandy was the preserve of the wealthy. The sale of beer was strictly controlled and there was a fashion for brown ale, which had a sweet taste. An increase in the duty on malt encouraged the brewers to introduce more hops, which became known as 'bitter'. Many thought it to be too bitter to drink, so it tended to be mixed with regular ale and the arrival of that old favourite, mild and bitter. The sale of pale ale became so popular many pale ale houses were established in the city. By the early 1720s a mellow beer brewed for up to five months was introduced. It became known as 'porter'. This was mostly drunk by the labouring classes and consumed at breakfast and dinner time. Brewed only in the city, it led to a class of beers generally known as stout. Here were heavy brown stouts and Irish stouts and one known as 'London particular'.

From the early 1720s London entered a period of madness prompted by the sale and vast consumption of gin, which quite literally brought large parts of London to its knees. It was introduced to the city by followers of William the Third arriving from Holland. 'Genever' shops were opened selling this fiery Dutch gin. Soon Parliament was lobbied by gentleman farmers who sensed good profits could be made by the distilling of English gin. The country was producing a surplus of grain and distilling it into gin was a relatively easy process. Parliament played ball by reducing the tax on gin, the duty set at tuppence a gallon and no retail licence was required. Stand by for lift off! Within months thousands of gin shops were opened and London entered a thirty year period of blurred vision, befuddled minds and personal disasters.

Gin was now so cheap that most could afford a noggin or two. 'Drunk for a penny, dead drunk for tuppence, clean straw for nothing' was the popular boast of gin shops. Much of the distilling and most of the drinking was confined to London. In the poorest areas the whole family joined in, including children and even babes in arms. Made from poor quality grain, much of London gin made 'Genever' taste like velvet. It was coarse gut rot, sometimes made more palatable by the addition of juniper. The powerful brew led not only to drunkenness but also to an increase in casual sex and a huge increase in bastard births. London society was shocked, as were foreigners confronted by marauding gangs set against a background stench coming from much of the city.

Matters had deteriorated so much that in 1736 a Gin Act was introduced aimed at reducing consumption. It was greeted by 'the execrations of the mob'. The effects of the Act were evaded by selling the gin as medicine or giving it misleading names like 'makeshift' or 'sangre'. Lord Lansdowne stated that gin 'offered the comfort of forgetfulness to prisoners and vagrants, it provided oblivion to the poor of St. Giles where one house in four was a gin shop'. Eighteenth century marketing came into play with the addition of cordials to mask the raw fiery taste that could burn the mouth.

A snapshot of the very worst effects of the witches brew represented by gin was provided by Judith Defour, who fetched her two year old daughter from the workhouse where the child had been issued with new clothes. The mother's desperation for gin prompted her to commit what must surely be one of the most depraved killings witnessed during this belated period. The child was strangled in order for her mother to sell her clothes, which fetched one shilling and fourpence. Having dumped the body, the proceeds were spent on gin. Henry Fielding commented later 'a new kind of drunkenness which if not put a stop to will infallibly destroy a great part of inferior people'. It was a poison called gin he reckoned affected over one hundred thousand people. Gin was now causing serious social problems. It was estimated that there were now over fifteen hundred small distilleries operating in London. Men were so raddled that they were unfit for military service and women were weaning babies on gin. By 1730 twenty five percent of all government revenues was due to alcohol.

William Hogarth again caught the mood with his paintings of 'Gin Lane' and 'Beer Street'. The word 'addiction' made its way into regular usage. Men staggered around and the streets were strewn with gin sodden women who had lost their last vestiges of self respect. A frightening madness had taken hold. Something had to be done and thirty years after the introduction of cheap gin the 1751 Gin Act was put into law. There had already been a tightening of the law with the Gin Act of 1736 when a fee of fifty pounds was required to obtain a licence to retail gin, but more was needed to quell London's insatiable thirst.

Acts could be passed but Londoners just ignored them, but not before serious rioting took place. There was an explosion in Westminster Hall and Joseph Jekyll became a figure of hate for the mob as being a major initiator of the hated Act. Informers found themselves in great danger. Five were identified and stoned to death in separate incidents, one being reported in New Palace Yard. The craze for gin and the madness resulting continued. Hogarth again caught the mood of Londoners with his print 'Night'. In it a figure closely resembling Sir Thomas de Veil (a man seen as trying to implement the Act) is pictured having a chamber pot emptied over his head. Two years after the Act was passed a mob gathered outside his house in Frith Street. They threatened to burn the house down and kill his team of informers.

Seven years after the Act became law only three licences had been paid for. This was a defiant London facing down authority and winning. Life was so dire for most of the working class and gin was seen as providing a temporary escape. Despite the dangers the number of informers mushroomed. Over a two year period almost five thousand people were convicted of selling gin without a licence. It became a game of cat and mouse with continued violence and killings. Gradually the increase in taxes was having the desired effect. Gin shops were closing down and the number of staggering and bemused drunks were no longer a common sight. What at its height had seen a whole section of society in London lose their minds and their dignity gradually subsided.

The closing of the gin shops did not stop Londoners' love affair with alcohol. In fact the reign of Queen Victoria saw a spate of new pubs being built. Many of them are still trading. They became very much a male preserve. No lady would think of entering a pub on her own, and there were those who never admitted women. Beer was now the drink of the working man whose thirst was catered for by a number of local breweries, whilst the largest started making deliveries outside their immediate area. Giant dray horses were a common sight hauling waggons loaded with wooden barrels. There was a pub on virtually all London streets. Segregation was introduced with the public and the posher saloon bars. Saturday night was the traditional time for a sing-song and a knees-up. It was time to take your missus out and buy her a couple of port and lemons. Then it might be off to the Metropolitan Music Hall in the Edgware Road or the Collins on Islington Green, or dozens of others scattered across London. Here we see raucous London again out to enjoy themselves. Shouting, cheering or giving 'the bird' to an Act that did not meet expectations. This was London in full voice, generous, funny but never far from good humour spilling over into a punch up. With the sounds of 'let's have another one', it was time to walk home. Then perhaps a nightcap of gin and orange. A link to those crazy days a century before. Now the gin is half the strength and produced in modern factories, but a reminder of the days when much of London went quite mad.

Chapter 10

Letting Off Steam

Living in London has always been rather like living in a pressure cooker, particularly for the poor. Crowded unhealthy conditions and economic hardship often prompted an outbreak of violence, particularly among apprentices. Political and religious differences could also prove to be inflammatory. Another constant thread was the hostility shown to people obviously different from the local population. This manifested itself as early as 1189 at the coronation of Richard I. Accounts vary as to the reasons but the end result was the attacks and murder of Jews. Some reports speak of leading Jewish figures bringing gifts for the King in an act of homage. Others say the Jews were banned from proceedings, whilst another story tells of Jews being ejected from the banquet taking place after the coronation. Whatever the truth, numbers of Jews were seized by a mob and killed. Again after all this time the facts are murky. Did the King actually set up the pogrom or was it true that he was incensed by the killings? Whatever, the attacks on Jews migrated north first to Stamford and then to the appalling attacks the following year in York.

The same xenophobia was still alive and well in 1527. May Day is traditionally a time for celebration, dancing and good cheer, but a group of apprentices thought otherwise. They resented an influx of foreigners, be they French weavers or Flemish cobblers. All foreigners were called strangers and as such different. There were about fifty thousand foreigners living in London during the reign of Henry VIII, many being Flemish but also merchants from across Europe together with increasingly powerful bankers. The trouble had been prompted originally by a Doctor Bell, a fiery preacher who claimed these 'strangers' were stealing the jobs of local people. He called on them to cherish their jobs and defend themselves. There were spasmodic outbreaks of violence by apprentices over the next couple of weeks, culminating in the May Day riots, which were to become known as 'the evil day' riots. A mob gathered in Cheapside releasing prisoners who had already been arrested for attacking foreigners. There was panic and hundreds of arrests and within a few days three of the rioters were executed at Tyburn. Although most of the rest were fully pardoned, it had been a really ugly and frightening outbreak, but suspicion of foreigners continued to be a source of trouble, which to an extent continues today.

The reasons behind what caused 'the brown dog riots' would find favour with many today. A number of live surgical procedures were carried out at the University College Medical School in front of students in a lecture hall. The operations were carried out without anaesthetic. The first operation on the terrier caused it to lose the use of its pancreas. Over the next couple of months other live operations were carried out, eventually resulting in the death of a dog in 1903. News of the events spread and was taken up by anti-vivisectionists. It was decided that a statue to the dog would be erected in Battersea. Whilst not a terrier, it was a rather noble looking brown dog. On a plaque was inscribed 'in memory of the brown terrier dog done to death in the laboratories of University College in February 1903 having endured vivisections....'.

The statue proved controversial, with threats coming from those in favour of vivisection in the furthering of medical knowledge. This movement continued to receive support from medical and veterinary students. In November 1907 a group of several hundred students attacked the statue with sledgehammers. Several were arrested and fined five pounds. Several weeks later the London students were joined by those from Oxford and Cambridge. They marched on the statue site carrying an effigy of the judge impaled on a stick. Locals and anti-vivisectionists were there to meet them. Skirmishes led to more violence and the riot that developed was reckoned to be the worst in London until the poll tax riots of the 1980s. Causes, noble or otherwise, would often lead to violence as tensions which normally bubble away just below the surface burst into life.

It did not appear to take much to get Londoners hot under the collar and take to the streets. Seven years after the massacre of the Jews following

Richard I's coronation, more trouble broke out. Over the centuries it was almost as if Londoners needed periodically to riot, almost embracing the excitement caused by rioting. In 1196 a preacher known as William the Longbeard incited violence by railing against the rich. Even watching a wrestling bout was enough to cause civil unrest and violence, resulting in three ringleaders being executed. The apprentices were not out of the limelight for long as fishmongers and skinners fought a pitched battle in 1340 after a fishmonger's servant was murdered. Short changing could also lead to serious disturbances. An under weight loaf or contaminated beer was all that was needed.

Easter, perhaps the most important religious holiday for Christians, invariably witnessed much violent and unseemly behaviour, never more so than in 1608. Was it really religious fervour that led to massive riots in London that became known as 'the bawdy house riots'. Certainly there was talk among levellers and their sympathisers of taking down 'the great bawdy house of Westminster' (Parliament). Whatever the reasons, March 22nd saw the start of five days of the worst riots ever witnessed in London, with at one stage forty thousand angry citizens supposedly involved. Attacks on brothels in the East End spread to the far more fashionable establishments in central London. There were real fears that these attacks were a prelude to an all out revolution. In the meantime prostitutes were attacked and premises burnt to the ground. As the riots continued unabated there were cries of 'we have been the servants but will be masters now'. Sentiments repeated over the centuries, but this mob were kidding themselves as gradually the ringleaders were arrested and executed. The King and his troops had quelled the fever and Londoners resumed their normal lives, possibly still asking themselves what all the disruption had really been about and whether anything of significance had been achieved.

Differences in religion and politics were always likely to cause dissent in 18th century England. The two came together in the form of a fiery preacher, Henry Sacheverell. He was a rather bigoted Tory high church Anglican. For once his barbs were not directed at Jews or Catholics but non-conformists, who were described as 'false brethren'. He reckoned that dissenters were a threat, not just to the Church of England but the very state. He underlined this view with a long sermon delivered at St. Paul's Cathedral. He preached against the glorious revolution of 1688. He had gone too far. He was charged with seditious libel and tried before the House of Lords in Westminster Hall. All printed pamphlets were to be burned.

It did not take long for riots to break out across London, probably encouraged by Tory sympathisers. Initially the target of the mob were Presbyterian meeting houses in central London. The rioting spread throughout the city and suburbs, with mobs demanding high church before spreading across the country. The continued violence and destruction in the years following eventually led to the passing of the Riot Act, giving magistrates far stronger powers.

Dorothy Orwell should surely claim a unique place in British history for being the first woman to be attacked for her choice of clothes. Traditional woollen clothes were heavy and uncomfortable to wear in summer. A fashion trend had led to the wearing of printed calico, which was light and available in stunning colours. In 1700 in an attempt to protect the weaving trade, a ban was introduced on the importation of calico. Many of the weavers were concentrated around the Spitalfield area and despite the ban unprinted calico was still finding its way onto the market. By 1719 the country was experiencing an economic downturn and silk weavers were being thrown out of work. They issued threats about the continued calico imports. In June 1719 their resentment boiled over. It was towards the end of the month that Dorothy Orwell was set upon by a mob whilst walking in Hoxton for wearing a calico dress. She declared that her dress and petticoat was torn and cut from her.

Now a war of words was added to the violence, with the weavers suggesting that any woman wearing calico had morals as loose as the clothes they wore. A verse from a popular Spitalfields ballad suggested that:

> 'None shall be thought
> a more scandalous slut
> than a tawdry calico madam'

As the weather cooled the problem of woollen dresses was again worn to fend off the cold, but the attacks continued the following year. Finally the Calico Act was passed in 1721 banning the wearing of calico clothes and also for furnishing fabrics. Here was an early example of how cheap imports could affect the livelihood of British workers. It became an ongoing problem that still persists today.

Spitalfields had been a traditional home for silk weavers since the early arrival of the French Huguenots. By the middle of the 8th century they had been joined by sizeable numbers of Irish weavers, who were frequently accused of undercutting prices and causing tensions between the two communities. Eventually they did get together to form associations, which were in effect illegal trade unions to protect themselves from cheap imports and masters who constantly sought to restrict their earnings. The weavers were a militant lot and there were frequent outbreaks of violence. In 1765 the House of Lords was forced to adjourn as a large mob of weavers demanded a ban on imports. That night they attacked the Duke of Bedford's London home, citing his support for the imports.

The resentment simmered on and two years later in 1769 trouble really came to a head. A raid was made on the Dolphin pub in Spitalfields where a group of weavers were meeting in an attempt to raise money for those of their number in particular need. Their masters were worried about any organisation which would weaken their control of the weavers. On entering the pub soldiers were met with resistance. Shots were fired and two weavers were killed, four others were captured, whilst the others fled. Two were sent for trial and convicted on the evidence of a married couple of Irish weavers who had been bribed by a Huguenot master weaver. The two men found guilty were hanged at Bethnal Green.

Some people seem destined to live extraordinary lives. John Wilkes was the son of a distiller born in Clerkenwell in 1725. Even as a young man he was described as being unattractive with a receding chin and a squint. This did not prevent him from becoming a relentless and successful pursuer of women. He did marry but the union was short lived, but did produce a daughter named Polly. Already wealthy, there is talk of him using bribery to gain a seat in Parliament representing Aylesbury. He went on to become Speaker of the House of Commons where he was not a success. Turning instead to writing, he started a magazine anonymously, called the 'North Briton', in 1762. The following year he used the magazine to attack the speech King George IV had made for the opening of Parliament. A warrant was issued to find the author of the article and it took only a few days for Wilkes to be identified and arrested. He was sent to the Tower of London, whilst his lodgings were searched and papers and correspondence confiscated. The authorities had not realised how popular Wilkes had become with the public. He argued that being a sitting MP he could not be arrested for libel. He pleaded his own case at Westminster Hall where he was followed by cheering crowds shouting 'Wilkes and liberty'. His defence was successful and he was released and awarded one thousand pounds in damages.

Despite the payment Wilkes was by now in financial trouble. He decided to print a composite volume of the 'North Briton', hoping it would bring in additional revenue. He also wrote a poem which was a spoof of Pope's 'Essay on Man' entitled 'Essay on Woman', which started 'Awake, my fanny'. Now he was in real trouble. He was called a coward and required to fight a duel with Samuel Martin in Hyde Park. Perhaps it was irony or retribution that Wilkes was shot in the groin. He took himself off to Paris, having been expelled from the House of Commons; he was tried in his absence and found guilty. In 1768 with funds exhausted and in danger of being arrested for debt, he returned to London.

Wilkes appears to be one of those remarkable (or annoying) men who bounce back from all kinds of scandal and adversity. On his return he was elected to represent the Middlesex seat in Parliament. Unfortunately he was still awaiting sentencing for the guilty verdict passed before he fled to Paris. He was sentenced to ten months in prison together with a fine of five hundred pounds. With news of his conviction crowds started to gather outside King's Bench Prison in Southwark. At its height there were reckoned to be up to fifteen thousand giving vocal support for this anti-establishment figure. They chanted 'Wilkes and liberty' and 'down with the King'.

The authorities called in the military, concerned that the crowd might attack the prison. They were greeted with insults and a volley of stones. One particularly stroppy demonstrator was chased into a nearby barn where an innocent boy was shot by mistake. News of the killing further inflamed the crowd, the Riot Act was read out and more troops called for. With matters about to escalate out of control, shots were fired and up to eleven people were killed in what became known as the 'St. George's Fields Massacre'. Upon release from prison Wilkes's extraordinary career continued its weird path. First he became an alderman, eventually becoming a city magistrate. The city loved playing the role of the defender of liberties. This culminated with John Wilkes, the plague of King and Government, being elected Lord Mayor of London in 1774.

It was as if the riotous behaviour of Londoners during the eighteenth century was just a warm up act for the main event. The Gordon riots of 1780 were by far the most destructive, with lawlessness in danger of running totally out of control. In 1778 the Catholic Relief Act was passed, with its aim to improve the civil rights of Catholics. It was generally unpopular, particularly in London. Opposition was headed by Lord George Gordon, who saw this as a cause to further his own political ambitions. St. George's Fields was again the setting for a mass meeting reckoned to be in excess of fifty thousand. Encouraged by Gordon they set off for central London. It was as if a mass madness had overtaken them and it was not just Catholics and their property that was the target of their fury. Certainly Catholic churches were burnt and ransacked, but so too were foreign embassies. Very quickly Gordon had lost control of the mob. Prisons became a particular target, with the forbidding Newgate torched and destroyed. King's Bench Prison fared no better, nor Bridewell, the fleet all were destroyed. Then the Bank of England and Lambeth Palace were attacked. Gin distilleries went up in flames as the mob sought new targets to attack. Seemingly the rage against Catholics had been widened as citizens hid in their homes or headed for the country. The riots continued for three weeks. Eventually some ten thousand troops were gathered. This was never going to end well. Given orders to fire on the rioters, over three hundred were killed and many more injured. Over four hundred arrests were made and gallows were set up all over London. Most of those detained were young, many under fifteen. Hugh Walpole reckoned that a handful of schoolmasters could have stopped the insurrection. What had started as an anti-Catholic protest had morphed into a rebellion against any form of authority. Eight prisons were destroyed, as were the homes of leading judges. Sponging houses for debtors were a particular target for the mob, as were houses used to retain pressed sailors, and yet not one Catholic was killed. Ironically the rebel-rouser John Wilkes took up arms to defend the Bank of England (a poacher turned gamekeeper). Eventually the lunacy that had taken over London declined.

Lord George Gordon was arrested for high treason but acquitted. In the years that followed, strangely Gordon became a Jew, calling himself Israel Abraham George Gordon. He was another strange unconventional character that London throws up on a fairly regular basis. Carrying on in much the same vein, he was jailed for libel and tried in 1787 in the rebuilt Newgate prison. He died of typhoid in 1793.

Surely now after all the blood-letting London could look forward to a period of calm and reflection. Well, not quite. In 1809 the price of theatre tickets was enough to cause localised rioting. Protests supporting the common ownership of land appeared a more worthy cause in 1819. Eleven years later the Duke of Wellington was attacked as he rode in his carriage for his continued opposition to electoral reform. Compared to the eighteenth century London now seemed by comparison almost tranquil. There was a riot in Hyde Park in 1886 with demonstrations both for and against a meeting of fair trade league. There was one last hurrah to see off the Victorian era with the 'bloody Sunday riots' of 1887. There had been a growing unrest due to an economic downturn and a ban on demonstrations in Trafalgar Square. Bans are never popular in London and a mass meeting was called. Troops together with police were ordered to break up the assembly, which resulted in two deaths. A march that started in Clerkenwell was met in St. Martins Lane by a massive force of about four thousand soldiers and police and the demonstrators dispersed as red flags were torn down. There were complaints about police brutality but although it was frightening for those caught up in the fracas, it would have hardly registered in the volatile frenzy of the previous century.

Life entering the 20th century was even further removed from the turbulent Georgian era, but Londoners were still all too willing to get involved in violence. 1930s politics were dominated for a time by the rise of Fascism. Sir Oswald Mosley was part of a social elite. Educated at Winchester and Sandhurst, he was elected Labour MP for Harrow. Helping his seemingly effortless rise, he married a daughter of Lord Curzon. A visit to Italy saw him make an extreme political turn by joining the British Union of Fascists. Styling themselves on the Nazis already ruling the roost in Germany, Mosley's black-shirted followers started inciting anti-semitic feelings on the streets of the East End. In July 1936 he addressed thousands of his followers in Victoria Park, Hackney. Viewing film footage of the event today, he cuts a comical figure ranting and gesticulating. The speech was followed by an outbreak of rioting.

He returned in October to lead thousands of black-shirts through the streets of the East End. The Labour Party had advised their supporters to stay at home, but by mid afternoon there were reckoned to be about one hundred thousand of anti-Fascists gathered in Whitechapel Road near the junction to Cable Street. A couple of thousand black-shirts found their route down Cable Street blocked by an overturned lorry. The violence that followed became known as 'the battle of Cable Street'. Belatedly Mosley was ordered to call off the march and the result was seen as a decisive victory for the Jewish community and its left wing allies.

Jews continued to be beaten up on the streets and their shops and businesses smashed up. On New Year's Day in 1937 a Public Order Act banned the wearing of political uniforms and tightened the law on marches. The Fascists retained a sizeable following in the East End, getting almost a quarter of the votes cast in the 1937 London county council elections, but any hope of continued growth was halted by the outbreak of war. The would-be dictator Mosley and his wife spent much of its duration in Holloway prison. After another gap of twenty years a new excuse for serious rioting shook London. As ever it revolved around newcomers and race rather than religion or politics and provoked serious rioting.

Liverpool had experienced a period of racial rioting in 1919, but generally with Britain being so predominantly white there had been few instances until the first arrival of West Indians in 1948. Actually black American servicemen had been surprised at how little colour prejudice there was in Britain compared to back home. All this changed with increasing numbers of people arriving from the Caribbean. Most of them were young men and it was obvious they were going to seek out some female company, which was resented by their white counterparts. There were wild stories about the sexual appetites of the new arrivals and complaints about noisy music and the crowded conditions these new arrivals lived in, which were forced upon them as so few landlords were prepared to let their properties to black men. All these problems grew along with the increased numbers of new arrivals. To make matters worse many young white women were attracted to the relaxed black men, who to some seemed so much more fun than the embittered locals. Something had to give and it did.

The trouble really began on August 23rd 1958 when a gang of white youths singled out a group of black men to verbally abuse and attack. The following day, a Sunday, a group of whites from Notting Dale and the White City Estate went 'nigger hunting'. They were armed with razors, knives and knuckle dusters, and a number of West Indians were seriously injured.

The following weekend there was more violence with a large group of Teddy Boys adding their number of those seeking out any black men they could find to 'rough up'. The worst rioting took place on Monday, September 1st. Mobs congregated in the centre of Notting Hill Gate, armed not only with knives and coshes but also bottles and bricks, with some carrying dustbin lids for protection. These yobs were joined by members of Oswald Mosley's Union Movement, acting mainly as agitators. Bicycle chains were wielded as the mob smashed windows and shouted 'kill the niggers'. They were egged on by women leaning out of upstairs windows. A terrified black youth sought safety in a greengrocer's shop where the owner's wife kept the chasing group at bay by threatening them with a kitchen knife, confirming that not all white people had lost all sense of decency.

By the evening West Indian men had organised themselves and they gathered in Blenheim Crescent with an armoury of weapons, including Molotov Cocktails. The white mob was ready for confrontation. They shouted 'burn the niggers out' and were met with a barrage of home made bombs. At last the police arrived to avoid what threatened to be all out war. A few arrests were made but it was really the British weather that came to the rescue as a massive thunderstorm broke out. The deluge dampened the ardour of both sides and it was left to the refuse cleaners to clear up what looked like a war zone.

The group who had chased the young student into the grocer's shop were sentenced to four years in jail. The judge summing up said, 'by your conduct you have set the clock back three hundred years'. Maybe he should have said 'even longer' as basically nothing had changed since medieval days when 'strangers and aliens' were attacked and abused. Riotous London had turned full circle. Little had changed, certainly not human nature. It would take time but gradually and grudgingly newcomers were accommodated and some even welcomed. London was starting its slow painful journey towards becoming perhaps the world's largest multi-national city.

Chapter 11

More Tea, Vicar

The demise of the News Of The World in 2011 denied Britons their traditional love of reading about influential figures falling from grace, either by financial misdeeds but more importantly sexual scandal. It was surely the reason why 'the screws of the world' enjoyed the largest circulation for a Sunday newspaper. Sundays would never quite be the same again. The naming and shaming of politicians, lawyers, doctors and particularly clerics was as much a part of a British Sunday as roast beef and Yorkshire pudding.

Of course there is no reason to assume that men of the cloth erred more than any other members of society, but over the years they do form an extremely colourful group. We assume that all priests have a genuine calling based on their faith. This should be even more apparent in those who reach the very highest office, but unfortunately this has not always been the case. George Abbott was born in 1562, and although never serving as a parish priest he soared through the church ranks based largely on his influential connections. The former Bishop of London was awarded the Archbishopric of Canterbury on March 4 1611. Extremely unpopular within members of the church, many stated that he was unfit for high office. He certainly lacked humanity, having a large group of Oxford undergraduates imprisoned for failing to doff their hats to him. Any dissent shown to his views or rulings was met with savagery. One such was Alexander Leighton, a preacher who really upset Abbott. Whatever he said or preached surely did not remotely deserve the punishment imposed. Leighton was first tied to a stake and given thirty six lashes. Then he was placed in the pillory for two hours on a frosty November morning. Next he was branded on the face, his nose split and his ears cut off before being carted off to prison for the rest of his life. The Archbishop was obviously not a man to be crossed.

Some were still prepared to defy him and three newly elected bishops refused to be ordained by Abbott. He was also implicated in the killing of a gamekeeper on a hunting trip. There was a concerted effort to unseat him and an inquiry held which failed to agree a verdict. It was then left to the King to decide the Archbishop's fate, but the King ruled in Abbott's favour and he was allowed to continue his calling. He died in 1633.

British monarchs were not always so forgiving. Despite having been chaplain to King George III, he decided that the death sentence passed on the Reverend William Dodd for forgery must be upheld. The reason given was that it would be wrong to make an exception or special case. It is more likely, however, that as the Earl of Chesterfield, a member of the nobility, was the victim of the crime, the King wanted to endorse the rights of the aristocracy.

Dodd was born in 1729, the son of the vicar of Bourne in Lincolnshire. Having graduated at Cambridge, he moved to London, and having taken holy orders became a curate at a church in West Ham. He built a reputation as an influential preacher, which eventually led to his appointment as a chaplain to the King. Mixing with rich and influential people fed his desire for the good life and increasingly he found himself in debt. He became involved in a number of property schemes, but his desire for money and status led to his first major error. The position of rector of St. Georges's church in Hanover Square would certainly fit exactly what he was looking for. What on earth prompted him to write anonymously to Lady Apsley, offering her money to help him secure the position, will never be known. It did not take long for all of London society to know of his involvement. He was subjected to such ridicule that he was forced to leave the country until the scandal faded.

Previously he had been tutor to a young Earl of Chesterfield and it was his connection to this family that tempted him and led to his downfall. His lavish lifestyle on a modest income led to a further escalation of his debts. At the beginning of 1777 he forged a bond for over four thousand pounds (a massive sum in the 18th century). The bond was presented to the Earl's bank and approved, with the money being given to Dodd. The Earl had not missed the money but a slight written blemish in the writing of the bond led the bank to request a signature on the newly written document. For an intelligent man Dodd was astonishingly naive. Confronted, Dodd immediately confessed and was imprisoned prior to his trial. From his cell he pleaded for mercy and even contacted Samuel Johnson for help. The case received wide publicity and over twenty thousand people signed a petition for clemency, but the King was unmoved. Dodd was not the first or the last to be seduced by the prospect of money. Despite devoting much of his life to good causes he was his own worst enemy.

A huge crowd, estimated to be about one hundred thousand, gathered at Tyburn. Dodd arrived in his own coach preceded by a cart containing his coffin. He still had hopes that he would survive the hanging. He had worked with the famous surgeons, the Hunter Brothers, on a theory that if a freshly hanged corpse was immersed in warm water the victim might return to life. Accordingly his body was rushed away to a nearby house where a bath had been prepared. Unfortunately the warm water experiment failed but money was not the only temptation to lead subsequent clerics from the path of righteousness.

It must be assumed that most Christian clerics are fulfilling a genuine calling to serve God. Over the years many have subjected their parishioners to long dreary sermons but there are others who are charismatic and inspirational. Then there are a number who stray and become involved in scandal, which usually sees them being defrocked or sent to a distant monastery to consider their sins. Added to this cast are those who rise to the highest positions in the church despite their obvious moral shortcomings. Of all the colourful and outrageous clerics over the centuries one stands out. How on earth did Lancelot Blackburne ever become an archbishop?

Blackburne's early life was conventional enough, attending Westminster school before going up to Oxford where he was admitted to Christ Church in 1676. He graduated and was ordained in 1681. So far so boring, until he took off for the West Indies. Some believe he was a ship's chaplain, but this was no ordinary ship but a privateer. He supposedly took part in a buccaneering expedition against the Spanish, taking his share of the bounty. Years later an old shipmate tracked Blackburne down and was astonished to hear that he had become Archbishop of York. On his return home from the West Indies we find Lancelot in service to the King. He is awarded a bounty of twenty pounds for 'secret services'. The citation reads 'to Lancelot Blackburne, clerk bounty for his transportation to Antego'.

By 1694 Blackburne was appointed as Sub-Dean at Exeter Cathedral. Rumours constantly followed him around. It was rumoured that he used a secret tunnel to enable him to have an affair with his neighbour, a Mrs Martyr. It was even suggested by Walpole that Blackburne was the father of another high ranking cleric, Bishop Hayter. What is certain is that the archbishop was an ardent womaniser. In 1743, the year of his death, he was still at it, apparently enjoying having two women sharing his bed. A contemporary satirist wrote:

> 'One had her charms below, one above,
> so I together blende either bliss
> Lydia laid on. Dolly had my kiss'

Quite an epitaph for an archbishop, but a testimony from memories of Horace Walpole paints a rather different picture. 'Blackburne, the jolly Archbishop of York who had all the manners of a man of quality, though he had been a buccaneer and a clergyman, but retained nothing of his first profession, except his seraglio'. So here we have an unconventional and lustful priest, but how did he really obtain such high office? Trying to peer through the mists of time, it appears most likely that his 'laxity of moral purpose' appealed to the King. More importantly it seems that Lancelot Blackburne was awarded the Archbishopric of York for secretly marrying King George I to his mistress the Duchess of Kendal. Certainly his religious life, such as it was, had been held hostage by his unconventional lifestyle. The be-wigged figure staring at us from a portrait painted of him gives no indication of his lurid past. As we all know looks can be misleading.

Reginald Bacchus was a well known theologian who for a time was a member of the Oscar Wilde set. He was married to the actress Isla Bowman, who as a child was invited by the Reverend Charles Dodgson (Lewis Carroll), the author of Alice in Wonderland, to spend holidays with him in Eastbourne. She was just one of a number of young girls spending time with him, but Isla obviously made a real impression, being the first to play Alice on stage

Whilst Bacchus was noted for his articles appearing in the religious press, he also became involved with translating French novels. This appears to have led him into the world of pornography and his writing of extremely erotic novels. These included 'Pleasure Bound Afloat' and 'Pleasure Bound Ashore'. Pornography was now big business and centred on Holywell Street in London. He died in 1921 aged sixty-three, another hiding his identity behind a respectable façade.

Jealousy is a powerful motivator which led the Reverend James Hackman to his death on the gallows at Tyburn in April 1779. Hackman is recorded as being baptised in December 1752. He was the son of a naval officer. It is possible that he attended Cambridge University, but at the age of twenty four he purchased a commission as an ensign in the army. Despite being promoted the following year he resigned and took holy orders. In 1779 he was ordained as a deacon in the Church of England. A few years previously, whilst still serving in the army, he stayed at the house of Lord Sandwich. It was here that he was introduced to Martha Ray, his host's mistress and so was set in motion the infatuation that would eventually lead to her death and his downfall. A portrait of her seated in traditional pose gives an idea of her attraction. Slim and poised, a book open on her lap indicating her knowledge and education. She is quoted as having 'sweetness of manners, and of remarkable judgement and execution in vocal and instrumental music'. Although she was older than Hackman, he was swept away and he quickly became besotted with her. She had been the noble Lord's mistress since the age of seventeen and had borne him several children.

It is quite possible that Hackman and Martha became lovers and he did ask her to leave Sandwich. For a time his hopes were raised, but eventually she turned him down. Just weeks after being ordained the impressionable young priest followed Martha to the Theatre Royal in Covent Garden. Horrified, Hackman realised that she was escorted by a man he suspected as being a new lover. It is not clear if James Hackman took two pistols with him to Covent Garden, or in a fit of rage he bought them locally. Whatever, the result was the same. Whilst the performance was running the jealous cleric waited in a nearby coffee house. As the couple were preparing to enter their carriage Hackman rushed forward, shooting Martha Ray at point blank range, killing her instantly. Then amidst the confusion he turned the second gun on himself. Obviously in a state of high emotion his aim faltered, only slightly injuring himself. Later he was to plead in his defence that he had only intended to commit suicide, this after he had changed his plea from guilty to not guilty. The evidence of bystanders was overwhelming. Hackman's defence lawyer submitted that his client was insane, to no avail.

The judge stated that the case against the cleric did not require 'a long form of deliberation' and he was duly sentenced to be hanged. A painting of Hackman pictures him in profile. He has a sensitive rather than a strong face, with a receding chin. Was this a case of premeditated murder or perhaps a genuine crime of passion? On his journey to Tyburn in a coach he was joined by the Newgate chaplain and a cleric friend, the Reverend John Villette. A slender figure dressed in black, Hackman stood a full five feet nine inches, well above the average height in the eighteenth century. It was reported that the prisoner conducted himself with great fortitude. The strange story of another erring clergyman was drawing to an end. There was to be no warm water bath for Hackman or faint hope of revival. After his execution the body was taken to Surgeons Hall to suffer the final indignity of public dissection.

Following his death in 1937 it was not just the News of the World that featured coverage about the colourful life of the Reverend Harold Davidson. Public interest was such that reporters from all the national press tried to put their spin on a story which even today is hard to believe, and many aspects are lately being challenged. Another mystery surrounding a prominent cleric which is difficult to unravel.

Harold Davidson was born in Southampton in 1875 to a Church of England priest whose family dating back many decades had all been clerics. His father hoped his son would also take holy orders, but at Whitgift school he showed a great interest in performing on stage. By his late teens he was appearing as a comic act at the Seymour Hall in central London. At about this time he talked a young girl from throwing herself into the River Thames. Shades of things to come. In 1898 he bowed to

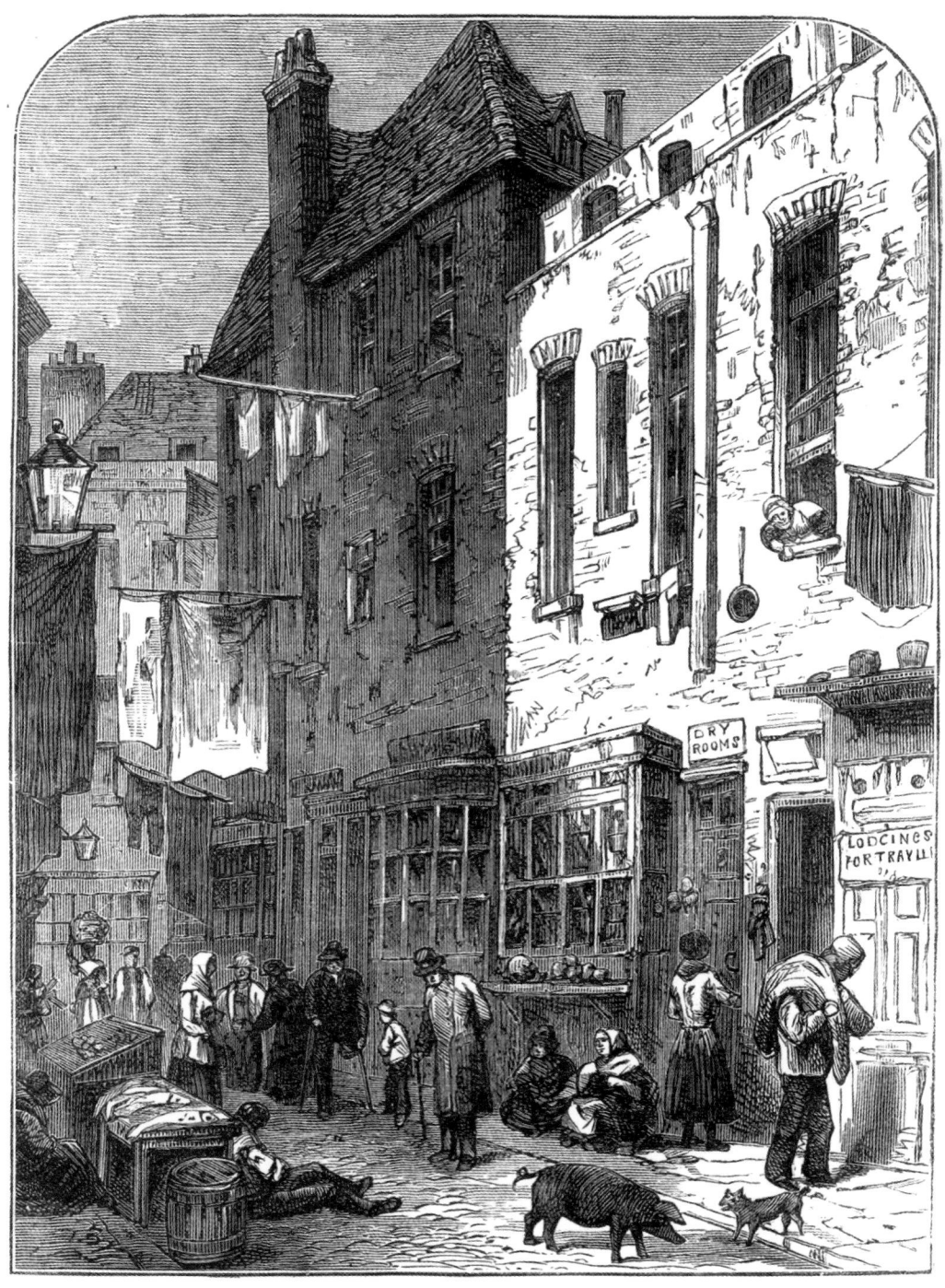
The foul and filthy living conditions in the London slums were a perfect breeding ground for crime.

Thousands gathered for public executions at Tyburn where the atmosphere was one of chaotic excitement.

Edith Thompson and Frederick Bywater, whose passion for each other eventually led to the gallows.

Burning at the stake was often reserved for those accused of heresy.

Jack Sheppard, the arch escaper from prison until even his luck ran out.

The baiting of defensive animals remains a stain that we find difficult to understand today.

The entrance to Newgate prison where prisoners were left chained in filthy conditions. It was also the starting point for a trip to Tyburn.

Slavery remains impossible for us to comprehend or defend. The conditions on the boats transporting these poor people were cruel and inhuman.

The strange and rather tragic Reverend Harold Davidson with one of the young girls he tried to 'save'.

John Gielgud, part of a very active London gay society, who was arrested for propositioning a policeman in a public toilet. Despite his concerns his public continued to support him.

Lily Langtry, 'The Jersey Lily', whose beauty entranced legions of admirers including King Edward VII.

Daisy, the Countess of Warwick, was one of a long line of ladies who caught the roving eye of the King. She was a particular favourite, having a mind of her own, but eventually her reckless spending caught up with her.

Brilliant Chang, the society drug dealer of the 1920s.

Whilst much of London was devastated by German bombs, the East End had to bear the brunt.

Spivs were regularly seen selling 'knocked off' goods in short supply.

The dapper, well connected but doomed spy, John Amery.

'Germany calling' but not any more. William Joyce photographed on his arrest. His sentence of death was much criticised.

West Indians arriving in London received a cold welcome and were subjected to frequent attacks.

The Messina brothers, who for a time controlled London's vice trade by violence and intimidation.

Pamela Green, remembered fondly by a whole generation.

The streets of Soho featured some of the best restaurants in London, but also an entire menu of sexual temptations.

The iconic Piccadilly Circus, a meeting point and the gateway to London nightlife.

The wayward Duchess of Argyll, whose graphic photograph with a headless man led to frantic speculation and many jokes.

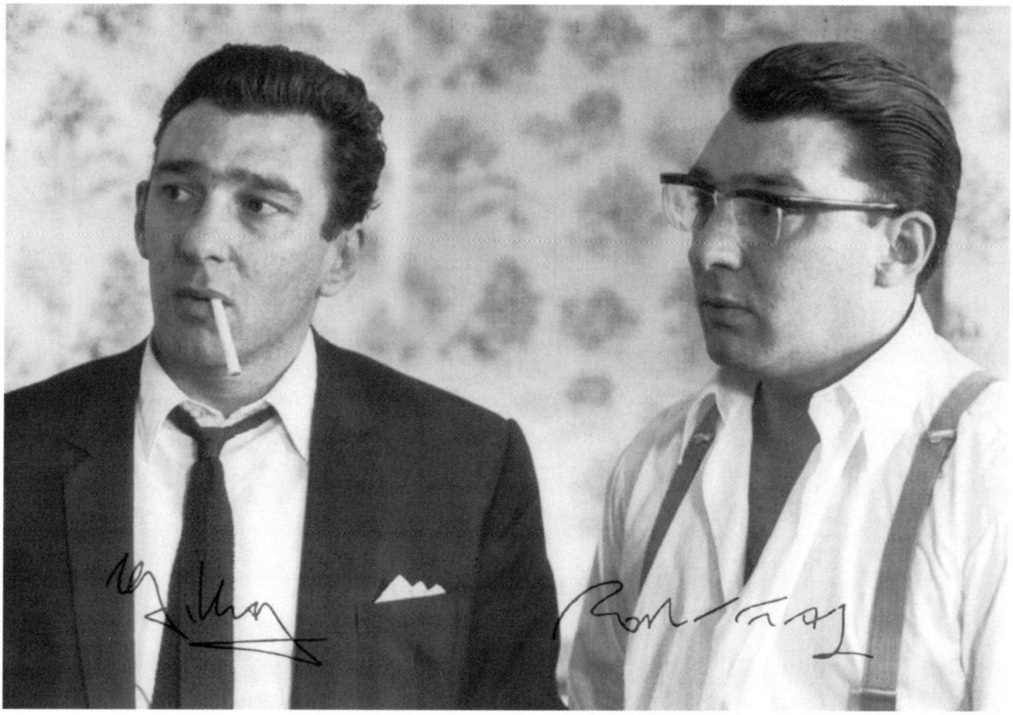

The notorious Kray twins, ruthless crooks but who for a time represented 'gangster chic'.

Eddie Richardson, sadistic leader of the leading rival gang to the Krays.

John Profumo, whose reputation was not ruined by his wandering eye but by him lying to Parliament.

his father's wish by entering Exeter College Oxford. After three years he was really struggling and left without a degree. In 1903 he finally passed the exams and was ordained. Three years later he was appointed rector of Stiffkey in Norfolk. Back in Edwardian England Norfolk was something of a backwater. His parishioners were either poor agricultural workers or farmers, and wealthy members of the squirearchy. The poor of his flock appear to have been genuinely fond of the man they called 'little Jimmy'. Davidson was only five feet three in height. The more influential villagers were critical of him from the start.

This unease deepened when the rector started to spend much of the week in London and soon rumours of his activities spread and multiplied. He became obsessed with the well being of young girls, particularly prostitutes. He spent much of his time trawling the streets and alleys of Soho. He wanted to save these 'fallen souls', befriending those as young as fourteen. He was quoted as saying that if Christ returned to Earth he would be found walking the streets around Piccadilly. Rumours reached fever pitch when he started bringing some of the girls back to Norfolk to spend the weekend with him. Back in London he started haunting the tea shops on Oxford Street, where he thought pretty waitresses might be in danger of prostituting themselves. He was banned from cafes and shops despite his protests.

For ten years a young prostitute called Rose Ellis took his fancy and there were suggestions that she became his mistress. It was her soul he insisted that interested him, not her body. A growing number of people did not believe him. In 1930 he was spending even more time in London, although he rarely missed Sunday services in Stiffkey. It was in this year that he met a sixteen year old street worker called Barbara Harris at Marble Arch. She was going to have a massive impact on his life but not in the way he wanted. On their first meeting he told her she reminded him of Mary Brian the film star. He increasingly became besotted by the girl and was forever forgiving her when she fell back into working the streets again. 'Sorry, Uncle Harold', she would coo, but he was fighting a losing battle.

With his behaviour becoming ever more erratic, news of his activities had reached the Bishop of Norwich. He started arriving back too late to take Sunday services and the number of girls staying at the rectory increased. A final straw was reached when Davidson arrived late for a Remembrance Day service and his bishop was said to have been incandescent with rage. He now took the unusual step of hiring a private detective to watch what Davidson was up to in Soho and Rose Ellis was interviewed. The noose was tightening. The aim was presumably to prove that his interest in these poor misguided girls was far from just spiritual. Barbara Harris wrote to the bishop accusing the rector of rape, although none of the other girls interviewed made any such claims. In fact they spoke of his kindness.

Despite a lack of concrete evidence Harold Davidson was called to appear before a consistory court in Westminster. By now the press had realised that they had a sensational story to report, resulting in huge crowds gathering in Westminster. Here he was accused of adultery with Rose Ellis and making improper suggestions to waitresses in a Lyons Corner House. He was also charged with 'habitually associating with women of a loose nature for immoral purposes'. Interest reached fever pitch with the release of a photograph of Davidson standing very close and staring at a nude fifteen year old, although she looks much younger. The girl, Ella Douglas, claimed that Davidson had told her he could help further her modelling career. It is claimed that the photo had been 'set up' but it is difficult to understand how this could have been done.

The most incriminating evidence together with the photograph was a letter supposedly written by Barbara Harris. It ran to a full fourteen pages and included the most intimate and lurid details. Subsequently Davidson's surviving relatives have claimed that the signature was different from others that she had sent him, all of which were entirely innocent and contained no sexual innuendos. As I know from my previous book 'The Hidden Letter' (which also centred on a vicar and an extremely erotic letter), getting any two handwriting experts to agree is seemingly impossible. Whatever, the church was determined to nail poor old Harold and he was duly found guilty. He was summoned to Norwich Cathedral and publicly stripped of his holy orders. The bishop told him he was to be 'removed, deposed and degraded'. Not much Christian kindness on show. An example had to be made. Was 'Uncle Harold' really a sexual predator or a kindly but naive cleric? We still do not know. Perhaps the answer lies somewhere in the middle ground.

Left with no money Harold reverted to his acting days as a means of making a living. By now a celebrity, he drew great crowds to Blackpool Promenade by exhibiting himself in a barrel. By 1937 he had moved onto Skegness, another popular seaside town. Here he appeared each night as a lion tamer. Freddy was a remarkably tame creature who was normally looked after by a young eight year old girl. Whilst Harold cracked his whip at the mangy lion, he ranted to the audience about the hierarchy of the Church of England. The crowd who came in droves whooped their support. Buses and charabancs swelled attendances as visitors from all over the country came to see the famous Vicar of Stiffkey. Wild animals, no matter how tame they appear, are always dangerous. Harold was getting older and his reflexes slowing. Complacency also probably played a part in his tragic death. As the lion grabbed Davidson by the throat most thought it was part of the act. As the lights were switched off it became clear something had gone dreadfully wrong. Harold was rushed off to hospital where he died several days later.

So ended an astonishing life, one that if written as fiction would be hard to believe. Like all unsolved mysteries it stays with us. The extremes of a well meaning devout man, or a sleazy child abuser, is impossible to fathom. What is your verdict?

Chapter 12

Bawd Games

With Paris known as the city of love and Venice as the city of romance, what of London? Perhaps the city of guilt. In Victorian Britain women were supposed to endure rather than enjoy sex. Becoming pregnant regularly reduced the constant need to get involved, releasing legions of outwardly respectable men to indulge themselves in the guilty pleasure of visiting prostitutes.

In mid Victorian London there were reckoned to be close on eighty thousand prostitutes in London, many of them young girls. In a city that thrived on trade a young girl from a slum background often had only her body to sell. There are reports of mothers selling their daughters. Hunger and poverty led to all manners of degradation. The life of a street worker was hard. Many looked old by the time they were thirty and had to retreat to dark alleys or roaming London's parks at night.

A few of those who were successful made enough money to open their own brothel. These ranged from filthy hovels to five star luxury, where a gentleman of means was welcomed and made to feel at ease. French wine and good food was on the menu as well as a wide choice of girls or mature ladies. Over the years the bawds who ran these establishments became known as 'mother', a comforting name for what were normally a steely hearted group of women who offered a warm welcome once terms had been struck. Mothers tend to forgive a few indiscretions from their favourite son and so the visitor felt a sense of comfort. 'Mother' also had a vaguely religious ring, thereby absolving their client of any fleeting guilt he may have felt, and be ready and waiting to greet him on his return. Many of course did return. From a stained and soiled couch to a luxurious boudoir, all were available with every taste catered for.

Prostitutes had formed a background to life in London since the middle ages, when in the twelfth century the Bishop of Winchester supplemented his income on the exertions of his 'Winchester geese'. In 1240 Cock Lane in Smithfield became the first designated 'red light' district in London. There was plenty of competition however with Ave Maria Alley a favoured spot for picking up whores. The city from Aldersgate to Gracechurch Street and Billingsgate all featured brothels. At this time bawds and prostitutes were routinely arrested and sentenced to being 'carted'. This was a vain attempt to restrict the number plying their trade on the streets. The unfortunate women were taken to the pillory, led by singing minstrels and a crowd beating on metal bowls. On reaching the pillory their offences were read out to the jeering crowd. Later they were again carted to Cock Lane and solemnly expelled from the city, no doubt reappearing for business days later.

Finding a suitable room to conduct their business often presented problems. At the very lowest end of the trade was a quick three-penny worth up against a wall. A step up was provided by accommodation houses. These were usually little more than hovels, but available for hire by the hour or night as may be required. A house owner in the Haymarket was able to retire to Camberwell on the proceeds. Tavern owners with an eye for business also rented rooms out, particularly in areas known for sex workers. Bagnios were ostensibly bath houses which tended to be situated in the Covent Garden area. Here a gentleman, having bathed and had a drink or two, could send out for a lady to help complete his evening's enjoyment. These places were expensive. A foreign visitor explained: 'the houses are often richly furnished with every device for exciting the senses'. If a girl did not please the client she was sent back with only her transport paid. The visitor also explained that in London everything was conducted with the utmost seriousness, unlike in Paris where the mood was much lighter. Guilt and a certain bleakness was the underlining impression.

Foreign visitors were horrified to witness children being sold to brothel owners in central London. What shocked most was the seeming lack of concern shown by passing pedestrians. It was as if a child's life was no more important than that of a dog. Children so young and so thin due to hunger, dressed in rags with no shoes on their feet. No doubt there would be a new 'mother' awaiting the child who would be schooled in the art of pleasing men, who would be prepared to pay a guinea or two for one so young. The bleakness and lack of joy continues periodically with outbreaks of venereal diseases. Sex in London is often a dirty business.

We all understand that being a mother is difficult but being a 'mother' running a brothel was even trickier. It required what today we would refer to as management skills. A head for money and keeping a firm hand on the purse strings was imperative, as returning a tidy profit was essential. Then there was the people skills, which were so important. How to keep a collection of feisty young women under control was not easy. Rowdy and aggressive clients added the need for the equivalent of a modern day 'bouncer'. Then of course the customers had to be made comfortable and at ease with their surroundings. Get all these essentials right and a small fortune beckoned. In the 17th century one 'mother' added luxury to the menu she was offering, tempting those with the deepest pockets to visit her unique establishments.

It did not take long for Elizabeth Holland to realise that working the streets as a common whore was not the answer. The sins of men would maintain her in providing them with a memorable experience, when she opened her first house in the city offering high standards of luxury combined with extreme services rarely available elsewhere. She provided food and wine of the highest standard, encouraging clients to stay longer providing they were still spending. By the early years of the 17th century her rivals were suffering from a loss of trade and joining together managed to get the authorities to act against her. She was arrested and sent to Newgate prison for a spell. Whilst awaiting trial her connections in high society obtained her release. Now to avoid city regulations she moved to Bankside, an area notorious for its brothels since the 12th century.

Elizabeth, or Beth as she was commonly known, was not about to become just another brothel owner and she saw an opportunity in a deserted Thameside mansion. Moated with a drawbridge and gate-house, she could see this wreck offered a great opportunity. It also had a range of outbuildings and extensive gardens. These were to provide a peaceful backdrop to the more vigorous activities that 'mother' Holland's ladies were offering in the lavishly furnished bedchambers. She attracted a clientele including King James I and many leading members of his court.

The prices charged were accordingly extremely high. The establishment was affectionately known as 'nobs island'. Each guest was met by Beth, as much to test their ability to pay rather than just being sociable. She extended no credit no matter how exalted the customer might be. Any violence was dealt with promptly and she insisted that her girls were treated with respect. Described as being small in stature but still handsome, she had made a blueprint for successful upmarket brothels in the years to come. A tranquil and sumptuous setting for the wealthy and influential to indulge their lust.

The arrival on the throne of King Charles I saw a reverse in fortunes for Beth. He ordered the suppression of brothels and there were reports of falling standards at the brothel. There were rowdy parties and the girls were giving up any pretence of genteel behaviour. By 1631 troops were sent to close the whole enterprise down. The girls fought their corner for a time, raising the drawbridge and pelting the invaders with anything they could lay their hands on. Reinforcements were sent for and the brothel closed down. There is no further news of Beth Holland, presumably like other successful whores since, she retreated in to a respectable and comfortable retirement.

By the 18th century there were numbers of up-market brothels in London, but as ever the rich clients were looking for something different, something that set this establishment apart. This was provided by Miss Harriott who ran an extremely exclusive brothel in King's Place, St. James. Miss Harriott was a black woman snatched by slavers from her home in Guinea and transported to Jamaica. It appears she was devastatingly beautiful but also extremely intelligent. William Lewis was a plantation owner and a captain in the Merchant Navy. He not only bought her but seemingly fell in love with her. Their story makes Eliza's in 'My Fair Lady' seem quite tame. Captain Lewis and Harriott lived as man and wife. He taught her not only to read and write but also groomed her to be able to mix in the highest social circles. Eventually they moved to London, living just off Piccadilly. They must have caused something of a sensation. There were few black people living in London at the time and certainly not in well to do society. This is where the fairy story ends as William Lewis contracted smallpox in 1772 and died. He had obviously not made financial provision for Harriott and she was promptly consigned to the King's Bench debtors' prison. It appears she was freed with the help of admirers whose admiration was probably more sexual than altruistic.

Known now as 'black Harriott' she took over 3 King's Place in 1774. Situated so close to Parliament, many of her clients came from the House of Lords. First white men enslaved thousands, now they wanted to enjoy them sexually. James Boswell refers to one brothel containing just black women. The business continued to flourish but it appears Harriott was a romantic at heart, not an attribute suited to running a brothel. Whatever, she appears to have developed a yearning for a young guards officer. Distracted, her girls kept the money due to her and even sold off the expensive contents of her house. Back to the debtors' jail, and although she tried to reinvent the success of her first brothel on her release it never took off in the same way. The British climate was beginning to affect her health. Slowly her condition worsened with the onset of tuberculosis from which she died. 'Black Harriott', whose real name we never knew. Just another extraordinary life that has been partly clouded by the passing of time. We get a glimpse of the woman and as you learn more you hope for hers to have been a happy ending, but you know this was not going to be the case in a harsh London that has a habit of dragging even the best well meaning people down.

Elizabeth Cresswell was the foremost 'mother' of the 17th century, with every taste catered for. She offered ladies of 'all complexions' from coal black to golden-locked beauties. Her first establishment was close to Lincoln's Inn Fields, with others including her largest which stood on the site now occupied by Moorgate underground station. She claimed that Charles I honoured her with his presence, although her pet phrase 'no money no cunny' was unlikely to encourage an aristocratic clientele to her door.

Sex workers may age prematurely but not all die young. The clever ones get out early, either moving on to run their own establishment or better still marrying well. Meeting an outwardly charming Irishman in the Fleet Debtors prison did not auger well for either Charlotte Hayes or Dennis O'Kelly, but both went onto prosper in their own fields. It is unclear if it was Charlotte or Dennis who financed her first brothel, but for a time their romance deepened. O'Kelly was a gambler whose fortunes varied widely. One thing is certain he had an exceptional eye for a horse, as did Charlotte for creating one of the foremost London brothels of early Georgian London. Born in slum conditions in Covent Garden, Charlotte Hayes used O'Kelly's aristocratic connections to help drive her business.

O'Kelly was three years older than his lover. Born in Tullow in County Carlow, he moved to London as a young man, taking a variety of menial jobs. It was rumoured that he was given money by a titled lady he associated with before he met Charlotte. He became known around the gambling tables, seemingly on a winning streak until his luck ran out and he found himself in jail where he met Hayes. Whilst she expanded her empire, returning to the religious connection by calling her girls nuns. Shrewd whilst kind, she kept them in order by hiring out expensive clothes and jewellery to attract wealthy clients, deducting the cost from their earnings. She also set up a network of agents to bring her fresh supplies of innocent country girls (they did not stay innocent for long).

Meanwhile O'Kelly's knowledge of horses led to him acquiring a stable in Epsom. An increasingly shrewd judge of horse flesh, he paid an astonishing six hundred and fifty guineas for a half share in an unproven stallion. Desperate to buy the other share, he made an unprecedented wager on naming the first five horses to finish in the right order in a race at Epsom. The horse he was convinced that would win was Eclipse. He won his bet as he had suspected because Eclipse came home a full furlong ahead of the second horse, and the rest tailed off, resulting in the rest of the field registered as unplaced. His winnings allowed him to purchase the other share and a racing legend was born. Eclipse went on to win every race he entered and subsequently O'Kelly made a fortune from breeding. He even achieved status by being made a member of the Jockey Club. Seldom out of trouble, he was subsequently ejected and also banned from other London clubs.

It is unclear how much he saw of Charlotte Hayes as their paths parted. He obviously was still very fond of her as he left her four hundred pounds a year for the rest of her life, together with many of his goods and chattels. She survived him by twenty five years, dying in her eighties.

'Mother' Hayes continued to attract her upper class clientele. One elderly gentleman suggested her 'nunnery' in Great Marlborough Street could 'make old dotards believe themselves gay, vigorous young fellows, and vigorous young men into old dotards'. Charlotte lived an extremely extravagant life and eventually found herself back in a debtors' jail. She was bailed out by O'Kelly's nephew in exchange for her remaining assets. She spent the last few years of her life in the Cannons Park Estate in Edgware, dying in 1811. Here was another case of seemingly ordinary people living extraordinary lives, but there was one bawd who offered a service totally new to 19th century London.

There was a discreet hotel just off the Charing Cross Road in the 1950s known for employing young, good looking waiters. Their duties late at night extended well beyond serving at table. Here ladies of a certain age could enjoy a late sexual adventure with little chance of discovery or social embarrassment.

Nothing is new in life. During the early 19th century an enterprising brothel owner spotted a considerable gap in the market. Why should men be the only ones to have some fun. Mary Wilson, who ran a number of establishments throughout central London, wrote a book, 'Eleusinian Voluptuary Cabinet'. Forget ancient Greek mysteries, Mary Wilson was offering discreet opportunities for ladies to indulge in a little 'off piste' sex. The building was split into two separate sections. One for married women to meet and enjoy their lovers, the other for more adventurous ladies looking for what was a random thrill. Mary Wilson informed her potential clients of the delights awaiting them, albeit written in the best possible taste. She explained that she has purchased what she described as a 'sensitive' property. This lay between two major thoroughfares and could be entered by shops 'devoted entirely to such trades as are exclusively resorted by ladies'.

Once inside her premises she boasted of elegant saloons surrounded by sumptious boudoirs. Next she finally got to the nub of what was on offer. She informed us that she had procured 'the finest men of their species'; so far, so very tasteful. The lady waited to make her selection surrounded by erotic murals to put her in the mood. She could now view the stallions through a window before making her choice. She had been informed she could enjoy her stud in the dark or with lamps burning. Some ladies chose to wear a mask to protect their anonymity. She could book the boudoir for just one hour or for a whole night. The price charged was huge and whilst the food and wine were excellent, these were charged as extras. It is unclear how successful this enterprise was for Mary Wilson, but any woman brave (or stupid) enough to get involved must have worried about the danger of blackmail.

In 1893 the Shaftesbury Memorial fountain was unveiled in Piccadilly Circus to a very mixed reception. Few at the time realised that it was soon to become one of London's iconic sites. It was as if this aluminium statue was acting as a magnet and unseen power that was drawing people from around the world. Theatres, restaurants and other places of entertainment sprang up. It was a meeting place for friends but also increasingly for easy pick-ups as street workers mingled with the crowds. London's centre of gravity had shifted.

Amongst the crowds it was also easy to spot those standing alone. Strangers, isolated and sad. Perhaps they belonged to a section of society which still faced discrimination in Victorian Britain not due to their colour or religion, but until recently the target for violence and verbal abuse. Despite this London has always been a queer city.

Chapter 13

Gay's the Word

There was a buzz of excitement in the foyer of the Saville Theatre in Shaftesbury Avenue. Outside taxis and chauffeur driven cars pulled up as the ladies in evening gowns or smart cocktail dresses joined the throng along with their dinner jacketed escorts. It was February 1951 and a rare chance to show off the latest fashions almost two years after clothes rationing had ended. This excited crowd was here to see the opening night of a new musical by Ivor Novello with lyrics written by Alan Melville. The show starred Cicely Courtneidge and was produced by her husband Jack Hulbert. The show was called 'Gay's The Word'. It had good reviews and ran for almost two years.

There is a poignant irony in that both Novello and Melville would have been known in the 1950s as 'queers'. The term 'gay' was not in common use for another twenty years. Gay was used in everyday conversation meaning light hearted and carefree. For a time there was a reaction against an innocent, rather lovely word having its meaning reassigned, but there is little doubt that Ivor Novello would have approved. Prejudice against homosexuals had a few years to run yet. There is no doubt that these men were perceived to be different, and as we have already witnessed, any form of difference in London was treated with suspicion and sometimes violence.

Gay men have always had to be careful living in London. Of course they had their own meeting places and 'molly houses' were in a sense the equivalent of modern day gay bars. Until 1533 any sexual acts between male adults were dealt with by ecclesiastical courts whose findings were invariably harsh. The 1533 Buggery Act did not just target men as it also related to acts performed by heterosexual couples. Bestiality was also outlawed and attracted the same death sentence. For the most part few executions were carried out but the potential loomed large. It took until the nineteenth century for the Act to be finally repealed. Not that this helped gay men particularly, as the Offences Against the Person Act of 1828 related to men only with the death sentence remaining. Seven years later John Smith and James Pratt became the last two men to be executed for homosexual acts. 'The abominable crime' remained firmly embedded in Victorian Britain and gay men had to live much of their lives either in denial or in the shadows. Eventually in 1885 the Criminal Law Amendment Act was passed. The Act was now targeted to prosecute those who committed 'any acts of gross indecency with male persons'. Those found guilty of gross indecency had to serve a term of at least two years' hard labour.

Molly houses had been around in London for centuries, with one opposite the Old Bailey, attracting attention in 1559 for men addressing each other as 'madam' or 'your ladyship'. In the 18th century a fountain in the Strand had become known as a likely meeting point for gay men. The owner of a male brothel in Camomile Street in Bishopsgate was affectionately known as the 'Countess of Camomile'. With so many molly houses operating in London there was a backlash in the form of The Societies For The Reformation Of Manners. This resulted in the closing of over twenty male brothels including the most notorious. 'Mother Clap's house was in the run down district of Holborn. It had become known as an area attracting homosexual men and Mother Clap had not been discreet. At her trial it was claimed that between forty and fifty men had been caught making love to each other. They also danced together, some dressed in women's clothes and mimicking the voices of women. There was a separate room where they carried out a marriage ceremony in all seriousness. The witness visited the house on three successive Sundays, witnessing much the same behaviour. It was reported that there was 'all manner of gross and vile obscenity', spoken in Mother Clap's hearing and she appeared 'to be 'wonderfully pleased with it'. She appealed to the court, insisting that as a woman she would 'never be concerned with such practices'. Not surprisingly the court did not believe her. Three of her young male prostitutes were hanged, whilst she was sent for a spell in the pillory in Smithfield before going to Newgate. The fury of the crowd, most of whom were women, was extreme and shocking. Eventually she was dragged away having had excrement, dead animals and stones thrown at her. She never recovered and she died three days later.

The vindictiveness of Londoners against convicted 'sodomites' was far more damming than any other crime, with a surge of cases coming before the courts during the early part of the 18th century. Many of those arrested were ordinary working men who were married. In 1726 it was recorded that an upholsterer, a milkman and a cowhand were among many who were convicted, most of whom had fathered children. Invariably they were sent to the pillory and assuming they survived that ordeal had to deal with the ongoing shame. These were not powdered effeminate men, suggesting that homosexual activity was taking place more widely than previously thought. It is the very ordinariness of those involved that strikes home. In 1764 the Public Advertiser reported that 'a bugger aged sixty was put in the Cheapside pillory…the mob tore off his clothes, pelted him with filth, whipped him almost to death. He was naked and covered with dung. When the hour was up he was carried almost unconscious to Newgate'. Ordinary many of these men may have been, but the rich and famous were not about to be sidelined for long.

Two sensational cases at the end of the 19th century led to a widespread belief that the British aristocracy had become corrupted by their inclination to get involved in homosexual relationships, which were still illegal at the time. As we have seen such activities were not confined to those high born. No matter, anyone convicted was liable to two years' hard labour, but worse suffering long lasting damage to their reputation. With prostitutes lining virtually every street in many parts of the capital, there was a feeling that the country was witnessing a dramatic moral decline.

Like so many scandals the Cleveland Street affair was a slow burner, but grew to implicate people of high standing, including those close to the Crown. In July 1899 a low key enquiry into a theft at the Central Telegraph office took on a life of its own. A fifteen year old messenger boy, Charles Swinscow, was found to have fourteen shillings in his possession. Good news, he was surely the culprit, but no. He was brought in for questioning, but came up with a story that the money he had received was payment for services he had rendered to a gentleman at a house in Cleveland Street. This was obviously way beyond the police constable's pay grade and so entered Inspector Frederick Abberline, nose twitching, sensing a scandal. The young messenger admitted making the money by acting as a male prostitute at what was obviously a brothel. The owner, Charles Hammond, was arrested along with a number of other young messenger boys. The wheels of justice were beginning to grind but very slowly. Why? Suddenly it appeared that some very powerful and influential men might be implicated. Time to tread carefully.

A post office clerk, eighteen year old Henry Newlove, accused Lord Arthur Somerset and Henry Fitzroy, Earl of Euston of being enthusiastic clients. Somerset was Equerry to the Prince of Wales and in charge of his stables. He was interviewed, but it is easy to imagine him denying any connection and frankly appalled that the detective had the temerity to suggest otherwise. The case appeared to have stalled until George Veck was arrested. Veck had worked at the Telegraph Office, but had been dismissed for sexual misconduct with other employees. The seventeen year old was arrested by Inspector Abberline, who was probably by now unsure of his line of enquiry. Letters were found on Veck from Algernon Allies. It was whilst he was being interviewed that Allies admitted that he had been paid for having sex with Somerset and that he worked as a prostitute for George Hammond at Cleveland Street. Somerset was interviewed for a second time by police before promptly leaving for Germany, where the Prince of Wales was enjoying one of his frequent holidays. It transpired that Veck's and Newloves's legal fees were paid for by Somerset and there was comment on how lenient the sentences imposed on the young men for their indecent acts were. The press were now beginning to show an interest and there were mutterings and mention of 'noble lords' being implicated during the trial of the young men.

Somerset made several visits back home, but by now the Commissioner for Police was pressing for action to be taken against Somerset, but Lord Salisbury the Lord Chancellor blocked the proceedings. Time to close ranks. Rumours regarding Somerset's involvement were now out in the open and he fled to France after hearing that a warrant for his arrest was expected. Somerset never returned, living a life of comfort on the Riviera. Despite rumours circulating, there had been relatively little coverage in the British press. This was about to change.

Articles in the foreign press were picked up by Ernest Parke, the editor of the North London Press, a radical paper printed weekly but with a limited circulation. Parke was aware of the speculation swirling around London. He was intrigued by the lenient sentences passed down to the messenger boys. Normally cases involving gross indecency warranted a two year jail sentence. In addition George Hammond, the owner of the brothel, had avoided arrest and slinked abroad. An American newspaper had claimed sensationally that Prince Albert, the son of the Prince of Wales, might be implicated as well as other leading members of society. There was more to this than met the eye. He sensed a cover-up.

Although Parke had no cast iron evidence he printed an article naming Henry Fitzroy, Earl of Euston, of being involved in an 'indescribably loathsome scandal in Cleveland Street'. He mistakenly said that Euston had gone to Peru to avoid further investigation and hinted broadly at the royal connection. Actually Euston was still in Britain and at once filed a case against Parke for libel. At the trial Euston admitted he had visited Cleveland Street on the understanding he would be able to watch nude ladies perform 'poses plastiques'. Having paid a sovereign to gain entry he was horrified to be confronted 'by the nature of the place'. The defence witnesses contradicted each other and were unable to describe Euston accurately. The jury found Parke guilty and he was sentenced to a year in prison.

What to make of it all? Certainly at the time it was felt that there was no smoke without fire. The case did leave an impression of powerful people using their influence to avoid the full weight of the law, a theme that is still relevant today. Prince Albert Victor certainly lived a disreputable life, but there was no direct evidence linking him to the scandal. Some, but not all, insisted he was ultra heterosexual, but they would, wouldn't they. Scandal involving the Royal Family was to be avoided at all costs. Luckily for his family and the country this flawed Prince died within a few years of the trial, and his dull but safe younger brother went onto become King George V in 1910.

In old age Lord Alfred Douglas received regular visits from the diarist and politician 'Chips' Channon at his home in Sussex. Channon was sorry to note how modestly Oscar Wilde's former lover was now having to live. Mind you, most people lived modestly compared to Channon's extravagant lifestyle. The scandal involving Douglas and Wilde had caused much soul searching in British society, with another homosexual scandal so soon after the Cleveland Street affair.

As a young man Douglas was beautiful, but spoilt and entitled. His relationship with Wilde infuriated his father, the ninth Marquess of Queensbury. He left a card at Wilde's lodgings accusing him of being a 'posing sodomite'. Against the advice of his friends Wilde decided to sue for libel, although Douglas, being young and petulant, supported the action. Although Wilde was famous for both his poetry and his cutting wit, these did nothing to further his case in court. The weight of evidence suggested that Wilde and Douglas were indeed lovers and the Marquess was found not guilty. Wilde was promptly arrested and charged with sodomy and gross indecency. During the trial a quote from a poem written by Douglas became etched into British consciousness with the phrase 'the love that dare not speak its name'. During the trial Wilde had spoken in defence of a romantic relationship between two men being valid and should not end in being sent to the pillory. This was probably the first public speech in support of same sex relationships, and as such remained influential in a gradual change in attitude towards gay men. At the time it fell on deaf ears and Wilde was sentenced to two years in jail. Later Douglas married and the couple had a child, although the marriage did not last.

Channon continued to visit Douglas into the early years of the war. A time when the diarist complained about being approached in the dark by male prostitutes as he walked home from the House of Commons. Irony was obviously not a strong point for 'Chips' as waiting at home at 5 Belgrave Square was his boyfriend Peter Coats. In the highest social circles anything was possible providing discretion was always observed.

Discretion was certainly not a strong characteristic exhibited by Quentin Crisp, who was trawling the streets of Soho at about the same time as Channon was leading his double life. Soho had always been more accommodating to minorities, but 'queers' still had to tread carefully. Not Crisp. Now in his thirties, he was rejected by the British Army on the grounds of him suffering from 'sexual perversion'. This left him free to trawl the blacked out streets and alleys, covered in make up and cheap perfume. For Quentin these were golden years as he set out to meet responsive GIs. Places like the Swiss Tavern in Old Compton Street tolerated rather than welcomed homosexuals. The pub was described as not being 'entirely straight' and of course today the street is one of the best known gathering points for gay men.

By the early 1950s attitudes towards gay men remained firmly entrenched. True, a blind eye was shown to the activities of celebrities like Noel Coward, but generally discretion was required. The star of film and theatre John Gielgud had recently been knighted to much acclaim in 'luvvie' circles. Although gay, he was always careful to protect the privacy of his personal life. That is until a night in October 1953 when he approached an undercover police officer in a Chelsea public toilet. He had just finished rehearsals for a new play due to open within days at the Haymarket Theatre called 'A Day By The Sea'. He was marched off to the local police station and ordered to appear in court the following day. There is some dispute as to whether Gielgud rang the impresario and stage manager Binkie Beaumont or not. Some say that Binkie's live in boyfriend said it was too late to wake the great man. Others say that Gielgud was too ashamed and retreated to a sleepless night. Beaumont was a very powerful figure with influential contacts who may have been able to divert the hearing to some suburban outpost where the case could go unnoticed.

In a central London court Gielgud said he was a clerk earning one thousand pounds a year. He told the magistrate, 'I cannot imagine that I was so stupid, I was tired and had been drinking. I was not responsible for my actions'. The magistrate fined him ten pounds and suggested kindly that it may be best for Gielgud to go and see a doctor. The feeling remained that homosexuality was an illness that could surely be cured. It is unusual for journalists from national papers to attend magistrate courts unless tipped off if there was a potentially juicy scandal about to break. There was no such indication and it was unlucky for Gielgud that a reporter for the Evening Standard was there by chance. Through an open door to the court he saw a familiar figure. He rang his office and the lunchtime edition headline had people rushing to buy their copy as a national treasure was exposed.

Gielgud's immediate reaction was to resign and leave public life, but he steeled himself to meet the company of 'A Day By The Sea' in the rehearsal room. Shaking with fear, there was an embarrassed silence as he entered. They had all been astonished by the news. It was Sybil Thorndike who broke the ice by saying in a loud theatrical voice, 'you have been a silly bugger!' Everyone including Sir John broke into laughter. Having completed a successful provincial tour and the opening night only days away, cancelling the show was impossible as the bookings were already well ahead of target. The show must go on. There were worries that there would be demonstrations and cat-calling of Gielgud. Public opinion was divided but many of the letters he received were vitriolic. Binkie laid on police and extra security to weed out any potential trouble-makers. He even arranged for stage managers from his other theatres to mingle in the bars before curtain up to winkle out any likely protesters. Among the cast and management there was tension and gloomy predictions. It was fifteen minutes into the play before Gielgud was to make his first entrance. He stood shaking in the wings. It was as if he was paralysed with fear. Once again it was Sybil Thorndike who came to the rescue. Walking off stage, she grabbed him saying, 'come on John darling, they won't boo me'. She was right. As he appeared the applause grew. People rose to their feet giving him a standing ovation. Overcome and with tears streaming down his cheeks, he stumbled into his first lines and the play continued.

After the final curtain calls champagne flowed in Gielgud's dressing room, the celebrations being cut short with news that hundreds of people had gathered outside the stage door. It was presumed that many of these would be hostile. It was suggested that Gielgud should escape by leaving by the front entrance, but the darling boy had discovered a back bone after all, declaring proudly, 'I am an actor and I will leave as always by the stage door'. Binkie arranged for a group to act as bodyguards, but once again Gielgud was greeted with cheers and people begging for his autograph. Once more he was convulsed with emotion because the public had defied expectations. Not so Buckingham Palace. There was talk of having his knighthood stripped from him. This did not happen but the Palace did let Binkie know that a proposed visit to appear on Broadway was to be cancelled, or at least postponed until the scandal had died down.

Here was a uniquely English scandal. A squalid meeting in a public lavatory. A suggestion that a visit to a doctor would help cure what continued to be thought of as an illness. A willingness to forgive (at least by a theatre going public), although much prejudice remained, but it was a tentative pointer towards reform. Within four years the Wolfenden report recommended the decriminalisation of gay sex between consenting adults. The government rejected the report and it was to take another ten years before homosexual acts between consenting men aged over twenty one was passed into law by the Sexual Offences Act of 1967.

Chapter 14

Your Money or Your Life

Highwaymen have a reputation for being 'gentlemen of the road', robbing people with a touch of gallantry. Whilst not a gentleman, highwayman Jack Collett can claim to have carried out some of the most outrageous robberies. Outrageous but not very bright. He had the luck (or misfortune) of holding up the Bishop of Winchester. Not content with his haul of fifty guineas he demanded that the Bishop take off his vestments. Presumably leaving the poor man in his undergarments, Collett rode off triumphantly. He then set about pulling off a number of successful robberies dressed in the Bishop's finery. He guessed quite rightly that few would be on guard approached by such an eminent figure. It should have been obvious that this ploy would be reported and he was bound to be caught eventually, but small time crooks are not normally that smart. Collett obviously thought the church would continue to help finance his lifestyle, as he was caught breaking into the vestry at St. Bartholomew's church in Smithfield. He was arrested and joined a long list of highwaymen executed at Tyburn. The charge of 'sacrilegious burglary' could hardly have been more serious in the eyes of the authorities.

Although London is not normally associated with highway robbery, it is to the capital that many involved headed for. The roads leading to London before the growth of the suburbs were prime locations for robberies, and it was easy to hide in the teeming city. London also offered a network of 'fences' prepared to pay a good price for stolen goods before selling them on. Jewels were re-set to avoid identification. Everything was possible in London.

As early as the mid 17th century there was a coach service between London and Chester. The trip was estimated to take five days and the cost an eye watering thirty five shillings. Until this time any lengthy journey had to be taken by horseback. Roads were little more than muddy tracks meandering through fields and meadows. The initial route was a success and others were laid on linking London to other major cities. Coaches were overturned and horses bolted and the ride in those early coaches was extremely uncomfortable, not to mention the need on occasion of having to get out and push, arriving at the destination days later, exhausted and vowing never to travel by coach again. By the beginning of the 18th century the commercial possibilities of travel began to dawn. The industrial revolution demanded manufactured goods as well as people needing to be moved. New roads were laid and coaches refined to offer faster and marginally more comfortable accommodation. New coaching inns appeared every few miles on the most popular routes. In a pre-Grand Prix spirit of speed it was possible to replace horses within two minutes so the coach could continue on its way. Speed was essential and 'flying coaches' in 1754 allowed the Manchester coach to arrive in London within four and a half days. Three years later the 'Liverpool flying machine' covered the two hundred and six miles in just three days, but it would set you back two guineas. Therefore only wealthy people could afford to travel by coach. Enter the highwaymen. They too became more sophisticated, making contacts in the ticketing offices and learning in advance of wealthy passengers likely to be carrying really worthwhile valuables.

By the end of the 18th century the Royal Mail began to run their own coaches. These took precedence as all other vehicles had to pull over to make way. By 1797 the Mail coaches were taking just twenty eight hours to travel from Manchester to London. The fastest private route took eight hours longer. By 1830 the coaches had achieved optimum speed. A whole new industry had developed, with coach builders improving both the design and comfort for passengers. Innkeepers kept their own horses which were hired out for an eight or ten mile stint. They would then be stabled and fed before making the return journey the next day. Coachmen normally travelled about fifty miles a day and their earnings relied heavily on tips. Each coach carried an armed guard who travelled the entire length of the journey, again expecting a hefty tip. The average coach normally carried four passengers, although some squeezed in six. The numbers travelling on the roof were governed by law with twelve being allowed on a stage coach, but only one on Mail coaches. For those relying on maximum speed outside passengers were normally restricted to just a couple. Despite the improvement in road conditions a long journey tested even the strongest constitutions, particularly travelling outside alongside the baggage. Assailed by wind, rain and snow in winter, the lurching of the coach made it impossible to sleep. Inside it wasn't much better. In summer it was actually better to sit outside rather than being seated between the other sweating passengers. There was always a fear of the coach tipping over, and to add to that worry there was the prospect of being held at gunpoint by a ruthless highwayman.

All highwaymen needed a steady nerve, a certain bravado and importantly a fast horse for their getaway. In character they were as diverse as those employed in any legal trade or profession. Some were little more than violent ruffians, whilst others prided themselves on their impeccable manners. These were the real 'kings of the road'. Whatever, most were caught eventually, paying for their audacity with their lives.

It was his meticulous planning that set William Page apart. Born in 1730, he came from a poor background with his father working on the Thames as a bargeman. His taste for the good life started when he was employed by an army officer as his valet. Eventually this led him to gaining a post as an under-footman at the house of the Earl of Glencairn. Attending lavish dinners and seeing how the other half lived created a feeling of envy. He realised he was never going to acquire any wealth working as a servant. His mind turned to robbery. All he needed was a pair of pistols and a horse. He had neither. He managed to persuade a colleague to let him have his pistols on approval for a day. Next he hired a horse from a local livery stable and set off for Highgate, an area he knew well. Here he pulled off his first robbery, but he was almost caught. He realised the only way to succeed was through detailed planning. He started drawing maps of areas close to London, but relatively isolated. He chose spots where the coaches would be at their most vulnerable, like at the bottom of a steep hill where when the weather was bad there was a danger of the over-laden coach tipping over. Quietly he carried out other raids before he hit on a most audacious plan.

At this stage William was joined by an accomplice who we only know as Darwell. Page made great play on leaving London in his own chaise and pair, dressed in fine clothes. At an agreed meeting place he linked up with Darwell, leaving his carriage in deep woodland. Then having changed into old clothes they lay in wait for the stage coach. Witnesses spoke of a polite robber but one wearing a very tatty black wig. Rushing off with the spoils, Page returned to London in his carriage dressed in his finery whilst Darwell rode off making contact with Page later to share the spoils. It is not known how many robberies the pair undertook together, but Page had a reputation for being lucky, narrowly escaping on a number of occasions. It is estimated that Page carried out over three hundred robberies before he was finally caught and sent for trial. Even then he had a final card to play. He had been identified as the robber by Earl Ferrers, but perhaps William Page would have been better employed as a lawyer. Cleverly he pointed out to the court that Ferrers had been ex-communicated for contempt of the Bishop of London's Consistory court, and that therefore he was not entitled to give evidence against Page on this technicality. The case was dismissed and Page released. Finally his luck ran out. Had he become over confident, thinking himself invincible? We will never know but within weeks he was caught attempting a robbery at Blackheath, a notorious hunting ground for highwaymen. He was duly hanged, dying before he reached the age of thirty.

Whereas William Page appears to have been of above average intelligence, Richard Dudley was surely just evil. Despite coming from a respectable home he was already stealing before he reached the age of ten. Whilst still a young man he became involved with a gang of violent robbers. Arrested, he was sentenced to death but his father obtained a Royal Pardon and bought his son a commission in the army and a marriage was arranged. Some people can just not be helped as Dudley walked away from his wife and life in the army to join another band of robbers. Caught again, his father was successful in getting the death sentence commuted to one of transportation. He escaped whilst the ship was docked in the Isle of Wight. Seldom out of trouble, he robbed a farmer of his horse and clothes as he continued to carry out a series of robberies. A reward was offered and it is thought he was betrayed by one of his own gang (so much for honour amongst thieves). This time his father was unable to help him and like so many in his chosen trade he was hanged.

Here are two outstanding characters who uphold the idea of there having been 'gentlemen highwaymen'. Claude Duval was born in France but on arriving in England obtained a post of footman in the court of King Charles II. It was during his employment for the King that as part of his protection duties he became an accomplished horseman and shot. Extravagant by nature and always short of money, he started taking to the road to boost his income. For a time he was successful, carrying out a number of raids in Holloway, an area covering low ground on the road from Highgate to the city of London. Always beautifully dressed, he never used any violence and whilst his French accent charmed the ladies it would eventually help in his capture. There is one often quoted instance of both his cheek and daring. Having held up a married couple in their carriage, Duval asked the husband for permission to dance with his wife. The scene, whether true or not, was immortalised in an 1860 painting by William Frith.

With a sizeable reward being offered for his capture, Duval returned to Normandy. What drew him back to take his chance in London again? A lady perhaps, but the outcome was predictable. Being easy to track down, Duval was arrested at a tavern in Covent Garden. He was sentenced to death and legend has it that legions of women wept at the prospect of his death. Because of his former association with the King, a Royal Pardon was sought. It was refused and Claude Duval joined a long line of highwaymen to be executed at Tyburn. It is believed that he is buried under the central nave of St. Paul's church in Covent Garden

There must have been hundreds of highwaymen roaming the roads leading to London over the years. Why then is it that certain characters still live on hundreds of years after their demise? James MacLaine was the last to be known as 'the gentleman highwayman' because of his courteous manner as he relieved victims of their money and valuables. More likely he was just a spoiled young man who squandered an inheritance and took to crime. No matter, it is not for us to moralise but rather try to piece together another extraordinary life.

It appears that MacLaine was born in Ireland to a Protestant family of Scottish descent. His parents died whilst he was young. His brother followed a long line of relatives by entering the church and became Royal Preceptor in Holland. There was little chance of James following the family tradition and on obtaining his inheritance he took off to Dublin where a love of the high life and gambling saw him squandering the money, much to the despair of his relatives.

They refused to give him any more funds. His brother was more accommodating, but he was only able to send limited money from his modest earnings in the Netherlands. He was forced to take a number of menial jobs before moving to London. A good looking young man, he set out to find himself a wealthy wife. Instead he had a scandalous affair with an army officer's wife and planned to leave for the West Indies in the hope of making his fortune there. This scheme was shelved when he found a young lady prepared to marry him. She was hardly out of the top drawer, being the daughter of a tavern owner. The dowry enabled James to set up in business but the venture was not a success. The couple had two daughters, only one of which survived. The marriage appears to have been a happy one, but James's life went badly wrong on the death of his wife, who died prematurely. Now down on his luck and vulnerable he became friendly with William Plunkett, an apothecary who had helped look after James's wife during her final illness. Plunkett was also Irish and they formed a bond due also to their financial difficulties. After much discussion they decided in desperation to try their luck at highway robbery. Their first attempt went well, catching a merchant returning from Smithfield and relieving him of sixty pounds. Feeling confident, they next held up a coach on the road to London from St. Albans. This was turning out to be easier than they had imagined. They continued their plunder, undertaking twenty successful robberies, brandishing pistols and with their faces covered by masks. Reports started circulating about the pair, one of whom appeared to be a gentleman. Hyde Park at night became a favourite hunting ground. If MacLaine ever felt in danger of being exposed he set off to see his brother in Holland until the rumours died down.

In November 1749 the writer and politician Hugh Walpole was travelling across Hyde Park by carriage when he was set upon by two men mounted on horseback. One wielding a blunderbuss was threatening, whilst his companion quietly placed a pistol through the carriage window. It appeared to go off by accident, grazing Walpole's face. They relieved him of money, his watch, sword and a leather purse. Later he received a letter saying that his belongings could be bought back for a price. The letter was well written in a time when relatively few people could read or write. It had become obvious that a 'gentleman' robber was at large. It would surely only take time before he was caught.

By now with his new found wealth, MacLaine was living in fashionable central London and mixing in high society. Women appeared to be constantly attracted to him. He had money and endless charm. Life was expensive and so he and Plunkett intensified their attacks. On one night in the summer of 1750 they held up a carriage owned by the Earl of Eglinton on Hounslow Common, before moving on to Chiswick where they held up 'the flying coach'. Details of the items stolen were now circulated and this led to James MacLaine's downfall. A stolen waistcoat he was wearing was recognised and constables called at MacLaine's fashionable lodgings where they discovered many items that had been reported as stolen. It was off to Newgate for James. The evidence was damning. Plunkett disappeared, presumably to Ireland assuming a different identity. Whatever, he was never captured and as time passed faded from the public's memory. Not so MacLaine, he had become something of a celebrity. His trial was attended by fashionable society and he was allowed to have dozens visit him in his cell in Newgate. At first he pleaded guilty, later changing it to not guilty. As the trial started a titled lady gave a character witness statement, stating she had always found him honest and she had never mislaid anything whilst he was in her company. Good effort but that was never going to change the minds of those convinced of MacLaine's guilt. He blamed Plunkett for everything, but it was no good. His brother pleaded for mercy. It cut no ice with the jury, who brought in a verdict of guilty without even leaving the court.

With no hope now of avoiding the rope, it was only left for James MacLaine to make a dignified departure. A huge crowd had gathered at

Tyburn. Despite some jeering his final words were heard by many close to the scaffold. He was calm as he said: 'Oh God, forgive my enemies, bless my friends and revive my soul'. He had broken the perceived understanding of a highwayman being just a common criminal, but with the inevitable final outcome.

Trust a highwayman to have the last word (well, at least at Tyburn). Unlike James MacLaine, John Austin made no pretence of being a gentleman. He was really little more than a footpad, but it was he who was the very last person to be hanged at Tyburn in November 1783. He was not a great act to end this long running show that had seen hundreds meet their death, but he did his best: 'Good people, I request your prayers for the salvation of my departing soul. Let my example teach you to shun the bad ways I have followed. Keep good company and mind the word of God. Lord have mercy on me. Jesus look down with pity on me. Christ have mercy on my soul'.

Unfortunately these cries went unheeded. As the cart jerked forward the noose slipped to the back of Austin's neck, causing this final 'Tyburn jig' to take an agonising ten minutes as his legs thrashed around seeking his final release. Gradually the number of highway robberies decreased with the increasing activities of the Bow Street Runners. Another major factor was the increase in the number of banks, resulting in people carrying less money on them. The last mounted highway robbery took place in 1831. There were now going to be more lucrative ways for criminals to thrive. Soon the masked highwayman would become a distant memory, but kept alive by popular culture.

Chapter 15

A Bit on the Side

We have all seen them. They stare at us from the inside pages of the national press normally on the arm of some Saudi prince, Russian oligarch or possibly an ageing pop star. It is as if these young women have been produced in some artificial intelligence factory. They all have long blonde hair, are slim and have legs that go up to their armpits. They will have worked hard to get to this point in their lives. Their south London or regional accents have been largely erased and they have learnt what cutlery to use at posh restaurants. For a few weeks or maybe longer they are introduced to a lifestyle they previously only dreamt of. Fast cars, swanky hotels and maybe a trip to Monaco or Barbados. These girls are street-wise, they know the score. Pay-back time comes later in a luxurious hotel suite. When the liaison has run its course the pay-off might be a bauble from their wealthy friend, but one possibly worth thousands. Then it is time to move on in the hunt for their next victim. These are the modern day version of courtesans and who can blame them for cashing in on their most obvious attribute. They would hate to be thought of as prostitutes. Mistresses maybe, albeit generally on a short lease.

To get a greater understanding of a fully blown courtesan in modern life we need to travel east. In Hong Kong it is not unusual for wealthy tycoons to have a lady comfortably housed in a fashionable apartment. Whilst ostensibly happily married, he rarely takes his wife with him when he entertains important clients. Whilst she stays at home living in extravagant comfort, it is time for the other lady in his life to take centre stage. She is far removed from the British equivalent. Whilst this lady also has stunning good looks, more is required. She will be expected to charm the guests with her wit and humour. It is also likely that she is well read and has a good grasp of world events. Her sexual favours are normally reserved for her one provider, although it is not unknown for two men to share the one lady, halving the expense. These arrangements are often tacitly accepted by the wives of these men. As with all of us, much of life is about compromise.

Courtesan, good time girl or mistress, mixing with nobility can bring its rewards. The Royal association goes back to Nell Gwynne, the orange seller who became the mistress of King Charles II. Our present Queen Camilla is the great grand-daughter of Alice Keppel, the long time confidante of Edward VII. Unfortunately not all those glamorous ladies who set their sights so high ended up wealthy and accepted in society. Sophia Baddeley certainly soared but then fell to earth with a terrible bump, and her story should perhaps be a warning for a modern young lady contemplating this perilous route.

Sophia Baddeley was born into the turbulent world of Georgian England. Her early life was conventional enough, giving few clues of the wild extremes of success and ultimate degradation to come. Music formed an important part of her early years. Her father and long time friend Eliza Steele encouraged her as she showed a real talent for playing the harpsichord. This was part of her genteel education, but by her teens Sophia was ready to rebel. Is extreme beauty a blessing or a curse? Her beauty it seems could turn a succession of influential and wealthy men to jelly, seemingly willing to finance her ever increasing demands. But as beauty fades and the money dries up the outcome is never going to be a happy one.

Fed up with incessant harpsichord lessons and attempting to be a decorous young lady, she was offered an escape route by a neighbour who introduced her to Robert Baddeley. He was an actor at the Drury Lane Theatre in central London. He was approaching forty, over twice her age. No matter, they eloped and were married in 1764. The marriage was a failure and although they never divorced, they were living separate lives. Four years later it was through her husband that Sophia was introduced to the stage. Being an actress in the eighteenth century was reckoned to be only one removed to being a prostitute. This stigma persisted even to an extent into the twentieth century. Sophia was generally considered a terrible actress, wooden and awkward on stage, but this did little to stop her rise. She was already having affairs early in her marriage and it was suggested that in effect her husband was pimping her and taking a financial cut, but Sophia did not need Robert anymore as admirers were queuing up just to be seen with her. Just when life appeared to be going well the unexpected happened, Sophia fell in love. John Hanger was the youngest son of an impoverished Irish peer. They moved to Soho and set up house together. We are told that he 'denied her no extravagance'. Shortly his money ran out and they were living on her relatively modest stage earnings. It could not last with them being pursued by numerous demanding tradesmen. Hanger obviously understood he faced ruin and decided to leave her. For the only time in her life she was on the receiving end of being dumped. She was devastated. For the first time she took to the laudanum bottle and was laid low for weeks.

Sensing her vulnerability, she was approached by Lord Molyneux who offered to set her up with an income of £400 a year. She hesitated as he was married, but added to her own earnings this offer allowed her to run her own carriage and employ servants. Her appearances at Drury Lane were now attracting full houses prompted by her beauty rather than her acting ability. King George III came to see her perform. She was now being invited to dine with some of the most influential in the land. No wives in sight, respectability to a point but no further. Lord Paget took a box paying £100 in the hope of attracting her attention. A succession of old men were losing their dignity, led astray by a pretty face, albeit an exceptionally pretty one. King George had even ordered her portrait to be painted by Zoffany, but it was time for the old timers to stand aside. Enter the young, good looking and extremely wealthy Lord Melbourne.

Although only recently married, Melbourne, like so many others, was swept away by Sophia. Not just her looks either, although she did exude a deep routed sexuality. His wife was a lady he was proud of, gentle and home loving, but this was different. By now Sophia was the talk of the town and considered to be the most fashionable in London. Melbourne approached her first through a friend, offering her a share in his fortune in exchange for 'the possession of her heart'.

In the first flush of their liaison Melbourne offered Sophia full access to his money. Now she was able to show her talent for extravagance. Here surely was the high tide of her life. Nothing was denied her, it was spend, spend, spend. Seen out, she was weighed down by jewellery. Melbourne even bought her a cream coloured mare so she could be seen riding side-saddle in fashionable parks. Sophia was not entirely vacuous, being extremely generous with friends. It really did not matter as long as she was spending. Now appearing on stage became increasingly tiresome. By now she was also finding Melbourne something of a bore. He demanded her attention whenever he pleased, interrupting her day. She began to resent him and he did not excite her sexually. She acquired a country house with resident servants. She was now a person considered close to the top rank (but not quite). Being the mistress of Lord Melbourne did nothing to dissuade others to seek her affection. The numbers leaving their calling cards represented a high proportion from the House of Lords. She was offered increasing inducements to break with Lord Melbourne. She was also worried that she had no legal agreement tying Melbourne to her, and offers were coming in promising protection for life in exchange for her commitment. One of the most interesting came from the Duke of Northumberland, a man of immense wealth. His persistence and money led to him gaining access to her bedchamber, which she instantly regretted.

Life for Sophia was an endless round of pleasure seeking and spending. Eventually any pleasure palls. The relationship with Melbourne had been cooling for some time. Her constant demand for money whilst going off on a trip to Ireland annoyed him. Eventually matters came to a head at a masked masquerade where Sophia discovered Melbourne in the company of Harriet Powell, who had been his mistress before he married. They argued, blaming each other for the breakdown. It was over and marked the gradual downfall of one of the greatest Georgian courtesans. Her obsessive spending had resulted in huge debts. These were reckoned to be in the region of eight thousand pounds. Time to pawn a few diamonds. None of her remaining suitors were prepared to pay up. How quickly circumstances can change. Her companion, Mrs. Steele, suggested that surely Sophia could dress well on a hundred pounds a year. Sophia replied: 'Christ, that is not enough for millinery....one may as well be dead as not in fashion'. Now the offers from her suitors were different in tone. She had lost the high ground (if she ever had it), now it was as if they were negotiating with a common whore. The worry of it all was affecting her looks. Debtors were clamouring for payment. She had been set adrift with little protection.

She returned to the stage but was now cut by men who had previously begged for her attention. She found some happiness in a relationship with a fellow actor and bore him two children. Increasingly ill health began to take its toll. Her last appearance at Drury Lane was in 1780. Her husband died the following year and this triggered a further decline in her health. Now she turned to a servant of her husband for love and support, much to the disgust of the ever present Mrs Steele. What followed was a spiral of debt, sickness and increasingly laudanum. She appeared in a play in York and in the biography of her life by Mrs Steele she was 'in truth reduced to beggary'. Sophia Baddeley died of consumption in 1785 aged just forty-two. An astonishing but in reality a thoroughly wasted life. Others who travelled the same route were more astute and able to retire from the bedchamber in comfort

Kitty Fisher and Sophia Baddeley were born within a few years of each other. Both were considered the great beauties of their day, fishing in the same pond, seeking out the rich and famous to keep them in style. It is quite possible the two met, but this is not recorded. There is a fine line being considered a courtesan and that of a high class tart. Kitty Fisher was what today we would call a 'celebrity'. She was simply famous for being famous. She had no aspirations of being an actress. She lived quite literally on her exceptional beauty. She was said to be witty, but essentially a hard headed business woman.

Strolling in St. James's Park she met Lady Coventry, who rather talked down to her and said: 'Why, a charming little gown, what is the name of the dressmaker?' 'I have no idea, m'lady', she replied in her poshest accent. 'It was a gift from your husband'. Ouch! A German visitor to London recorded that Kitty could command one hundred guineas a night 'for the use of her charms' and she was never short of takers. Following a visit from the King's brother, the Duke of York, he left fifty guineas on her dressing table. Kitty was deeply offended, letting it be known that he was not welcome to return. To prove her point she ate the offending note. Now we get the sense of the girl, free spirited, hard and bolshy. Perhaps twinned with her great beauty is why the great portrait artist Sir Joshua Reynolds, who painted her several times, admitted that he had failed to capture her unique allure. Instead we see a rather pudding-faced young woman and have to question what all the fuss was about, but then ideas of beauty do shift over generations.

Eventually Kitty got her man. Not a lord as she had hoped, but John Norris, the son of an MP. They lived in some style in the house which is now home to Benenden school. It is unclear whether Kitty caught smallpox or fell victim to consumption, but within months of her marriage she was dead aged just twenty five. What was it about her that lives on today over and above thousands of other 'good time girls'? Perhaps the very quality that Reynolds and other artists who painted her failed to capture. She remains of interest because she above most others represented a London girl from a poor background who used whatever talents she possessed to better herself. As well as being hard headed she could also be kind and generous to those around her. She was witty and took no nonsense from anyone, no matter how exalted. This characteristic is carried on today by countless other 'cockney sparrows'.

Harriette Wilson was born in Mayfair in 1786. The area had yet to have the cachet it enjoys today. Harriette was one of fifteen children and whilst three of her sisters went on to have respectable lives, Sophia, Fanny and Amy joined her in the oldest profession in the world. Harriette's fortunes fluctuated wildly and when things got particularly tough she hit on an idea of publishing her memoir. Before it went to press she made contact with her many wealthy and outwardly respectable 'friends', suggesting sending her £200 by return to avoid any embarrassment. She went through the card, Dukes, Marquesses, Earls, honourables and even a few rich commoners. It appears almost all of them coughed up except the redoubtable Duke of Wellington. He returned her letter, telling her 'publish and be damned'.

The book caused a sensation, with barriers having to be set up in the Haymarket to control the crowds outside the publisher's premises. Although he and Harriette both made a fortune from the enterprise, it did not end well for either of them. Stockdale the publisher was embroiled in endless court cases, whilst Harriette was shunned socially and eventually left London to live in Paris. Before leaving she was physically attacked on Dover pier by a lady whose husband had presumably been exposed. With lumps of her hair pulled out it was definitely time for Harriette to take her leave.

Later in a different era we will meet other more discreet courtesans who went onto enjoy riches and social standing. They were generally accepted as guests in the country's finest houses and drank cocktails at the Ritz. These ladies were the clever ones. What was on offer was very much the same as it had always been, but many of their relatives are now considered to be amongst the country's elite.

Chapter 16

Turning a Pretty Penny or Two

In 1945 the Andrews sisters had a huge hit with 'Money is the route of all evil', written by Alex Kramer and Jean Whitney. Simple lyrics but strangely profound as the desire for more money (or the lack of it) is often the major drive in crime. For centuries mad would-be alchemists have sought to change base metals to gold. Coiners in their turn sought to pass off dud coins posing as gold sovereigns. Today as national banks close numerous branches and cash machines, the internet is proving fertile ground for a new more sophisticated group of scammers. Earlier the introduction of paper money encouraged enthusiastic counterfeiters to print their own money, although normally they were eventually caught.

During the eighteenth century the serial fraudster Charles Price largely avoided detection. Outwardly he lived a respectable life, neither drinking nor gambling. His activities were successful enough for him to run three houses. One was for his wife and family, the second for his mistress and a third as headquarters for his bewildering range of swindles, even posing as a devoted preacher to rob the unsuspecting followers of their money. He was always a dedicated and resourceful crook, paying great attention to detail. Sensing an opportunity to make big money, he set up his own printing press to produce very convincing counterfeit notes. He made his own plates, paper, ink and watermarks. Then he needed a method of distribution. This he did by employing a number of young boys who were to spend some of the dud notes and keeping the legal tender change. Of course there was a danger that his accomplices would just run off with the proceeds, but he saw to it that they got a good cut for their work.

The notes he produced were really good, initially raising no suspicion. He always met the boys at a pre-arranged venue sitting in his coach. To them he was something of a mystery, a seemingly ordinary looking, middle aged man. They had no idea where he lived or anything about him other than he provided them with an income in excess of their wildest dreams. It could never last. The boys were arrested and Price disappeared, closing down his press and moving onto his next scam. It was estimated that he made well over one thousand pounds from this scheme alone, a vast sum in those far off days. He continued to live a charmed life, generally just keeping ahead of the law. He advertised for a partner to join him in a new brewery he was supposedly opening in Birmingham. For Samuel Foote it seemed too good an opportunity to be missed. His desire for a quick return cost him five hundred pounds and so the bogus schemes thought up by Price continued. All good things tend to come to an end in time. Price was finally arrested. Seemingly unable to face the shame, he committed suicide in Tothill Fields Prison in 1786. The crimes undertaken by Charles Price seem almost feeble compared to one of the most audacious frauds attempted in the twentieth century.

To enter the world of Horatio Bottomley is to enter a fantasy land of his own making, albeit a very lucrative one for much of his life. Repeatedly exposed as a serial swindler, he still managed to persuade people to invest in his latest bogus scheme. He was born in 1860 in Bethnal Green to parents of humble means. Soon afterwards his father was admitted to Bethlehem Hospital following 'a fit of mania'. Within three years his mother died, leaving the young boy being endlessly shuffled around family members and institutions. It was a chaotic upbringing and he frequently ran away. On leaving school he took a number of menial jobs, but interestingly joined a debating society. It was his gift for speaking that helped make his considerable fortune, but ultimately led to his downfall.

Aged nineteen he enrolled at Pitman's College to learn shorthand, gaining employment as a legal shorthand writer for a firm in central London. This in turn allowed him to enter the world of publishing as a proof-reader. Bottomley married Eliza Norton in 1880. Although he became notorious, his love of women was second only to his desire for ever more wealth. By now his next step was to become a journalist. He formed a number of journals and magazines known as the Catherine Street Publishing Association. With growing ambition he helped establish the Financial Times. In 1889 he founded and floated the Hansard Publishing Union. Within a couple of years he was filing for bankruptcy and so started his wildly fluctuating financial career. Charged with conspiracy to defraud, he was against all expectations found not guilty. He conducted a brilliant defence with his increasing ability to convince people with his gift for persuasive rhetoric.

Now Horatio moved into overdrive. He founded the Joint Stock Trust and Institute, which he used as a vehicle for promoting Western Australian gold mining companies. Seemingly this scheme transformed Botttomley's fortunes as by 1897 they were referring to him as being 'a man of millions'. At last he was able to buy properties suitable for a man of his standing and he also set up homes for a number of mistresses. Next it was a house in Pall Mall and the purchase of racehorses. A successful owner, winning the prestigious Cesarewitch. By 1906 with the backing of the mighty Odhams Press he launched the John Bull Magazine, a title designed to appeal to the patriotic beliefs of most of the population. The magazine claimed it was written 'without fear or favour, rancour or rant' in the interests of the common man.

Despite his growing wealth Bottomley craved acceptance and a place in society. He was elected as an MP for Hackney South in 1906, representing the Liberal Party, but rumours were already beginning to circulate about his business dealings. He managed to fend these off until 1912 when he had to admit his liabilities ran into hundreds of thousands of pounds and he was declared bankrupt, forcing him to resign his seat in Parliament. John Bull had been running competitions where most of the proceeds ended up in Bottomley's bank account, but still not enough to bridge the gap caused by his reckless spending.

The outbreak of war allowed Bottomley to cash in on the undoubted patriotic fervour sweeping the country. He started addressing public meetings, calling on young men to volunteer for military service. News of the power of his oratory spread and he addressed a mass meeting at the Royal Albert Hall. He even had the cheek to contact the Prime Minister Henry Asquith with a proposal that he should be appointed the Official Director of Recruitment. Knowing of his reputation, Asquith declined, but realising Bottomley's popularity he encouraged him to continue in an unofficial capacity. His fee for speaking ranged from fifty to one hundred pounds depending on the venue. It is reckoned that Horatio addressed over three hundred recruitment and patriotic meetings. Despite his insistence that he would not benefit financially from his lectures, it is estimated that they brought him earnings in excess of twenty thousand pounds. The historian A. J. P. Taylor put a much higher figure of around seventy eight thousand pounds brought in from his recruitment and patriotic meetings.

The 1918 election saw Bottomley again returned to represent Hackney South. Again doubts were being voiced about the Victory Bond Club promoted through his John Bull Magazine. It became obvious there had been very little financial oversight and few records kept. By 1922 there was a rush from the public to withdraw funds. Again it was proved that many of the supposed winners from the scheme were spurious and that Bottomley had spent as much as ninety thousand pounds of subscriptions on his own lavish spending. He was arrested and again conducted his own defence, but to no avail. He was found guilty and sentenced to seven years, serving just five. Released from jail, he once again tried to reinvent himself, launching various schemes. This time he found no takers. He fell from public view, dying penniless in obscurity aged seventy three. If he had lived in the previous century he would surely have been executed. There are plenty of Bottomleys praying on the unsuspecting today. It is quite extraordinary how vulnerable we all still remain to plausible rogues. Horatio Bottomley would certainly have approved. Three years before he was born the phrase 'as safe as the Bank of England' was blown out of the water by a gang carrying out a series of well planned scams.

George and Austin Bidwell's parents were grocers who lived in New York. Finding it tough to make a living in Brooklyn, the family moved to the Mid West before finally opting for Grand Rapids by the mid nineteenth century. Initially successful, the business expanded too quickly and ran into financial difficulties. The brothers saw their father working all hours but still struggling to make a profit. There had to be an easier way and the brothers were prepared to cut corners. George went back to New York where he found a job working for a wholesale grocers. He was obviously a bright young man as he was trusted to go on buying trips abroad. He started mixing with Wall Street brokers along with his younger brother. Austin had striking good looks and was charming, quickly gaining the confidence of new acquaintances. The brothers set up a series of financial swindles, but they were naive and both spent a spell behind bars.

Whilst inside they met George MacDonell. An interesting man who had qualified as a doctor but had chosen a path of crime. He was a convicted forger. Together the men began to formulate a plan that they were convinced would transform their lives. It was during their time in prison that they also met Edwin Noyes, who was to become the fourth member of the gang.

He was involved in the forgery of bills of exchange. These bills were issued by banks to their customers, promising payment by a given date as a form of secure credit.. Astonishingly they discovered that in Britain the checks as to the validity of these bills were largely taken on trust, unlike in America. It appeared that if they could build up a good credit record the possibilities to pull off a dramatic fraud was really possible. The four men arrived in Britain in 1872, but not before making about six thousand pounds from swindles involving French banks. The plausible Austin made contact with the Bank of England posing as a businessman involved in the building of Pullman cars in Birmingham. In December 1872 a series of genuine bills of exchange valued at just over three thousand pounds were paid into their account. These were posted from Birmingham establishing the account. A letter was received from the Bank stating that the bills had been cleared and accepted. Next Austin Bidwell travelled to Paris where he bought another bill of exchange from Rothchilds Bank valued at over four thousand pounds. Now forger MacDonell started weaving his magic. He bought blank forms for bills of exchange whilst Austin acquired forms identical to those used by Rothchilds in Paris. With the genuine Rothchilds bill safely banked, the forgeries began to flow. They had a very limited time as the bills would be presented in three months at the end of March for payment when the forgeries would be discovered. The plan therefore was to present as many bills as possible within the time frame and withdraw the cash. At the end of January they presented their first batch of bills valued at four thousand, two hundred and fifty pounds. Imagine their delight as these were passed and the cash withdrawn. Gaining in confidence, the next batch was for just over eleven thousand pounds and still no suspicion raised. By the end of February their haul was in excess of one hundred thousand pounds. Mac the forger had certainly worked his magic.

The gang were converting the proceeds into gold coins and negotiable bonds, both of which were untraceable, which they moved into foreign accounts held in their names. On February 26th they presented their last batch of bills prior to a planned departure. They had come all this way without a hitch when an alert clerk noticed that two of the bills were undated. The bills had been forged in the name of Blydenstein, a small London bank. Assuming it was a simple oversight, a Bank of England official sent the bills back to Blydenstein's for a routine authentification. They reported that they had no record of these bills and assumed them to be forgeries.

Noyes was designated to pick up the cash but found an unwelcome reception party waiting for him. He was promptly arrested. George Bidwell, who had been waiting for Noyes, saw he had been detained and made a swift exit, but was arrested later. MacDonnell managed to board a ship to America and probably thought he had slipped the net. He was wrong, being arrested in New York on his arrival. Austin Bidwell managed to make it all the way to Havana where he was arrested at the end of March. They had very nearly managed to rob the Bank of England apart from one careless error which brought them down.

Their trial was a sensation, with rumours of an armed breakout and bribes paid to warders. These proved to be just distractions and all four men were sentenced to life imprisonment. 'A gentleman's word is his bond' had run its course. The world of business was never going to be the same again. Victorian Britain was scandalised, but within years the arrival of a new King was to witness a change in accepted morals. A loosening of the country's stays in more ways than one.

Chapter 17

Bertie

When King Edward VII called on a lady who had caught his eye it was more a case of submission rather than seduction. A time to perform for King and country. Much had changed since the death of the reclusive Queen Victoria, who had hidden herself away from public view. Edward dedicated his life to one of extravagance and pleasure. For him it was an endless round of champagne, huge cigars, fine food, racehorses and curvaceous women. Despite these weaknesses the great British public appeared supportive. His appearance at events was often accompanied by shouts of 'Good old Teddie'.

His need for female company was prompted by a visit to a young Irish prostitute arranged for him by army colleagues when he was stationed in Dublin. This at a time when women were denied the vote, and yet his short reign being dominated by Mrs Pankhurst and her legions of suffragettes whose activities brought civil unrest and chaos to the streets of Britain. Britain was on a cusp as the first signs of an empire in decline were signposted by the Boer War. No matter, it was time to have fun. The Royal court was transformed. He liked the company of successful wealthy men, Jewish financiers and business tycoons. Even as Prince of Wales he had enjoyed an allowance of ten million pounds a year. Now his love of the good life went into overdrive. Despite his acceptance of people, his mother would have ignored Bertie as she was a stickler for protocol. Beware anyone who became over familiar.

Queen Alexandra was beautiful, charming and also very popular. She was also very accommodating in turning a blind eye to Bertie's frequent romances. Together they presented a united front and he always remained a dedicated father and family man. Most aristocratic marriages were arranged. Money, titles, status all intermingled in an attempt to form a new family dynasty. After the birth of a couple of children both partners were free to enter a bewildering procession of bed-hopping, providing of course there was no hint of scandal. It was generally accepted as being normal behaviour amongst those of aristocratic breeding. To think otherwise was to have middle class values. Better to be called common rather than bourgeois. It was to this background that 'good old Teddie' set off on his lusty journey. Although there were countless ladies who succumbed to his charms, there were a select few (for a time at least) who found their way to his heart. It was also true that his lifestyle led to a number of scandals that rocked the very foundations of the monarchy.

It is easy to understand why Bertie kicked over the traces after the repressive upbringing imposed on him by his parents. As a young man he had a reputation for being charming and informal, putting people he met at ease. A trip to Paris made when he was in his teens left a lasting impression and a lifelong love of France. Here the court was stylish and fun compared with the gloom of Victoria's London. There were already rumours circulating about his amorous affairs when in 1870 he found himself embroiled in a sensational divorce case.

Lord Mordaunt had only been married to his wife Harriet for four years when she confessed to him that she had been unfaithful to a string of lovers including the Prince of Wales. Arriving home unexpectedly, he caught his wife riding in a carriage with the Prince. Enraged, he ordered Bertie off his estate and for good measure shot the horses involved. Divorce in Victorian England was extremely rare. Most could not afford the expense, whilst no self respecting aristocrat would want to wash their dirty linen in public. Then in 1870 the unthinkable happened when the Prince of Wales was called as a witness. He had been indiscreet enough to send Harriet a series of letters. Whilst they were just friendly in tone, the fact that Bertie had laid himself open to derision had the courtiers and politicians scrambling to find a solution. It seems likely that even the Prime Minister was involved. Whatever, the case was dismissed. It was Harriet who was to suffer for her unladylike behaviour. She was apparently the victim of a mania. Ostracised from society, she spent the rest of her life being shuffled from remote houses to various asylums for the insane.

It seems unlikely that Bertie ever really fell in love with anyone but himself. He did however have a number of long standing affairs. These women were all beautiful, but importantly confident, intelligent and able to stand up for themselves in any company. Lillie Langtry was twelve years younger than Bertie and in a sense his first official mistress. The daughter of a philandering Jersey cleric, ambitious and desperate to leave Jersey, she chose marriage as an escape route, but her husband soon ran into financial problems. Trying to impress his beautiful wife, Edward Langtry bought a large house and a series of yachts. With the money running out, they moved to London where Lillie hoped to gain entry to fashionable society. Her initial season was a disaster. She was unable to dance well and was not able to afford expensive clothes.

It was her beauty that got her noticed. She had a milky white, flawless complexion and was soon being referred to as 'the Jersey Lily'. It was Lord Sebright who introduced her into society. Importantly his friends included a number of writers and artists. It was they who were now lining up to paint this outstanding beauty. Millais and Edward Burne-Jones arranged sittings. Lillie had arrived and it did not take long for the Prince of Wales to find out what all the fuss was about. Was she really as stunning as everyone seemed to think. She was. Lillie was now attending up to three parties a day, and it was at one of these held by the Arctic explorer Sir Allen Young that Lillie was introduced to Bertie. She was everything he looked for in a woman. She exuded sexual allure, but she also spoke her mind and was in no way intimidated by him.

It did not take long for them to be seen in public together. She was a free spirit, vivacious and able to share his interests. Importantly they became firm friends as well as being lovers. Still famous artists sought permission to paint Lillie, but in spite of an impressive roll call, it was Whistler who best captured the essence of 'the Jersey Lily'. With her husband sidelined, Lillie bought a modest house in Norfolk Street just off Park Lane. There she regularly entertained Bertie 'to tea'. They rode regularly together along Rotten Row. Whilst everyone guessed their relationship was anything other than platonic, this did not matter providing there was no outward hint of scandal, but Lillie still had the power to bewitch. One foolish wealthy young lover bought her a yacht and for a time maintained it with a crew of thirty.

Wealthy now in her own right, Lillie became a leading racehorse owner, a passion she shared with Bertie. In a nod to the importance of their relationship, Bertie bought Lillie a substantial property in Bournemouth known as the 'Red House'. He continued to 'have tea' with countless other ladies. His carriage parked outside fashionable houses in London was a sure sign. Lillie was special, but so was Daisy Maynard.

By 1880 Bertie's infatuation with Lillie had cooled, although they continued to be good friends. Despite endless affairs it was to be a number of years before Daisy Maynard became central to his life. Having known her since she was very young, even as she reached maturity, initially she was not attractive to him. She was petite, sharp featured with dark blue eyes and an attitude rather unbecoming for one so young.

Unlike Lillie, Daisy was born to an established aristocratic family of great wealth. Being born in 1861 in Berkeley Square signposted a privileged life. Privileged but turbulent. Her father Charles Maynard was the youngest son of the 3rd Viscount Maynard, but Charles died three months before the Viscount and so it was that in 1865 Daisy inherited all the estates that included the ancestral pile Easton Lodge in Sussex, and an income of £30,000 a year. Daisy was educated at home, which was centred on a command of foreign languages and British history. It was obvious from an early age that Daisy had a mind of her own, a trait that she carried on throughout her life. Her mother had strong royal connections and at the age of seventeen she was taken to Windsor Castle to meet the Queen, who thought Daisy could be a suitable candidate to marry her son Prince Leopold. Daisy had other ideas and instead married Lord Brooke, the son of the Earl of Warwick. The marriage at Westminster Abbey was attended by the Prince of Wales and his wife. The couple moved into Easton Lodge and spent a fortune on renovations. Daisy quickly became a leading social hostess and a fearless rider on the hunting field.

It is possible that only the first of Daisy's children was fathered by her husband as she was already taking a succession of lovers, and it appeared her husband was too much of a gentleman to object. She had a passionate affair with Lord Beresford. Ever the spoilt child, Daisy was infuriated to learn that his wife was pregnant. What was good for the goose did not extend to the gander as far as she was concerned. She sent Beresford a letter accusing him of disloyalty. Unfortunately Lady Beresford opened the letter and forwarded it to her lawyer. Daisy, now Lady Warwick since her husband's father had died, now appealed to the Prince of Wales for help and avoid a scandal. Bertie put pressure on Lady Beresford to return the letter, but she refused. She did make the concession that if Daisy left London for 'the season' then the letter would be returned. Daisy refused and it took the intervention of the Prime Minister Lord Salisbury to negotiate an agreement, allowing all concerned to save face.

But now finding time between her many lovers, Daisy was tacitly acknowledged as the Prince of Wales's semi-official mistress. From his initial reluctance he now seemed besotted by her. Lavish parties costing thousands were thrown at Warwick Castle and criticism of Bertie's lifestyle was growing, particularly by the church establishment. This all came to a head at a party taking place after the Doncaster races at Tranby Croft. Once again Bertie was drawn into a case taking place before the Lord Chief Justice in London. It concerned a member of the party being caught cheating at Baccarat. Whilst not directly involving Bertie, it drew attention to his lifestyle and the rakish company he kept. Bertie was subpoenaed to appear and tongues wagging went into orbit.

In exchange for lavish parties at Warwick Castle, Daisy had to endure endless shooting parties at Sandringham that she hated. She had by now been affected by criticism of her own lavish spending, and had acquired a social conscience that was to be a feature of the rest of her life. Whilst Bertie had no time for women's emancipation, he was not unaware of the terrible lives many of his subjects were forced to live. She even arranged for him to visit workhouses with her, but it was only a token nod as far as he was concerned, but Daisy was now on a mission. She dedicated much of her later life to good causes. She championed women's rights and even stood against Anthony Eden as an independent Labour candidate in 1923.

After Bertie's death in 1910, Daisy's reckless spending on social soirées and good causes had led her close to bankruptcy. She threatened to publish Bertie's letters to her, which it was feared would illustrate the huge cost of his wasteful and lavish lifestyle and the number of mistresses he had acquired over the years. She was offered enough money to clear her debts, but the Crown claimed copyright. In 1928 she was jailed in Holloway for her debts and only released on condition that her memoirs had to be submitted for approval before publication. Years later when the letters were finally released they were hardly sensational. Rather just friendly and chatty considering the influence Daisy did have for a time with Bertie.

By the time Bertie met Alice Keppel in 1898, he was known behind his back as 'Edward the caresser'. According to Catherine Walters (known as 'Skittles', another of his mistresses), during his latter years he had become impotent. If this was true, meeting the alluring Alice stoked his fires again even if only temporarily. She was twenty nine, twenty seven years younger than the Prince of Wales who was still waiting patiently to take over from Queen Victoria. Alice was different from any of his other conquests and possibly the only woman he ever really loved. Queen Alexandra gave him stability at home but was rather dull. By contrast Lillie Langtry had been truly exciting but here obvious unbridled love of all things lavish and frivolous were just a touch common. Daisy on the other hand was to the manor born but not truly discreet and Queen Alexandra hated her and refused to be seen in her company. Whilst Alice was beautiful, she offered so much more for a man soon to take on the responsibilities of King. Alice was brought up in Scotland, the daughter of a Baronet. Dark with piercing blue eyes, a tiny waist and an ample bosom, she also had a deep sexy voice. Bertie was immediately drawn to her, not only by her looks but also her intelligence. She was even tempered and exuded happiness, guiding conversations to please him. With her he felt content. A sense of homeliness spiced by her dark beauty, attributed by many to her partial Greek heritage.

Alice was married to George Keppel, a serving officer in the British Army. He was tall, attractive and a perfect gentleman, but he was relatively poor. They could only afford to employ seven servants despite him being the son of the 7th Earl of Albermarle. A way to improve their finances was for Alice to take a number of wealthy lovers, seemingly with the tacit approval of her husband. They had two daughters, but it seems likely that one was not fathered by George. He also took a number of lovers in this never ending merry go round of aristocratic bed hopping.

Alice had already built something of a reputation as being a leading hostess by the time she met Bertie. She was the near perfect partner. She indulged him and yet was strong enough to stand her ground if they did disagree. Increasingly he began to value her counsel, being well informed and wise. Her influence increased after his coronation, which had to be delayed due to him having appendicitis. Increasingly she tried to restrict his vast intake of food, champagne and cigars with little effect. She was also a smoker, seldom seen without her fashionable long tortoiseshell cigarette holder. Sir Harold Acton reckoned no one could compete with her as a society hostess. She was glamorous, witty but kind, and could in his opinion be a true representation of Britannia. Her charm was such that even Alexandra approved of Alice, if only for the fact that she seemed capable of calming the King's increasingly volatile mood swings.

The cosy relationship Bertie had with George Keppel was improved further when a job was arranged for George to act as an agent for Sir Thomas Lipton, the tea magnet. The Keppels' finances were further improved by the King getting leading financiers to advise Alice on her investments, in addition to giving her shares from his own portfolio. Alice certainly had a weakness for money and what it could buy. It enabled her to move from Portman Square to the grander Grosvenor Square. All appeared calm, the King had never been more settled. Alice advised him wisely, calmed him and was engaging company. George, far from being the cuckholded husband, was on excellent terms with the King, and even the Queen completed this happy circle until the King's health took a turn for the worse.

There are conflicting reports about Bertie's last hours. Some suggest that Alexandra invited Alice to be at his bedside, but his doctor insisted that it was Bertie who demanded that Alice should be at his side. Whatever the truth, Alice rather let the side down in the final moments, becoming quite hysterical with grief. She was led from the bedchamber by staff, leaving the Queen alone to grieve. Alice was allowed to attend the funeral, but with the decorum she had shown during her relationship with Bertie she entered and left by a side door.

Bertie had turned out to be a surprisingly successful monarch. He was diligent in attending daily to his red boxes, showing particular interest in foreign affairs. His Queen was held in genuine affection by most of the population, and his own lavish lifestyle somehow considered suitable for Britain as a great world power. His demand for correct social etiquette extended to a fastidiousness regarding service dress and the display of medals, a trait continued by King George V.

What of the Keppels after Bertie's death? They bought a wonderful palazzo in Florence where they entertained on a grand scale. Returning to London, they were still welcomed into society, but not the royal circle. Astonishingly their marriage lasted fifty six years. He had always maintained that he did not mind what his wife did, providing she eventually returned to him, which she did. Alice died in September 1947, to be followed a couple of years later by George, who spent his last years at a permanent suite he had at the Ritz.

The death of Bertie marked a change in mood throughout the country. Strangely the new King had more in common with Queen Victoria than his father. Perhaps it was as well because the prospect of war was increasing. The time for frivolity had passed. Few could have guessed at the carnage about to be unleashed. A time that wiped out a generation of young men and left others scarred, both mentally and physically. Edwardian England, in retrospect with all its faults, increasingly felt like a golden age.

Chapter 18

The Long Weekend

It was Robert Graves who referred to the period between the wars as the 'Long Week-End'. Whilst Edwardian England was thought of as a golden age, the Great War was one of the bleakest. It witnessed the culling of an entire generation of young men, with fatalities numbering almost nine hundred thousand. Hardly a family was left unscathed. The highest percentage of deaths were amongst junior officers, with leading aristocratic families being affected like everyone else. War memorials in towns and villages bear testament to the savage effects on whole communities. Air raids by Zeppelins and Gothas killed over five hundred civilians, creating the spectre of worse to come in any future conflict.

Much of the grieving and worries about the future was put to one side with the ending of the war on November 11th 1918 (at least in London, elsewhere the celebrations were more muted). Relief rather than exhilaration was the over-riding emotion. Duff Cooper, the diplomat and politician, recorded in his diary whilst awaiting his demob: 'We had a motor meet us at Liverpool street. All London was in uproar – singing, cheering and waving flags. In spite of real delight I couldn't resist a feeling of profound melancholy looking at the crowds of silly cheering people and thinking of the dead'. That night some of his chums gathered at the Ritz were in lighter mood. Champagne corks popped and the dance floor was covered in balloons and streamers. At the Savoy any sense of inhibition was given over to paper hats worn askew, jackets removed and over two thousand glasses smashed by the well-heeled guests. If this behaviour had taken place in a pub down the road the police would have been called, but this was surely a time when a chap could let off steam.

A couple of weeks later a giant Victory Ball was held at the Royal Albert Hall. Time to dust off the silk topper and for the ladies to dig out their ball gowns and pearls. The ball was seemingly a great success, but the next morning the body of actress Billie Carleton was discovered by her maid in the swanky Savoy Court. Tongues wagged, there was a sniff of scandal here confirmed when it emerged that Billie had died of a drugs overdose. Billie had been plucked from the chorus line by C. B. Cochran and appeared to be heading for stardom. She was very beautiful, but unfortunately her acting ability was more suited to silent films and her voice lacked depth. These shortcomings could be fixed, but Cochran became aware of her drug habit and fired her.

Questions started to be asked. How could a relatively minor actress afford to live in such an expensive apartment and who was supplying the drugs? She was obviously 'a kept woman'. The Tatler was really catty about her, stating: 'she had cleverness, temperament and charm. Not enough of the first and perhaps too much of the latter'. A gold coloured box was found at her bedside containing cocaine. The inquest found she had taken a lethal cocktail of drugs. The supplier was a dance instructor called Reggie de Veulle, a man who had recently been implicated in a homosexual blackmail case. He maintained that he in turn had purchased the drugs from a Scottish woman called Ada. Further investigations revealed she was married to a Chinese man, Lau Ping You, who lived in Limehouse. Cue for the popular press to go into overdrive. 'Beware the yellow peril' screamed the headlines. Once again Londoners' suspicion of foreigners reared its head. A beautiful British flower killed by an inscrutable Chinaman. The trial unleashed a huge surge of anti-Chinese sentiment despite there being only a few hundred living in London. They were accused of running opium dens and smuggling English girls abroad to face 'a fate worse than death'.

The circumstances surrounding the death of Billie Carleton led indirectly to the Dangerous Drug Act of 1920 that implemented controls on the supply of cocaine, morphine, opium and heroin. Previously the drugs had been freely available and taken mainly by those from the upper strata of society. Duff Cooper became increasingly worried by his beautiful wife Diana's reliance on a variety of drugs.

Far from a sense of euphoria at victory, Britain was a place of brooding resentment. Demobilisation was taking far too long and there were riots and outbreaks of violence. There was a real fear that war had brutalised a whole generation. A spate of robberies and murders suggested that Britain was in the grip of a crime wave. If not brutalised, our brave soldiers were returning home, many of them having contracted VD from those shocking French girls who enticed them into their squalid brothels.

Worries about the increase in crime were not misplaced, particularly in London. War and its aftermath offered rich pickings, particularly if backed up with extreme violence. A number of gangs emerged, but by far the most feared was led by Charles Sabini (known as 'Darby'), an unusual gangster in many ways. Born in Saffron Hill in Clerkenwell (known as 'little Italy'), he was the youngest of six brothers. Darby had avoided military service and used the war years to build up his power base and was acknowledged as the gang's outright leader. Although of only medium height and slight build, he had the reputation as being the most feared man in London. Always dressed in dark suits with a waistcoat and a spotless white shirt with no collar and a cloth cap. His mother was a strict Catholic and this was reflected in his behaviour towards women, who he always treated with respect. He disliked swearing and always avoided blasphemy. Interestingly, despite his wide range of criminal activity he never got involved with prostitution. Here we have a complex man. Although he and his gang used extreme violence, Darby never used a razor as it made him feel squeamish. Give him a knuckleduster, cosh or even a chair leg and he would wade in with the best of them.

Between the war years when his gang usually reigned supreme, Darby was assisted by his brothers Harry Boy, George, Fred and Joseph. They recruited tough Jewish gangsters living in their area and at times imported recruits from Italy. It was rumoured that Darby had links with the Italian Mafia. What is certain is that the Sabinis had a grip over London that made the Krays look like beginners. Their contacts included the police, politicians and leading lawyers. Their success initially revolved around the racetracks of southern England. They offered 'protection' for bookies, offering a range of services that all had to be paid for. Anyone declining their offer ended up in hospital. They would sell off the best pitches to the highest bidder, but everything the bookie required for him to operate, even down to the chalk to mark up prices, had to be paid for.

A normal day down at Brighton could clear a profit of about five thousand pounds for the gang. On Derby Day they budgeted for between fifteen thousand pounds and twenty thousand pounds return. This trade was too lucrative not to be challenged and one gang willing to have a go was a Birmingham outfit led by Billy Kimber. There were a number of pitched battles, normally ending up with the Brummies being arrested. Sabini was so powerful in London that successful robberies carried out by other crooks had to make a contribution to the gang. Darby used a pub in Old Compton Street as his headquarters. He would sit in a back room behind the saloon bar holding court. Clubs and shops throughout the West End also paid their dues to the gang. Refusal to comply resulted in swift retribution, with premises being wrecked until normal service was resumed.

The 1920s are remembered fondly as the jazz age and the vacuous 'bright young things', but there was trouble brewing. With the mass demobilisation of troops, a huge number of firearms had found their way into the country. This combined with an unemployment rate of over two million by 1922 provided a perfect background for an increase in gun crime. Motor cars were being used to speed the gunmen away from the scene of the crime, and questions were being raised in the House of Commons. Darby Sabini had always been very wary about the use of guns and he warned members of his gang accordingly. You can imagine his annoyance in 1922 when he received news that his brother Joseph had been arrested for causing an affray involving a gun.

Joseph had gone with four henchmen including Simon Nyberg to confront bookmakers George Gage and Frederick Gilbert, who had witheld money due for their 'protection'. It was claimed that four shots had been fired and an array of other weapons were found nearby. These included a hammer and the incriminating pistol. The use of a gun elevated the offence to another level. Enter a smooth lawyer retained by Sabini, but this time their influential contacts failed to help. The boys were remanded in custody and subsequently jailed.

It was probably unlucky for them that a week previously had witnessed the execution of two men found guilty of shooting Field Marshall Sir Henry Wilson. Whilst this had been a political assasination, the public was becoming increasingly alarmed about the use and availability of guns. Sir Henry Wilson was the former head of the British Army and Ulster Unionist MP. Two men, Richard Dunne and Joseph O'Sullivan, were members of the London Brigade of the Irish Republican army. O'Sullivan had served in the British Army, losing a leg during the Battle of Ypres, and this was going to be significant in their capture. Wilson was shot outside his house at 36 Euston Place. He had just returned from unveiling a war memorial at Liverpool Street station. Dressed in full military uniform, the Field Marshall drew his sabre in a vain attempt to protect himself as the gun was pointed at him. A brave gesture matched by Dunne refusing to abandon O'Sullivan, whose chance to escape was hampered by his disability. The men were executed on August 12th 1922. Three sad deaths to be added to an increasing number as the 'troubles' in Ireland rumbled on for another century. Too much killing and violence, it was time for a juicy scandal and they did not come much jucier than a case that was heard at the Old Bailey in 1929.

To a background of jazz and the roaring twenties the gang spread its control. Visitors from the suburbs and the provinces were drawn rather than being put off visiting the West End. Particularly in Soho they were aware of shady looking foreigners smoking on street corners, of ladies of the night plying their trade. It just added to the excitement and there was seldom any trouble as the gangsters appeared to restrict their violence to other criminals. So it was against the huge events of the day the Sabinis went about their business, seemingly seldom bothered by the police or the authorities. Questions were asked about criminal elements in the House of Parliament and then seemingly forgotten. People could leap off rooftops during the financial crisis of 1929 or the General Strike years later, but the gang continued to thrive. Or did it? As war threatened once more, Darby seemed to lose his control. Respectability beckoned but he was devastated by the death of his son, of whom he was so proud. The young man was a pilot, having gained a commission in the Royal Air Force. On Darby's death in 1950 it was a surprise to many that he left very little money. Perhaps he had the last laugh sheltering his assets from the taxman. If not all, his scheming and violence showed a very poor return. In future, brains rather than brawn would be increasingly important for savvy criminals

Advanced technology would eventually open up new opportunities for criminals, but for the time being violence predominated. The fear about the availability of guns was confirmed early in the 1920s by a series of attacks. With the death penalty still in effect for murder, Darby Sabini always emphasised the use of guns was more of a threat, but the Times reported an affray in 1922 involving his brother Joseph. Together with four henchmen including Simon Nyberg, they were charged with maliciously shooting at George Sage and Frederick Gilbert, a bookmaker who had obviously tried to withhold the money owed for his 'protection'. On being arrested Nyberg was seen to drop a hammer, and an array of other weapons were discovered nearby including a pistol. It was claimed that four shots were fired. Enter a smooth lawyer to defend the boys, but on this occasion they were remanded in custody.

A week earlier witnessed the execution of two men found guilty of murdering Field Marshall Sir Henry Wilson, the former head of the British Army and Ulster Unionist MP. Two men, Reginald Dunne and Joseph O'Sullivan were members of the Irish Republican Army and the assassination was a prelude to a century of death and violence that still lingers today. Huge crowds gathered outside Pentonville jail, but the execution had been switched to Wandsworth prison. A new wave of armed robberies were recorded, aided by the use of a speedy get-away car. The press were now reflecting public concern. The Times thundered: 'The people of this country have not been cowered ….as has unhappily been the case in Ireland'. They reported that recently there had been six incidences of shootings in London, referring also to 'murderous gangs who infest the racecourses in many parts of the country', but neither the gangs nor the IRA impacted much on most people's lives. They were more interested in a good juicy scandal and they did not come much juicier than a case that was heard at the Old Bailey in 1929.

It was in February of that year that Leslie Barker was arrested at the Regent Palace Hotel for failing to appear at a bankruptcy hearing scheduled for the previous December. Barker, variously known as Captain or Colonel Barker, also claimed to have been decorated with the DSO for bravery. He also had a reputation as a boxer and something of a womaniser. He was carted off to Brixton jail where he underwent a standard medical. The doctor was in for a nasty shock. Leslie Barker was found to be a woman. It was off to Holloway women's prison pronto! Although he was separated from his wife, they had shared a marital bed together and she had attributed his impotence down to his supposed war wounds. The popular press could hardly contain themselves by the time the case came to be held at the Old Bailey. For days it dominated the front pages.

Barker had been born in 1895 and registered as Lillias Irma Valerie Barker. As a young woman she had shown a keen interest in horses and found employment in a number of racing stables. In 1918 she met and married an Australian, Harold Arkell-Smith. For whatever reason the marriage only lasted a matter of weeks. Not deterred and attracted to Australians with double-barrelled names, she set up with Ernest Pearce-Crouch, with whom she had two children.

By 1923 Barker emerged as Captain Leslie Barker, soon to promote himself to a full blown Colonel. At this point he won the heart of Elfrieda Hayward, the daughter of a Brighton dentist. The marriage ran into trouble as Barker drifted in and out of a variety of jobs. Boxing, manager, cafe owner and farm manager, but he showed an inability to stick to anything for long. In 1927 he was arrested for being in possession of a firearm with a forged certificate. He appeared in court with his eyes covered in bandages, claiming he had been blinded in the war. Without checking his story he was found not guilty.

The jury two years later were not so gullible and Barker was sentenced to nine months for perjury, which she served in Holloway Prison. It is a case that resonates today with all the ongoing debate on transgender rights. Within months of her release she was living with an actress as man and wife, and had other relationships with women. For a time Barker worked as a butler and received references referring to him as a 'perfect servant', even after being arrested for stealing five pounds from his employer. He settled in Norfolk, still posing as a man, and served in the Home Guard during the war. When she died in 1960 her true identity shocked her neighbours, who had no idea. Those with longer memories however recalled one of the most sensational trials of the inter war years.

Running the Barker trial a close second was that of Marguerite Fahmy. Earlier in July 1923 the national press headlines screamed 'murder at the Savoy'. In the early hours of July 8th three shots rang out, leaving Marguerite's husband Prince Ali Kamel Fahmy Bey lying dead on the floor of their luxury suite. Earlier they had been heard having a violent row in the restaurant on their return from the theatre, where they had seen Evelyn Laye star in 'The Merry Widow' (I know, you just couldn't make it up!). Here were two wealthy foreigners involved in a sordid crime committed in one of London's most prestigious hotels. The press went into overdrive. For once the British cast aside their traditional distrust of the French. Here seemingly an attractive young French woman had been subjected to outrageous humiliation by a dissolute playboy Egyptian Prince. It was time for ladies in the suburbs to reach for the smelling salts. The Prince had apparently shown more interest in his male secretary than his new wife, whilst subjecting her to the most perverted sexual practices. Middle England took in a collective breath and waited for further revelations. Defended by Sir Edward Marshall Hall, it took the jury less than an hour to find sallow, sultry, sexy Marguerite not guilty. Summing up, the judge said: 'We in this country put our women on a pedestal. In Egypt they have not the same views'. The defence case had been racially prejudiced and led to a diplomatic protest from the Egyptian embassy.

After the trial the public perception began to change somewhat. It was claimed that Marguerite, who was ten years older than her husband, had worked as a prostitute in Paris and was a gold digger. If she was it did her no good as she was left nothing in Fahmy's will despite her best efforts to claim his estate. The great British public felt vindicated. For a time they had been taken in by her sob story, but it just underlined the widely held view that all foreigners were distinctly suspect.

By the 1930s London was dubbed the murder and drug capital of Europe. The excitement and frivolity of the 1920s jazz age had gone, to be replaced by strikes, unemployment and the increasing spectre of war. Oswald Moseley's fascists were not just supported by thugs, but also by a fair chunk of the high society.

The prospects for the country were looking really grim and forcing vulnerable people to act out of character. It appeared that unemployment and destitution forced Marguerite Eastwood to throw her eight month old baby out of a train heading for Barnes. Obviously desperate, Eastwood was found guilty and sentenced to death. This was later commuted to life imprisonment, but somehow this sad case underlined the problems and mood of the country. With sandbags being placed outside banks and government buildings and guns being installed in Hyde Park, 'the long weekend' was ending badly. On September 3rd war was declared with Germany. Despite the late summer sunshine the country waited nervously, but war was going to create wonderful opportunities for criminals waiting in the wings.

Chapter 19

Dodging the Bombs

Two days before the outbreak of war in September 1939 blackout restrictions were imposed on the British public. This required all windows and doors to be covered with material so no light was able to be seen at night. This was rigorously imposed by neighbourhood wardens to the point where lighting a fag was likely to be reported. As people crept around the darkened streets of London, a familiar area suddenly became a dangerous jungle. Dangerous, as it was reckoned by 1942 twenty percent of the population had been involved in an accident. An added danger was the possibility of being attacked and robbed before the assailant melted into the all enveloping darkness. Serial criminals thought that the blackout was a perfect gift from Hitler and boy, how they exploited it.

Further legislation included the National Registration Act, requiring each citizen to carry an identity card. These were soon being faked and sold on the black market. It appeared that each restriction imposed opened up opportunities for dishonest people to prosper. Food and particularly petrol coupons were soon traded illegally. The early imposition of the National Service Act imposed conscription on all men aged eighteen to forty-one. Hard core criminals just ignored it. Military service was for mugs. There was serious money to be made. These men just failed to turn up for registration and although the government vowed to track these shirkers down, in truth they did not have the manpower and there were more important matters to attend to. Suddenly forgers were much in demand. Copies of medical discharge papers were available (at a price), and one doctor was struck off for providing a fake certificate. Men trying to avoid military service were described as 'traitors' or 'saboteurs'. It also did not take long before racketeers were being harangued in the press.

Middle England was outraged, but would normally turn a blind eye if they were offered black market goods.

With an influx of French, Dutch and colonial troops arriving in London, the mood lightened. The threatened bombing had not started and many thought it a time to party. With licensing laws so strictly imposed, bottle party clubs became all the rage with after hours drinking. There was reckoned to be between two and three hundred bottle clubs in London at the outbreak of war. Some were quite exclusive but many little more than clip joints where a squaddie had to pay an entrance fee on the promise of 'a good time'. Once in the club he would be joined by a hostess, who flirted with him until his money ran out, as she drank fake champagne charged at thirty shillings a bottle. Here the unwary were also relieved of their money by sleight of hand or marked cards. Again it was unwise to complain if you did not fancy a visit to the local hospital. The blackout claimed its first major victim when Ciro Pearls were relieved of their entire stock at their Bond Street store in February 1940.

Meanwhile the downstairs bar at the Ritz was attracting what the Duchess of Marlborough referred to as 'a lot of old queers'. Many remembered this bar with affection. Felix Hope-Nicholson referred to it as being 'notoriously queer', with an outrageously camp atmosphere and a reputation for easy pick-ups. Some women did infiltrate this male preserve, one particularly being welcome. Edomie Johnson was plump, middle aged and a serious drinker. Her great advantage for 'the boys' was that each night she appeared with an attractive young serviceman on her arm. He would be swiftly disgorged into a flock of welcoming admirers. She was happy to be known as 'the buggers' Vera Lynn'. Considering homosexuality was deemed an offence and liable to fines or even imprisonment, it is surprising the bar flourished for as long as it did.

The phoney war was over. September 7th 1940 had been quite a glorious summer's day. A day when any troubles gave way to the wonders of nature, until suddenly all hell was let loose. Glancing skyward, it was possible to see a swarm of menacing bombers and fighter planes. It was five o'clock when this menacing fleet reached its target. An hour later the planes had gone, leaving a trail of death and burning chaos. By eight o'clock a second wave of bombers arrived to pulverise the docks lining the River Thames.

Warehouses were ablaze and the Tate and Lyle sugar factory set on fire, which gave out a horrible sickly smell. The Thames itself was alight, not to mention the rows of terraced houses smashed to smithereens. Wailing ambulances and cries for help were a template set for horrors to come. West Ham, Whitechapel, Bow and much of the East End were to bear the brunt, but before long it was the more fashionable areas of London that would also be randomly bombed, including many landmarks like Buckingham Palace. The bombing continued almost nightly until May 1941, by which time thousands had died and the ancient architecture of London re-arranged.

Even amongst all this misery and horror there were those prepared to take advantage to line their own pockets. Gangs waited in cars rushing to be the first on the scene. As the destruction spread to the West End, shops and department stores offered rich pickings from among the debris. Rationed goods and luxuries were able to be sold off at a handsome profit. Worse were those posing as ARP wardens, who arrived at newly bombed buildings driving a mocked up ambulance. They would come out with a stretcher supposedly covering a dead body, but actually laden with valuables lifted from the building. The Cafe de Paris, the fashionable night club near Leicester Square, advertised itself as being the safest venue in London, situated well below ground. It was an exact replica of the doomed liner, the Lusitania, which maybe should have been a warning. At 9.30pm on that fateful evening, just as the band struck up, a bomb fell, falling directly down an airshaft, and exploded on the dance floor. Mayhem. Bodies everywhere, a scene of total destruction. Enter the ghouls. Through the dust and rubble two men were spotted pulling rings off the dead bodies of young women. In the confusion they sneaked away. The local Honeydew restaurant was used as a mortuary. The death toll was eighty, just one of so many similar tragedies witnessed across London during the Blitz, but a shocking example of some ready to benefit from others' devastating loss.

On December 7th 1941 the Japanese attacked the American fleet at Pearl Harbor, followed by the German declaration of war against the United States that led to an invasion of Britain. This was not to be jack-booted Nazis, but an altogether welcomed appearance of the Yanks.

Britain was at a low ebb, soon to be emphasised by the loss of Singapore. The tide of war was about to change. Increasingly the Americans flooded into central London. It was not just for their military might that the troops were welcomed, but also by legions of young (and not so young) women. They appeared to be awash with money, being paid four to five times more than their British equivalent. Here were opportunities for London cabbies and seasoned criminals to cash in.

Whilst the American officers were housed in over twenty hotels in London, including the ballroom at the Grosvenor House Hotel, much of the activity centred on the Rainbow Club situated on the corner of Shaftesbury Avenue and Denman Street. Built on the site of the former Delmonico restaurant, the club was an attempt by the US authorities to offer a sense of home for these young GIs trying to come to terms with this strange place called London. It had bars and restaurants offering all kinds of food not available elsewhere. The club acted like a magnet, drawing not only young women, but spivs and small time crooks who bought goods from the GIs to be sold on the black market. That arch snob Evelyn Waugh complained that the Squares of Mayfair and Knightsbridge were being invaded by the type of women who had normally only gained access as servants. They were throwing themselves at American servicemen in exchange for nylon stockings, or even as something as mundane as razor blades. He was horrified.

It did not take long for trouble to break out. It was not just about discrepancy in pay and the fact that the Yanks were bagging all the best looking girls, there was racial trouble too. Troops from the southern states took exception to British girls walking out with black men. The posher restaurants started to refuse entry to blacks, frightened to offend their better customers. The streets of central London were awash with prostitutes, some as young as fourteen. Tales circulated of soldiers being relieved of their wallets by light fingered young women, who disappeared before the soldier realised he had been duped. Another favourite ploy was for two girls to team up with a couple of GIs. Then they said they had arranged to rent a swanky suite in a fashionable block of flats. Having fed them with the delights they could expect that night, the girls left the men in the foyer having taken money supposedly to pay the landlord.

They explained that if the landlord or his agent saw the men they would realise that the apartment was being let for immoral purposes and refuse them entry. Whilst the young men waited anxiously, no doubt thinking of the pleasures to come, the girls slipped out of the back entrance never to be seen again. Many of these young men had never left their home town or state, they needed to wise up.

The London Evening Standard ran a number of leading articles bemoaning the state of London being in danger of becoming an expanding red light area fuelled by the huge number of servicemen roaming the streets. A survey carried out rated the Dutch troops the most welcome with a rating of almost seventy percent, whilst the Americans languished with a rating of just over thirty percent, lower even than the Free French. There was growing concern about the number of deserters, known euphemistically as 'absentees'. It was reckoned that these numbered in their thousands and most chose the anonymity of crowded London to hide away. The problem became more acute as the war dragged on. Friday, May 21st 1944 witnessed a huge dragnet designed to catch the offenders. British and American military police first targeted amusement arcades followed by Lyons Corner Houses. Surely the word would have spread, but the searches continued at the Astoria Dance Hall in Charing Cross Road, a favourite of GIs looking for a pick up.

A week earlier uniformed and plain clothes police joined their military colleagues in another sweep of the West End. Some estimates put the number of deserters to be as high as twenty thousand. These huge sweeps, that included some MPs carrying rifles and fixed bayonets, only had modest success. As late as 1946 it was reckoned that there were still around eight thousand deserters still avoiding arrest.

The number of stolen goods available in London swelled as the war progressed. Dockers were now supplying whisky and a vast range of goods due for export. Just as the Brits and Yanks were getting on better terms as their differences were accepted rather than challenged, suddenly the GIs were gone and the gravy train ended following the D-Day Landings. Restaurant owners looked anxiously down deserted streets for customers. Part time street workers applied again for their office jobs. In a time when good time girls had become tarts and respectable young ladies good time girls, a period of re-thinking was required. London now appeared drab and wounded. Great tracts reduced to rubble whilst rationing restrictions were tightened further. For many the Yanks had been something of a tonic, bringing a colour and vibrancy to the old city. Now they were gone, leaving memories and thousands of illegitimate babies. It had been fun while it lasted and now many of those young men were going to die in another foreign country. The Rainbow Club was finally closed in January 1946 and the world moved on, leaving just memories.

Suddenly in 1942 the headlines were not devoted to the progress of the war but to a series of gruesome murders. A black-out ripper was at large. In the early hours of February 9th the body of a forty year old chemist's assistant was found in a surface air raid shelter. It appeared Evelyn Hamilton had been strangled and the motive assumed to be robbery, but the plot thickened. Within days there was a far more worrying discovery. Evelyn Oatley was found dead in her Wardour Street flat. She had been horribly mutilated. The papers claimed she had once been a Windmill girl, although this was never proved. She certainly had been a dancer who had recently turned to prostitution. Detectives found that a tin opener had been used on the poor women and deduced the killer was left handed. A re-examination of Margaret Hamilton's body, confirmed by the marks on her neck, indicated that here too the killer was left handed. Within three days another victim was discovered, in Gosfield Street. Margaret Lowe had been working as a prostitute. She also had been strangled and her body defiled. Alarmed now, the police called on the services of the famous pathologist Sir Bernard Spilsbury for help. Whilst he was still examining Margaret Lowe the sensational news came in that a fourth body had been discovered. Doris Jouannet was described as a part time prostitute, being married to a hotel manager. It was in their flat that her body was discovered. She also had been strangled and savagely mutilated. The country demanded answers. The police had none, there was a maniac at large. The papers were in full cry, 'West End search for mad killer'. Frighteningly the man appeared out of control. On February 12th Greta Hayward had a very lucky escape. She had been picked up by a young officer and taken to the Trocadero for a drink. Later they sauntered down the Haymarket where the young man offered Greta money if she would have sex with him. 'No, no, thank you', or words to that effect, she replied. 'Well at least give me a goodnight kiss', he suggested. Pulling her into a side alley, he grabbed her, dropping his gas mask. As he attempted to strangle her he was disturbed by a delivery boy. Startled, he ran away leaving Greta unconscious, but importantly he had left his gas mask, which contained his service number.

By now many of the street walkers in central London decided to take a few days off until the killer was found. Others worked in pairs, taking a good look at each client so they would be able to give a good description if something terrible did happen. They hoped their scrutiny would deter the mad killer, but the net was closing on him. The police by now had been able to establish that the killer was Officer Cadet Gordon Frederick Cummins. They waited for him at his billet that night, but he did not return. They found two cigarette cases and a fountain pen belonging to three of the murdered women. His fingerprints were also identified at each murder scene. They desperately needed to find him, but where was he? He had picked up a prostitute at a restaurant in Regent Street and went with her to a flat in Paddington. He apparently had a confident, almost haughty manner. Cummins wasted no time in trying to strangle her with her own necklace. As they struggled she landed a hefty kick with the high heeled boots she was wearing, knocking him off the bed. He was losing his touch. Embarrassed, he apologised and insisted on giving her ten pounds before making a swift exit. His time was up, or was it?

Despite having established fingerprints belonging to Cummins at the scene of the crimes, he still maintained his innocence. What is more, he appeared to have a watertight alibi. The billet passbook indicated that Cummins had been back on every night the murders occurred. He explained the gas mask away by stating that these were always picked up randomly by cadets without checking if they had the right one. He remained confident, even arrogant under questioning, but not for long. It soon became obvious that the cadets had a system of signing each other in to avoid being put on a charge. Cummins was arrested and sent for trial at the Old Bailey.

Even here there was a hitch. English law decreed that a suspect was only able to be tried for one murder. Some botched evidence by the police meant that the first jury was dismissed, but a new jury took little time in finding Cummins guilty. The evidence against him was damming. Despite this Cummins remained confident that he would receive a reprieve. He was wrong. Being articulate and arrogant was not enough. To a background of thunderclaps and flashes of lightning, Cummins was hanged on June 25th 1942 at Wandsworth jail.

The government was keen to illustrate that no company or individual (no matter how famous) was beyond the law. As such, household names like Sainsbury's, Woolworths and department stores Swan and Edgar and D. H. Evans were taken to court for breaking regulations. In 1941 public attention was focused on Noel Coward, whose drama 'Blithe Spirit' was playing to full houses despite the danger from bombing. One of the charges brought concerned dollars that he had brought back from the States not being offered to the Treasury. Although during his visit he had been acting as an unofficial ambassador drumming up support for Britain, he was fined two hundred pounds. He was later fined a further six hundred pounds for not declaring other US investments. As an excuse he said that his London office had been bombed, destroying all his financial details of his various investments. He was obviously believed as otherwise the fine would have been much higher.

By 1944 it was the composer Ivor Novello who fell foul of the authorities. He was a proud owner of a Rolls Royce and in an attempt to stay within the rules he converted the vehicle to run on gas to avoid the use of petrol. Despite a gas bag being fixed to the roof, a small amount of petrol was required to prime the system. In 1943 he applied for permission to take the car home to the country at weekends (he was currently appearing in his latest musical 'The Dancing Years'). Permission was refused. Subsequently he arranged to transfer ownership of the car to a company of a friend who could apply for a licence to use petrol. Novello continued to use the car, which was driven by his chauffeur. Obviously someone reported him and he was sentenced to eight weeks in prison. The conviction was upheld in May 1944 and the sentence halved on appeal. He received huge sympathy from the public and it was rumoured that he was treated harshly, as it was widely accepted that he was gay and prejudice against homosexuals remained very strong at the time. On his return to 'The Dancing Years' after release from prison, he received a standing ovation.

Whilst well known celebrities like Coward, Novello and Cecil Beaton fluttered on the fringes of high society, they were never really accepted. Some of those high born aristocrats who talked disparagingly about 'powdered pansies' were not averse to a little intimate male company themselves. The worst conceivable crime at a time of war was treason and unbelievably the culprit was drawn from a family very close to the centre of government.

Chapter 20

Traitors

The Treachery Act of 1940 resulted in sixteen spies being executed for their actions against Britain. Being a spy operating on foreign soil warrants a grudging acceptance of their bravery, even if it was directed against Great Britain. Sympathy for those guilty of treason was harder to justify. It is necessary to understand the mood in Britain during the 1930s. Looking at newsreels of Oswald Moseley ranting appears comical to us today, but it is important to realise how many were attracted to the Fascist cause. Whilst it was mostly working-class men who threw themselves into pitched battles against the Jews in the East End of London, they were supported (in spirit) by many of the social elite. Visits to Germany to witness Nazi rallies initially drew much favourable comments from those who feared communism and were often weirdly anti-semitic.

Within two weeks of each other two men seduced by Fascism ended their lives by having an appointment with Albert Pierrepoint in Wandsworth prison. Controversial characters, their stories continue to fascinate. William Joyce was born in Brooklyn, New York on April 23rd 1906 to Irish parents who had emigrated to the States. Staunch Unionists, they returned to Ireland whilst William was still a baby. Even as a youngster William sought out strange company, being friendly with a group of the infamous Black and Tans. It is even suggested that he served as a junior intelligence officer for the British Army combating the growing threat of the IRA. At the age of sixteen he moved to Britain. Later he attended London University where he gained a first class honours degree in English literature. Obviously intelligent, he retained a love and knowledge of Shakespeare. He flirted with Fascism before joining Oswald Moseley's British Union of Fascists in 1932. Within a couple of years his power of public speaking led to his appointment as director of propaganda.

His dislike of Jews was not helped when he was slashed in the face by a razor wielding communist Jew during a march in the East End. By 1937 Joyce had fallen out with Moseley and formed his own party, the National Socialist League, which was short lived. Just before the outbreak of war he left for Germany with his wife Margaret. He used a fraudulent passport he had obtained in 1933, despite him never having obtained British citizenship (this was to prove vital in his eventual conviction). Within a year of his arrival he had become a German citizen. It is at this stage we need to introduce the exotic figure of Anna Wolkoff. Four years younger than Joyce, Anna was the daughter of Admiral Nikolai Wolkoff, aide-de-camp to Tsar Nicholas II. The family arrived in London after the revolution and were forced to live in reduced circumstances. Anna visited Nazi Germany regularly during the 1930s and had meetings with Rudolph Hess. She opened a Russian tea room in South Kensington, an unusual setting for the regular meetings of a spy ring.

Members of the Right Club met regularly at the tea shop in Hartington Road. It provided good cover as they were joined by elegant ladies and their large and lumpy counterparts, seeking respite after an exhausting morning shopping at Derry and Toms. The club was formed in May 1939 and initially attracted many of Britain's leading aristocrats, including the Dukes of Wellington and Westminster. The group was founded by the Scottish Unionist MP Archibald Ramsay. He like many of the establishment had a hatred of Jews, who they maintained were trying to 'oppose and expose the activities of organised Jewry'. This obsession seems somewhat strange as he was unlikely to have encountered many in his Peebles and South Midlothian constituency. It was here in the tea shop that William Joyce met Anna Wolkoff before he slipped away to Germany.

The motto of the Right Club was 'Perish Judah'. It was attracting members with extreme right wing views, who saw much to admire in Nazi Germany. Ramsay began addressing meetings and rallies emphasising the need to end Jewish control, adding 'if we don't do it constitutionally we will do it with steel'. The audience hooted their approval. During the 'phoney war' Ramsay struck up an alliance with Oswald Moseley. Ramsay and his followers began distributing leaflets stating that 'the phoney war being converted into an honourable negotiated peace'.

Meanwhile Anna Wolkoff was attracting the attention of MI5. As early as 1935 there had been concern expressed about her friendship with Wallis Simpson (the future wife of King Edward VIII). They suspected that the two women might be involved in passing secret information to the Germans. With the war newly underway, Anna Wolkoff met Tyler Kent in February 1940. Tyler was a low ranking member of the American Embassy where he worked as a cipher clerk. He became a regular visitor to the tea room, attracted no doubt not just by Anna's politics, but also her glamour and deep sexy Russian accent. It appeared that Tyler was concerned that the American President Roosevelt might commit the US to join the war against Germany. He reckoned he had evidence to prove it as he had made copies of correspondence between Roosevelt and Winston Churchill. He invited Anna and Archibald Ramsay back to his apartment to view the papers. These included assurances that America would support France if it was invaded by Germany.

Wolkoff had not realised that the group had been infiltrated by members of the Secret Service. Joan Miller and Marjorie Amor later testified that these documents were passed to the Assistant Naval Attaché at the Italian Embassy. Next Anna asked Joan Miller to use her contacts at the Italian Embassy to pass on a coded letter to William Joyce in Germany. The letter contained information for him to include in his regular 'Germany calling' broadcasts. Miller showed the letter to her MI5 contact before forwarding it onto Joyce. Maxwell Knight, who was in charge of monitoring political subversion within MI5, was made aware of what was going on within the Right Club. There was a snag however, because American Tyler Kent was involved, it was left to Guy Lidell, a senior Secret Service officer, to arrange a meeting with Joseph Kennedy, the American ambassador. He agreed to waive Tyler Kent's diplomatic immunity and on May 20th 1940 Special Branch raided Kent's flat. Here they found a number of classified documents, including correspondence between the American President and Britain's Prime Minister. In addition they found Ramsay's Red Book, which he had given to Tyler for safe keeping. In it were listed all the sympathisers and supporters of the Right Club. A truly influential list indicating how widespread the support for the Fascist cause was, but the game was up. Kent and Anna Wolkoff were arrested and charged under the Official Secrets Act. The American was sent down for seven years whilst the mysterious Anna was sentenced to ten years. She was furious and vowed to kill Joan Miller. Presumably a lengthy spell behind bars weakened her resolve and after the war she moved to Spain, where some years later she was killed in a car crash. Back to William Joyce, who was broadcasting daily from Germany.

The reason Joyce had gone to Germany was twofold. Firstly he had been offered a contract to be an announcer for the German Radio English Broadcasting Service. In addition his own political prospects in England had taken a knock with his defeat in the London County Council election in Shoreditch. So just before the outbreak of war he and his wife Margaret flew to Berlin. Although English by birth, Margaret needed little persuading as like her husband she was a dedicated Fascist. It is quite possible that on arrival they were treated with some suspicion as possible 'plants' by MI5. It did not take long for them to get clearance and William started writing scripts for the German broadcasting service.

Soon he became one of several men referred to as 'Lord Haw-Haw', a name coined by Jonah Barrington (a pseudonym, his real name being Cyril Carr Dalmaine). Joyce had a rather false stylised posh accent and his regular broadcasts began with him saying 'Germany calling' whilst encouraging Britain to surrender. His sneering delivery enraged some whilst others found it ludicrous. Whatever, it is reckoned that he had a regular audience averaging six million and much higher during the early months of the war. The government was concerned about the effects of the broadcasts on morale. Whilst the broadcasts were boastful and far fetched, many found them concerning and not a little menacing. One East London woman spoke for a substantial minority, stating to mass observation: 'I think he is very good … he's very interesting and a lot of what he says is true'. Many took Joyce's threats seriously, making for the shelters when he warned of increased raids. There were rumours that the government was going to ban the broadcasts, but they realised this would cause uproar. Far better to ridicule than censor, but opinion remained very mixed. A Lambeth housewife was enraged: 'He makes my blood boil, I feel inclined to smash the set saying what he does about England'. The effect of Willam's broadcasts was insidious with a cumulative effect, but as the tide of war changed they became increasingly hysterical and unbelievable. That is until the buzz bombs arrived, threatening London and the south east again. There were hints of Germany possessing a super bomb and nerves remained on edge, despite the allied landings in Europe.

Joyce recorded his last broadcast in Hamburg the day Hitler committed suicide. Still defiant, he fled with his wife to a small village called Kuffermuille near the Danish border. Margaret had also made broadcasts from Germany and was known as 'Lady Haw-Haw'. A photograph depicts her with short cropped hair. Not unattractive, she had a rather prissy look with thin lips and the hint of an enigmatic smile. A biography authorised by their daughter Heather probes into the characters of this unusual couple. Margaret is described as flirtatious and something of a nonchalant personality. William is described as being droll and intellectual, with a particular love of Thomas Carlyle. Apparently theirs was a tempestuous relationship, increasingly fuelled by alcohol as Germany's fortunes worsened.

By May 1945 rumours spread of a British couple living in a cottage in Kuffermuille. At the end of May they were confronted by intelligence officers. Thinking Joyce was reaching into his pocket for a gun in a misunderstanding, William was shot. He had actually been reaching for his passport. Photographed as he was being taken away on a stretcher, Joyce stares unblinkingly, maintaining a look of supercilious defiance. He was driven to the border and handed over to the military police. He was taken to London where he was tried on three counts of high treason. Many legal minds felt that what subsequently happened was a blot on British law.

William was born in America and although his parents were naturalised, they were American citizens under British and American law. Joyce, although having lived in England for most of his life, had never taken out British nationality. Importantly he had fraudulently obtained a British passport, which allowed him to travel to Germany. Then in 1940 he took out German nationality. None of this was to help him at his trial. The government needed a conviction, which mistakenly they thought the public demanded. In truth there was quite widespread sympathy for Joyce mixed with apathy.

At his trial he pleaded guilty to fraud and the judge directed the jury to acquit him on two counts of treason. On the third count it was maintained that Joyce had committed treason by broadcasting German propaganda between September 1939 and July 1940, when he officially became a German citizen and still owed allegiance to the Crown. Although the BBC had no record of his broadcasts covering these dates, Joyce was convicted purely on the anecdotal evidence of Detective Inspector Albert Hunt of the Special Branch. So concluded a somewhat murky trial. Joyce was executed on January 3rd 1946. He apparently met his death with dignity and bravery. He was buried in an unmarked grave in the grounds of Wandsworth prison. His daughter conducted a campaign for the release of his body, which was finally agreed thirty years after his death and transferred to the family grave in Galway. An interesting footnote to this story relates to his wife Margaret never being charged, despite her activities in Germany, including broadcasting. Strange, but then much relating to this couple is. Perhaps William struck some sort of a deal? Less well known but even more astonishing relates to the treason taken by the son of a serving British government minister.

From a very early age John Amery was the cause of worry, stress and ultimately shame for his parents. His father, the Tory politician Leo Amery, became famous for his speech in September 1940 in the House of Commons which led to the resignation of Prime Minister Neville Chamberlain. 'In the name of God, go', he demanded, which in turn led to Winston Churchill being appointed and the future of Great Britain being re-set. Subsequently Leo Amery became Secretary of State for India and Burma.

His eldest son John was born on March 14th 1912, no doubt to great celebration and anticipation that the child would live to achieve great success. His early childhood misbehaviour was hopefully just a passing phase, but by the time he started attending school at Harrow there were more deep rooted concerns surfacing. Was there some bad blood lurking in the family's past? Today it seems likely that John was autistic. An early school report tells us 'he resented discipline and scoffed at the current conventions'. He stole from fellow pupils and local shops, not showing a shred of guilt. By his early teens he would leave the school to visit night clubs. He was a loner, making few friends, and thoroughly disliked by his classmates. His headmaster wrote: 'Of all the boys whom I have known, John Amery was the most abnormal. Just because John Amery was morally imbecile it was not possible to make anything of him at Harrow'. His father arranged for him to see Doctor Maurice Wright, a leading psychiatrist, who suggested that he had no sense of right or wrong and he concluded that John's condition was incurable. He was increasingly moody, introspective and violently abusive if obstructed in any way. His language was foul and whilst at Harrow he even accused a housemaster of a sexual assault. His parents really did their best and on leaving Harrow sent him to an exclusive private school in Switzerland. That didn't work as he was expelled in short order. A private tutor was engaged, who noted John's 'entire lack of normal feeling'. Neither did he have any sense of obligation to anyone or anything. He harangued his father, saying he was a fool not to be dishonest and make money from his position. It was noted that he had a superficial charm but no affection. A photograph of him taken in his early twenties pictures a young man with matinée idol good looks, but with a hint of the demons that lurked within.

On leaving school he went into business and promptly went bankrupt. He picked up over seventy speeding fines, none of which he paid. He married a woman described as a prostitute, before moving to Spain in 1936. Whilst there he fought for Franco in the Spanish civil war, serving as a gun runner. Already attracted to the Fascist cause, he served as an intelligence officer with the Italian volunteer forces. It was during this time that he met the French Fascist leader Jacques Doriot. They travelled across Europe together and in 1941 Amery was recruited by the Nazis making propaganda broadcasts to Great Britain. Unlike William Joyce, Amery's delivery was wooden and awkward. Being the son of a British politician, he was initially feted by the German hierarchy.

By now his family must have been squirming in disbelief and shame, but his disastrous lack of judgment continued with him forming the Legion of St. George in April 1943. This was his attempt to get British prisoners of war to fight for Germany against the Soviet Union on the eastern front.

Very few were that mad and his attempts were futile. Returning to his broadcasting duties, he lectured verbosely, stating: 'I dared to believe that some ray of common sense, some appreciation of our priceless civilisation would guide the councils of Mr. Churchill's government. Unfortunately this has not been the case', and so he droned on with few taking any account of what he was saying (not even the Germans).

As the war progressed it must have dawned on Amery that he had backed the wrong horse. He moved to Italy where still as a devoted Fascist he made a series of propaganda speeches and broadcasts, but the net was closing in. Whilst in Milan he was captured by Italian partisans. He was taken into custody by Captain Alan Whicker, who was attached to the British Army's film and photographic unit. Amery appeared to be in denial about the seriousness of his situation. Detectives from Scotland Yard were flown out to interview him. He was confident he would not be charged and if he was he inferred to the police that his father would sort things out for him. He was wrong. Back in London he was charged with high treason at Bow Magistrates Court on May 9th 1945. He was remanded in Brixton prison awaiting trial. Six months later there were gasps of disbelief when he pleaded guilty on eight counts of high treason. This left the judge with no option other than imposing the death penalty. Was it possible that John Amery finally discovered a conscience to protect his family from prolonged agony caused by a protracted trial? His mother made a direct appeal to the King, whilst the South African Field Marshal Smuts lobbied Prime Minister Clement Atlee, to no avail.

Enter the hangman Albert Pierrepoint. He noted that Amery was a heavy smoker. He was five foot seven inches tall and weighed one hundred and forty pounds. Apparently Amery was reported as saying: 'Mr. Pierrepoint, I have always wanted to meet you but of course not under these circumstances'. John Amery requested that four photographs in his possession should be given to his mother. Hopefully not the one presumably taken on his capture. His former good looks had taken on a rather haunted expression, not helped by him being unshaven. John Amery was hanged at Wandsworth prison on 19th December 1945. He went to his death aged thirty three with great dignity. Albert Pierrepoint claimed that Amery was 'the bravest person I'd ever hanged'. In death he at last reached out for a form of redemption. In April 1948 a letter was sent requesting that Amery's mother should be given permission to visit his grave. Permission was refused by the Home Office.

It is John Amery's mother-in-law who features in a bizarre footnote to this sad story. Despite his constant warnings about the dangers of Jewish domination of the world, there was a secret tucked away in the Amery family background. It is possible that Amery knew that his father's mother was a Hungarian Jewess at a time of rampant anti-semitism in the establishment and to an extent within the Tory party. Successfully burying the fact allowed Leo Amery to navigate his way to the top of the political jungle. Truth is stranger than fiction.

William Joyce and John Amery, two misguided zealots executed within a fortnight of each other. Could life in London get any stranger? Maybe not quite, but it is time to meet the Messina family.

Chapter 21

Sex and the City

In horse racing breeding is the essential ingredient to obtain success. A track record that points the way forward. So it was in establishing the Messina brothers as the dominant players in London's sex industry during the war and into the 1950s. Their credentials were gold plated. Their father, a Sicilian, moved to Malta as a young man, learning his trade helping to run a brothel in Valetta. He married a Maltese girl who gave birth to Salvatore and Alfredo before moving to Egypt. There gradually the couple built up a chain of brothels. Whilst in Egypt the family grew with the birth of two more boys, Attilio and Eugenio. It was Eugenio the youngest who was the first to arrive in London during the 1930s. It was a time when most of the street girls worked freelance under the control of a boyfriend or pimp. Many were French or Belgian, who were fondly known as 'Fifis'. Many had married British men, enabling them to work in London. Eugenio was able to claim British citizenship as his father was a Maltese national. He married Colette, a French girl, and had her working the streets within weeks of their wedding (obviously our Eugenio was no romantic). Next his brothers arrived to join the happy couple. They in turn set about recruiting more girls from the continent, with a sprinkling of British girls added to the Messina team. They were often tempted with promises of marriage and expensive gifts. Once on board the girls were ruthlessly exploited. Whilst the sex trade in London had flourished since the Bishop of Winchester's 'Winchester geese' roamed Bankside, it is through the prism of the Messinas and an astonishing investigative journalist that we can view the rise and fall of the family that ruled London's sex industry for over a decade.

With the outbreak of war the Messina boys, like all self respecting criminals, failed to register for military service. Instead they set about organising their team of girls. In the Spring of 1942 single women were required to register for war service. The girls were instructed to tell the truth. They were prostitutes, they said. Cue for hands to be thrown up in horror and general disapproval. These woman were certainly not suitable to work in government offices and certainly not in the land army. So it was that they returned to the not so loving embrace of the Messina boys.

Back in Soho the ladies now had their entire lives controlled. They were not allowed to mix socially and even had to be escorted on shopping trips by their maids. They endured something akin to a monastic life. Swearing was frowned upon, blasphemy banned and, bizarrely, low cut dresses also forbidden. After all, the boys regularly attended mass at St. Patrick's church and standards had to be maintained. Any breaking of the Messina code was met with the threat of violence. Regular transgression was punished by a beating or the kiss of a razor. During the early years of the war there was competition on every street corner, both professional and part timers. Some order was required. Soon only the Messina girls controlled all the most lucrative pitches, a virtual no-go area. Anyone having the temerity to encroach was violently attacked. Average takings for each girl was one hundred pounds per night They were paid fifty pounds a week (still a high wage in wartime London) and the boys were raking in a fortune.

Next came the introduction of new rules. The average time allowed with each punter was seven minutes and the girls had to return to their pitch within ten minutes. The boys toured the streets in their expensive cars ensuring their instructions were carried out to the letter. Time and motion study had arrived in the sex trade. Exemptions were made for discerning clients who required more than the basic service. All tastes were catered for at a price. Fines were imposed on girls who did not stick to the script. As the money rolled in the boys invested in property, which because of the dangers of falling bombs was very inexpensive.

It was too good to last. Another Maltese gang tried to muscle in on the Messina kingdom. Carmelo Vassallo was already feared and even considered unstable. He demanded one pound a day for each girl as protection. Many of the girls became too frightened to appear on the street. Martha Watts, one of the most trusted Messina girls, went to the police. She need not have bothered for retribution was both swift and brutal. Eugenio Messina confronted Vassallo supported by a couple of associates. Carmelo left howling minus a couple of fingertips. Problem solved. Well, not quite. Eugenio was sentenced to three years for the attack whilst Vassallo and four of his side kicks were sent down for four years in a trial held at the Old Bailey. Demanding money with menaces was obviously considered worse than slicing off a finger or two.

By 1946 the boys' weekly earnings had soared to ten thousand pounds a week but they were worried that business would tail off with fewer servicemen thronging the streets. There were questions in Parliament demanding action against the brothers, but nothing was done. Gradually conditions were becoming more difficult for the Messinas and upon Eugenio's release they decided to go underground. Competition was threatening more violence, the police were beginning to make things more difficult and then there was some journalist snooping into their affairs. Publicity was the last thing they wanted, but it was this strange reporter called Duncan Webb who would finally bring them down. His close ties to the mobster Billy Hill was also a worry.

Duncan Webb was weird, obsessive and outwardly sanctimonious. His career started in the 1930s as a cub reporter on the South London Press. During the war he was in the army in west Africa before being invalided out in 1944. On his demob he joined the Daily Express, no doubt influenced by its famous editor Arthur Christiansen. He subsequently went on to hone his skills at the London Evening Standard. Duncan Webb became obsessed with the effects prostitution was having on the country, but he had form. He appeared at Great Marlborough Magistrates Court charged with grievous bodily harm. He had apparently refused to pay the prostitute Jean Grewes the agreed fee of two pounds. She followed him out onto the street and got a passer-by to ring the police. The man (Robert Wadham) continued to follow Webb, who then showed him what appeared to be a warrant card and then hit him in the face. Still arguing, Wadham found a genuine policeman and Duncan Webb was arrested. The charge was reduced to one of common assault and later one of impersonating a police officer was dismissed. He was bound over and fined two pounds. We don't know if poor Jean Grewes ever got paid, but the readers of his exposé of the Messinas would have been shocked to learn that their white knight had succumbed to his baser instincts.

After his conviction Duncan Webb moved onto The People, a Sunday broadsheet and a rival to the News of the World (often referred to as the 'screws of the world'). Webb's first article exposing the Messina gang appeared on September 3rd 1950. This was explosive and a dangerous enterprise as Webb was about to find out. The headline screamed:

'Arrest these men. They are the emperors of a vice empire in the heart of London. The Messina gang exposed.'

He then went on with his strangely stilted copy: 'Yesterday I made the final entry in a dossier uncovering the activities of a vice gang operating in the West End of London on a scale that will appal every decent man and woman'. He went on to offer Scotland Yard his detailed dossier. There were mug shots of the brothers and a photo of their headquarters in Bruton Place.

He gave details of women married off to Englishmen to allow them entry and to ply their trade in London. The article caused a sensation and the paper's circulation soared, but it came at a price. The following week's edition of The People gave details of how Webb and a lady companion were attacked by two men and taken to Charing Cross hospital. The attackers were heard shouting: 'The Messinas are pals of mine, it's about time you journalists were done proper'. No matter, our intrepid investigator was back on the case the following week. He tells us that for three months the gang had been lying low but living in a luxury flat in Kensington Park Gardens. By October 1st Webb reported that Messina gang women were flouting the authorities with a photograph of two street walkers. He kept the story going, being outraged as the girls were only fined two pounds despite repeated convictions.

It was time for Carmelo and Eugenio to leave. Having loaded up their Rolls Royce, they set off for Paris where they were joined by Salvatore. The brothers continued to run their London operation from France. In March 1951 Alfredo was arrested at his Wembley home and charged with living off immoral earnings and attempting to bribe a police officer, whom he had offered two hundred pounds. With Alfredo sent down for two years and the other brothers out of the country, it appeared on the surface that the gang had been broken. Strange as ever, Webb placed an advertisement in the Times giving thanks to Saint Jude.

It did not take long for Webb to understand that the Messinas were still in control of the sex trade in London, albeit whilst based abroad. June 24th 1952 saw him launch a second batch of reports designed to bring the Maltese down. Although Webb was supposedly a devout Roman Catholic, rumours started circulating about him consorting with prostitutes. Certainly he often referred to himself visiting their flats in his hunt for new evidence before excusing himself. Was he a hypocrite as his detractors inferred? His zealous application to exposing what he called 'this sordid trade' is debatable, but no one can doubt the effect of his campaign on the future of investigative journalism.

His article of June 24th is headed 'Vice in London', Duncan Webb's second report to the Home Office of how the gangs brought in women from Paris. His articles were having an effect, with questions being asked in Parliament, but more widely there was concern amongst the public. Was it right that a whole area around Leicester Square and Soho was swarming with street walkers. The swisher area around Curzon Street and Shepherds Market was similarly affected. Church leaders were appalled. It was impossible to walk through whole areas of London without being accosted. Was this the image the greatest city in the world wanted to project? The more liberal minded disagreed, girls lurking on street corners added a certain frisson and colour in drab post-war London. Young girls meeting a boyfriend in London were advised by their mothers to keep walking to avoid unwelcome attention from men seeking a prostitute. The streets needed cleaning up, but not for a while yet.

Keeping up the pressure, the following week Duncan Webb filed a story with the headline 'One gang made a million in ten years'. If anything, for once Webb is underestimating the amount made by the Messinas. The article also features a photograph of a woman known simply as 'Colette'. He writes: 'On occasions she dresses like an ordinary housewife, but in fact this woman known as Colette is depraved and in a vice ring with a terrible record. For the present she is out of the country on holiday.

Will she dare to come back here?' The articles were having the opposite effect than intended. Droves of men headed for London, if only to look or maybe sample what all the fuss was about. It even inspired one very old street worker to employ a new strategy. Lisle Street just off Leicester Square was dimly lit and where the older and less attractive women were forced to seek their trade. This particular woman hit on the idea of dressing like a county lady, all tweeds, woollen stockings and flat shoes. She also affected a posh accent and acted as if reluctant to accompany the punter. Suddenly she was in constant demand. A frolic with the lady of the manor was too hard to resist. This was marketing the Messinas would have appreciated.

With Webbs's disclosures in danger of running out of steam, the edition of July 8th contained a far more serious and worrying allegation, under the headline 'These two women were murdered by vice gangs'. He was careful not to name the Messinas on this occasion, as the editor was obviously worried about possible court action, but the inference was clear. The murders of these two women remain unsolved today but do pose questions, particularly that of Rita Green. She was shot three times in what looked like a contract killing and a warning to any girl stepping out of line. Rita lived in a small flat at 42 Rupert Street in Soho. She was killed on September 9th 1947 at about seven o'clock in the evening. Within minutes of the killing a crowd formed in the street outside her flat and the road was shut on the arrival of the police.

She had been shot in broad daylight by a revolver in the stomach and chest. Two of her friends were quickly on the scene and initially the killer was reported leaving clutching a music case. She was still fully dressed and so there was no sexual motive for the attack. It was reported that at least five people had seen the killer, but all gave different descriptions. He was apparently aged between twenty five and forty. Not much help there then. Worse, his height ranged from short to tall. Were people deliberately misleading the police as there was a general fear on the streets at the time as various criminal factions waged war against each other. His clothing was variously described as being dark or possibly a tweed suit. All agreed he wore a trilby hat pulled down over his eyes and that he carried a despatch or music case. Rita had striking looks, being six foot tall and had stunning black hair and eyes. She was shot by a .45 revolver and a week previously it was noticed that she had a black eye. The police concluded that she was killed by a stranger. Most locals disagreed but kept quiet.

Webb waffled on in his article about the fact that 'black Rita', as she was known, worked on her own but was difficult, independent and refused to pay protection money. The inference was that an example had to be made of her. He described the person seen leaving her flat as foreign looking. Despite his best efforts Webb had been unable to add much other than the suspicion that if anybody did know the truth no one was prepared to come forward. A combination of fear and corrupt police who did not consider the death of a street walker demanded more attention. Time to move on.

Webb's series of articles carried on until the end of August. During the intervening weeks he claimed to have smashed the Messina vice ring. The paper photographed some of the houses they had bought under headlines like 'The long trail of filth that led them to London luxury'. The persistent investigator even followed them to Italy, exposing them further. His final article recorded how a woman called Sally Wright was enslaved by Attilio Messina. His pursuit of the Messinas had long become more of a crusade, driven perhaps by his religious beliefs. Still the brothers continued in business. By 1953 Attilio was making regular trips to London, but he was picked up by the police and sentenced to six months in jail. Still Eugenio, Carmelo and Alfredo continued to control operations from Paris. In November 1953 Eugenio was kidnapped and only released when a ransom had been paid. Rattled, the brothers moved their headquarters to Lausanne. Eugenio managed to obtain a British passport under the name of Alexander Miller and bought a very expensive property in Curzon Street in fashionable Mayfair to be run as a brothel. A police raid found fourteen thousand pounds in the safe.

The brothers were now scattered across England and the continent. Attilio appears to have been the nastiest of a rotten bunch. Using his veneer of charm and the good life, he then adopted violent tactics to get Edna Kallman to work the streets. This was much against her will but she was terrified of receiving another beating. She was allowed to keep just seven pounds a week of her considerable earnings. Plucking up courage at last, she fled to her parents' home in Derby where the police were called. In April 1959 Attilio was sentenced to four years' imprisonment. On his release he skulked off to Italy. Salvatore was living in Switzerland enjoying a comfortable retirement, whilst Alfredo, who had managed to obtain British citizenship, was living in Bedford where he died in 1963. Eugenio lived in San Remo and married Maria Theresa Vervaere, who had worked for him in Curzon Street where he still owned property. The story goes that he died on the day of his marriage and when his brothers arrived they found an empty safe. Maria Theresa wanted a share of his fortune. It is unclear if she was successful. Much of the Messina reign is clouded, but it involved corrupt policemen that allowed them to carry on for so long. To get some idea of the money floating around it is reckoned that even a constable on his beat in Soho was receiving sixty pounds a week for turning a blind eye. As the Messina boys drifted away there were others willing to take up their mantle, still controlling young women with threats of violence, but none have achieved the dominance of the 'famous five'.

There had to be and there is a final twist to this weird and sad battle between a gang of ruthless crooks and the man who set out to bring them down. Already terminally ill, Duncan Webb set off to Bala in north Wales to get married in a registry office, thus hoping to avoid any publicity. His bride was the former wife of the notorious acid bath killer John Haigh. Why? Again we will never know, but within three weeks of the wedding Duncan Webb was dead aged just forty-one. The distinguished journalist and editor Roy Greenslade described Webb as being 'larger than life'. He continued: 'A movie scriptwriter would find it hard to make his career credible'. Importantly he went on to say: 'For a period of eight years until his death he was the most famous investigative journalist in Britain'. In 1955 Time Magazine described Webb as the 'greatest crime reporter of all time', quite an epitaph. Had he lived, perhaps he would have investigated others who were also prepared to scrape the bottom of the barrel to make their fortunes.

Chapter 22

Where There's Muck There's Money

Pornography has existed since men lived in caves. It received a boost with the arrival of the printing press. By 1688 Samuel Pepys was sitting down to read 'L'Escole des Filles' and recorded that it was the most bawdy and lewd book that he ever saw. He confessed he felt ashamed for reading it. It came with a plain cover and he decided to burn it lest it be found in his library. Pornographers continued to take advantage of technology and the next leap forward came with photography. The repressed Victorians were seduced and beguiled as the business boomed.

Interestingly, my book 'The Hidden Letter' concerns perhaps the most explicit content I have ever read. Written in 1893 it was discovered recently hidden in a former saddle room of a country vicarage deep in the heart of rural England. Supposedly written by a young woman, it still has the power to shock today. It was authenticated by the curator at the British Library and was considered to be the most important handwritten pornography to be discovered. As such it was restored and now can be viewed in the Library in central London. Was it the vicar? We all love mysteries.

By the beginning of the eighteenth century we need to meet Edmund Curll, one of England's foremost pornographers. He often fell foul of the law but insisted that many of his titles were scientific rather than titillating. He was twice dragged before the House of Lords for including well known members in his rakish tales. In 1719 he published 'A treatise of the use of flogging in venereal affairs'. This was in no way thrilling, he claimed, rather it was a stark warning to those who might be tempted. He cited a case where a man died whilst being flogged in a London brothel. Having sex with a nun is a constant theme favoured by writers of pornography. By 1728 Curll was up before the King's Bench again. This time his offence was publishing 'Venus in the cloister', subtitled

'The nun in her smock'. Unable to cite a scientific content, he received a hefty fine but not one sufficient to stem his output. He was pushing his luck and his book concerning the 'Reverent Abbé Claudius Nicholas des Rues for committing rapes on 133 virgins' saw him sentenced to a spell in the pillory. Once again he avoided his sentence by circulating pamphlets bizarrely claiming the book was actually a tribute to Queen Anne. He continued publishing a wide range of books until his death in 1747, including biographies like 'The Black Plaque Guide to London'.

The dirty book shops often associated with Soho of the 1950s had a forerunner situated not far away in Victorian London. Visitors and tourists to London, particularly those from country towns and villages, were drawn to Holywell Street to be exposed to the type of publications never encountered in Bath, Harrogate or Tunbridge Wells. The street was soon to be swept aside by the beginning of the twentieth century to make way for the grand sweep of the newly built Aldwych. The Times described Holywell Street as the most vile street in the civilised world. It was also referred to as 'a sink of iniquity, a place where dirt and darkness meet and make mortal compact'. At first glance the visitor may have been impressed by a certain old world charm. Here was old London with half timber framed buildings complete with bow fronted windows. Nostalgic Christmas cards come to mind, but the stench coming from Half Moon Alley was foul and off-putting, but still many men lingered before taking the plunge and entering the dark, dank interior. Here books normally with plain covers but enticing titles could be purchased. Often the most provocative titles contained stories that would not have offended their Aunt Agatha. The more discerning buyer was welcomed into a back room where hard-core books, prints and, increasingly, photographs could be bought at a price. William Dugdale was the leading exponent of printing innocuous books with sexy titles, making more money from first time mugs than the explicit stuff. Anyone complaining on returning to his shop would be allowed entry into his inner sanctum.

The location of Holywell Street allowed outwardly respectable gentlemen to make their purchases, before mingling with crowds along The Strand and back to their hotel, lodgings or club within a few minutes, trusting that no one recognised them in that street of shame. There was, however, a growing backlash against London being turned into a cesspit of prostitution and pornography. Punch Magazine joined the fight, declaring that it wished Holywell Street could 'be swallowed up by an earthquake'. A police inspector tasked with attempting to stem the tide of pornography, which would surely still shock today, suggested that the Holywell shopkeepers should be 'nailed by the ears to the nearest gatepost'. William Dugdale was eventually arrested and sent to prison. The trade in Holywell Street continued until it was finally demolished, but market forces dictated that the trade merely migrated to Soho.

The general unease about London's declining reputation because of its seemingly out of control sex trade was taken up directly by Prime Minister William Gladstone, but doubts were expressed about his motives. He was convinced he could bring about change and reform some of the young street walkers. He referred to one as 'a most lovely stature, beautiful beyond measure'. Unkindly, fellow MP Henry Labouchère commented: 'Gladstone manages to combine his missionary meddling with a keen appreciation of a pretty face. He has never been known to rescue any of our East End whores, or for that matter is it easy to contemplate him rescuing any ugly woman'. The street girls referred to him as 'old Glad-eye'.

Girls were being sold by their mothers for a few pounds prior to them being sent abroad to act as prostitutes. The worry about young girls was emphasised by a particularly disgusting book published in 1887 by Edward Avery. 'The Autobiography of a Flea' chronicles the degradation of a young child at the hands of three priests. Whilst obviously only fiction, it did underline what was going on in London. The connection to the church also fed into the theory that celibacy was widely considered to be something of a sham.

During and after the Second World War, dirty book shops sprang up in Soho, but initially what was generally on offer was pretty tame stuff compared to the late Victorians. Most of the magazines were imported from the States. Following the example of William Dugdale, their enticing covers were not matched by the contents. Spicier fayre was soon being imported from Paris under the general term of erotica, giving a certain respectability to the trade.

Enter 'the dirty dustman'. Ron Davey was employed by Hammersmith Council and he hit on the idea of selling photographs of nudists and women wrestling before moving on to more explicit material. He sold packs of three photos produced on a primitive printer and was unable to keep up with the demand.

George Harrison Marks was a photographer who had learnt his trade the hard way, snapping holiday makers on Brighton Pier. Whilst there he had photographed the comedian Norman Wisdom, and it was through his introduction that he got to photograph the cast of a show being produced by Bernard Delfont. He started dating one of the chorus girls called Pamela Green and shortly afterwards they moved into his flat in Gerrard Street. Pamela had already done some nude modelling for another photographer and like the 'dirty dustman' was packaging them and selling them to the shops. Switching her allegiance to her new boyfriend saw the gem of an idea grow into a huge business. Sex sells. Harrison was entering a massive potential market. He advertised for models and was astonished by the positive response. His first applicant was an ex-Windmill girl and many others followed. In 1957 he took the plunge, launching his first magazine. Forget the tame competition, this thirty two page magazine entitled 'Kamera' was launched just a couple of weeks before the opening of Raymond's Revue Bar. A new liberalism was sweeping London. Harrison's initial print run of fifteen thousand sold out within days. The first edition featured fifteen girls in extremely provocative poses, far raunchier than 'Lilliput' or 'Spick and Span'. The format was simple, a provocative colour front cover and increasingly erotic photos inside, keeping within a whisper of the existing law. By the 1960s, with a large American car and a huge bank balance, Harrison entered the world of outright pornography and this marked the end of his relationship with Pam Green, who really disliked the path he was taking, expanding as he was to mucky movies. Many men who were schoolboys at the time look back on Pamela Green with a glow of nostalgia.

Where George Harrison was heading was already occupied by hardened criminals like Bernie Silver. Prostitution, pornography, all merging in a dark money making trade helped by a change in public outlook. This was emphasised by the failed attempt to suppress the publication of D. H.

Lawrence's 'Lady Chatterley's Lover', followed by Roy Jenkins' Obscene Publication Act of 1960. Sorry, Mary Whitehouse, but times they are a-changing and much appreciated by a new set of hard men seeking to control the fleshpots of London.

Chapter 23

The Godfathers

During the 1930s when Oswald Moseley and his followers were causing trouble and violence in the East End, one of their fiercest adversaries was a young Jewish man called Jack Comer, known as Jack Spot. He was fearless, wading in even when severely outnumbered. Later in life he traded on this reputation, claiming star status in the Jewish community long after the pre-war brawls were largely forgotten. He boasted that for a time he paid nothing for food and drink (he never touched alcohol), even his clothes were gifted to him by grateful Jewish traders. Of course this was not entirely true, his 'protection' came at a price. Spot was one of a number of war-time and post-war criminals whose lives sometimes crossed paths. Cooperation on occasions, whilst others were a foretaste to violence. These were the last of the Neanderthal gangsters who relied on brawn rather than brain. Today savvy crooks sit behind computer screens, making the sort of money that Spot and the Krays could only dream about.

There are many myths surrounding this group of thugs seeking to control parts of London. What control? Certainly the race tracks, but other than that it was about taking a cut from clubs, spellers, cafes and shops, prostitution and pornography. No doubt important to these men at the time, but their actions today would be considered at the lower end of criminal activities. The really successful modern villains never draw attention to themselves. They live in swanky houses, send their children to private schools, give money to charity and sometimes get a gong presented by the King. They would view the activities of the thugs operating in the post-war period with distaste, as they set about each other with razors, knuckle-dusters and coshes. Worse still, the use of guns, which sometimes led to murder charges. Not very bright when the death penalty was still being applied.

Whilst Darby Sabini sunned himself on his balcony overlooking the promenade at Brighton, there were those anxious to take over his concessions, particularly on the race courses. It was natural that these should be taken over by the White gang from Islington, who had been allies of the Sabinis. Their leader was big Alf White, a much feared figure. He tried to extend his influence to the West End where he was opposed by an alliance between Billy Hill and our friend Jack Spot. Billy Hill was one of the few gangsters of this era who showed a veneer of sophistication and intelligence. Born in 1911 to a well known criminal family, he referred to himself as 'the boss of the underworld'. He was the organiser of major robberies and specialised in jewellery heists. Always well groomed, he attempted to appear to be something of a gentleman, but he was also ruthless and not someone to upset. In his autobiography (actually written by Duncan Webb), he claims to have seen off the White gang as they sought to infiltrate the West End. The war had offered huge opportunities to form a power base, with money obtained by a number of smash and grab raids. Like his leading contemporaries he avoided military service, saying only mugs volunteered.

By 1947 his successful showdown with the White gang led to a couple of years' relative peace amongst the various London gangs. Money was flowing in and culminated in his organising a mail bag robbery in Eastcastle Street, netting almost three hundred thousand pounds. With his book raising his profile to celebrity status, Billy now sought the company of the notorious Lord and Lady Docker, winning their doubtful friendship by securing her Ladyship's jewels which had been stolen from their home. He fell out with Jack Spot, who appeared jealous of all the attention Hill was receiving. Unlike many criminals, Hill knew when to quit whilst he was ahead. He travelled between his house in France whilst making regular visits home. He even opened an upmarket club in swanky Sunningdale. When he died in 1984 Jack Spot reckoned he was the richest man in the graveyard.

Jack Spot was born in Whitechapel in 1912 to Jewish Polish immigrants. Growing up in the East End, it was vital to be able to look after yourself. The area spawned numbers of very tough Jewish youngsters, many of whom sought their fortune in the boxing ring. The 'Star of David' on a boxer's shorts was a regular sight at fight venues. If you did not fancy boxing or had a head for legitimate business, then maybe it was time to turn to crime. His stock was already high in the Jewish community, when in 1937 he was jailed for six months for viciously attacking a 'blackshirt'. Later Spot boasted that a call from a local Rabbi anywhere in the country resulted in the anti-Semites being sorted. During the war he served for a time as a marine, with his toughness being acknowledged. Unfortunately, he had a number of fights with anti-Semitic marines and he was dismissed from the service, stating his mental instability. He set up a working agreement with Polish criminals. His fearless physical bravery earned him respect in the London underworld and he started running a protection racket at race tracks.

He won the backing of powerful Jewish bookies prepared to pay for his protection, making enough money for him to open a couple of dodgy clubs. He was great at self promotion and although he did not drink, he was usually seen smoking a cigar, the size of which Winston Churchill would have approved. Whilst unlikely, he claimed he was regularly making three thousand pounds a week. Certainly his gambling clubs were proving very profitable.

The problem of trying to maintain control through force is that age becomes a factor. Nobody doubted Spot's bravery, which at times was reckless, but middle age brought about a perceived softness. There were new young bloods prepared to take him on. Now it was Jack who needed protection, particularly on the racecourse. He had heard about a couple of young men making a reputation for themselves in the East End. He approached the Kray twins, who were prepared to help for a cut of the take at Epsom on Derby Day. They just stood by Spot's pitches drinking, talking, taking the whole exercise as if it was all a bit of a joke, but the day passed off successfully. The Krays looked on Spot with a touch of pity. He was an old man, he was past it.

It was obvious that Spot's place in the sun was fading fast. Unlike his sometime friend Billy Hill, Spot was really just a violent thug. He had no mental capacity to plan or organise. He conceded that Hill had his own ideas and plans that occasionally led to clashes, but he still boasted that he had made Billy Hill, but no one was listening anymore. With his takings falling away and furious at Hill's claim to be boss of the underworld, he went searching for the journalist Duncan Webb, who had made Hill sound like the archangel Gabriel. Finding Webb drinking in a Tottenham Road pub, he attacked him with a knuckle-duster, breaking his arm. Hill was cross and Duncan Webb was not overjoyed either. This attack showed everyone that Spot was losing control, a fact he appeared to accept, stating he was retiring to a life of contentment with his wife Rita. Despite this, Spot heard that Billy Hill was planning to attack him. Returning home to their Hyde Park flat, they were set upon by a group of men led by Frankie Fraser. They were both knocked to the ground and Spot was badly slashed with razors that required some eighty stitches. Despite his injuries Spot was not prepared to grass, but Rita was. Frankie Fraser and Robbie Warren were both sent down for seven years and Spot wore his scars as a badge of pride, but he gradually fell on hard times. Rita left him and with little money to show for his lifetime of violence, he occasionally came to London, but was largely not recognised or ignored. Criminal life in London had moved on. He certainly outlived his part friend, part rival Billy Hill, finally passing away in 1996 in a nursing home in Sussex, unloved and forgotten.

The lunchtime rush was over. I had just finished a ploughman's when the door opened and four men entered. Two following the leaders like supplicants. The chatter in the bar stopped. I knew at once who these men were. The twins leant against the bar eyeballing each of us in turn. They were not as big as I expected, but were dressed in smart Italian style suits, white shirts and sober ties. Dressed as if about to attend a church service or more likely a funeral. The hush was broken by an invitation to have a drink with them. The offer was made in a dull monotone, which was somehow threatening. A few customers went nervously forward to take up the offer. I was sitting by the door and I slipped out, half expecting to be called back for not showing due respect to the leaders of 'the firm'. It was the only time I ever saw the Kray twins in the flesh. They certainly exuded an air of menace, endorsed by their reputation for violence and unpredictability.

Ronnie and Reggie Kray were born on March 17th 1933 in the East End to a feckless father and a dominating mother. They had an older brother Charles and a sister Violet, who died in infancy when the twins were three. Moving to Bethnal Green just before the war, the family were very inward looking, seemingly not needing or wanting close friends. Their father was called up for military service but deserted in short order, thus endorsing their reliance on their mother. In their teens the boys took up boxing, but their success has been overstated, neither was championship material. By this time Ronnie was showing a temper that he found difficult to control. Some have attributed this to a feeling of guilt about his sexuality.

Like their father, service life was never going to appeal to the brothers. They simply refused to obey orders. No punishment that the army could devise made any impression on them. They remained defiant and eventually were given an dishonourable discharge. It was time to make some money. Their first venture was to acquire a run-down snooker hall. Mixing constantly with serial criminals led to their starting their own protection racket. By the end of the 1950s they already had a reputation for extreme violence to anyone not meeting their demands, or even taking umbrage at some perceived insult. It was their unpredictability that caused alarm. Their influence widened to include dog and race tracks where protection came at a price. They also took over businesses that failed to meet their demands. As their sphere of influence widened they came up against the feared Richardson gang from south London. At first there was enough money for both parties to thrive until clashes became inevitable.

By the early sixties the twins were becoming minor celebrities in their own right. They started being seen in the company of well known actresses like Diana Dors. Dodgy homosexual politicians, including Robert Boothby and Tom Driberg, who seemingly got some sort of kick mixing with gangsters, particularly with Ronnie Kray who had similar sexual leanings. The Krays were seduced by publicity, the minor celebrities by 'gangster chic'. Ronnie no longer hid his gay leanings, which shocked the criminal fraternity. There were also rumours about Reggie. He was briefly married but the rumour was that the marriage was never consummated.

In 1960 the property racketeer Peter Rachman was paying protection money to the twins, and in an attempt to ingratiate himself with them he gave them a lead about a prestigious gambling club in Wilton Place,

Knightsbridge. He reckoned this would be a soft target for a takeover. A down payment of one thousand pounds and some blood curdling threats were enough for them to get a controlling interest. This proved to be one of their best investments, netting them a cool forty thousand pounds a year. Life was good.

They now employed Leslie Payne as their financial advisor. The money was rolling in and they needed help on where to invest it. Payne reckoned that by the mid-sixties up to half of the illegal gambling clubs in London were paying protection money to the Krays. Their tentacles were now spreading out to the suburbs and other major British cities. Were they beginning to stretch their resources too thinly? They received a visit from representatives of the New York Mafia who were interested in becoming involved with upmarket London clubs and casinos for money laundering. They returned not convinced that the Krays were the right partners, thinking they relied too much on thuggery rather than brain power. Realising there were few other options, they invited Ronnie to New York. Although he was almost childish in his admiration for the American gangsters, they awarded the Krays a contract to provide protection for the prestigious Colony Club in central London.

They became part of a scam involving bearer bonds. Payne demanded a greater share of the profits as it was he and his corrupt city contacts that were taking the risks. This was denied and there was a major fall-out and he parted company with the twins. Threats were made to kill him, which he laughed off. Payne, a survivor of the battle of Monte Casino, was one of the few who refused to be intimidated by the brothers.

There is some confusion about the killing of George Cornell at the Blind Beggar pub in Whitechapel on March 19th 1966. Cornell was a member of the Richardson gang, but had not been present the previous day when in a shoot-out at Mr Smith's club in Catford where Richard Hart, a friend of the Krays, had been shot dead apparently by Frankie Fraser. The killing led to the arrest of almost all the Richardson gang except Cornell. Ronnie heard that Cornell was drinking at the Blind Beggar and set off to confront him. Versions of what happened vary. What is not in doubt is that Cornell referred to Ronnie as 'a fat poof'. Some said that related to a previous meeting. Whatever, Ronnie shot

Cornell dead in broad daylight in front of numerous witnesses. Things took a worse turn the following year when Reggie killed Jack 'the hat' McVitie, who had failed to the agreed contract killing of Leslie Payne.

The wheels had fallen off the Krays' empire and the worries expressed by their New York contacts were borne out. The twins were unstable and not that bright. They were arrested and subsequently sentenced to life with a recommendation that they serve a minimum of thirty years. They were only aged thirty five. They made money in the short term, but what else could they claim? Ronnie died in Broadmoor in 1995. Reggie was eventually released on compassionate grounds whilst suffering from terminal bladder cancer. He received a typical East End gangster send-off. But what of the Richardsons? They were even nastier than the Krays, worryingly so.

The Richardson brothers ran the foremost criminal gang south of the Thames. Unlike the Krays they did not seek publicity to preen their egos, but they received it anyway in April 1967 at the Old Bailey in a hearing dubbed 'the torture trial'. They always considered themselves a cut above the Krays, liking to be known primarily as business men. In essence both were just thugs who were bound to cross swords as both gangs set out to expand their control.

The Richardson brothers were of similar ages to the Kray twins, Charles being born in 1934 and his brother Eddie two years later. Strangely Charles first met the Krays at an army camp in Shepton Mallet. He also refused to accept orders and was dismissed from the service. The brothers started off as scrap metal dealers before resorting to violence to get into running down-market drinking clubs. They progressed to insurance fraud and a profitable scam at London airport. The brothers drew other fraudsters to them like moths to the light. One Jack Duval was a tough Jew who had once been a foreign legionnaire and served in the RAF during the war. Ultimately none of these credentials were going to help him. Duval had been running an airline ticket fraud that was netting him huge returns. Apparently the Richardsons bought into the scheme claiming a half share. In March 1963 Duval was forced to leave the country to avoid the law. The trust in the partnership, always fragile, had broken down by the time Duval returned from Italy. Charlie beat him up as a warning, but became enraged when he discovered that Duval had given him a number of dud cheques. Not very clever. Retribution hovered in the air but Duval had gone to ground, so Charlie decided to take it out on one of Duval's associates, the unfortunate Lucien Harris. What happened next ultimately led to the Richardsons' downfall.

Criminals frequently fall out and often resort to violence to settle the disagreement, but seldom cold blooded torture. What was in the brothers' make up that encouraged them to torture and humiliate? Leads from a crude generator were attached to the most sensitive parts of Harris's body and as the handle was turned he was flung to the floor by the shock. Despite their empire spreading into the West End, stories of the torture being handed out by the Richardsons began to spread, as did the fear of who would be next. They started giving unwarranted beatings as a warning, thriving on the fear and injuries they were inflicting. James Taggart, who had been tortured by the gang, went to see the Chief Constable of Hertfordshire with his complaints. Others were also going to the police, fearful for their lives. After the shoot-out at Mr. Smith's club there were a number of arrests, including Eddie Richardson, who was jailed for five years.

Evidence continued to be gathered by the police on torture allegations. On Saturday, July 30th (the day England won the football world cup) Charlie Richardson and members of his gang were arrested. The 'torture trial' at the Old Bailey was sensational. How was it that humans could sink so far. Prosecuting counsel Sebag Shaw spoke for the majority when he said: 'This case is not about dishonesty and fraud, it is not about violence and threats of violence, nor let me say at once casual acts of violence committed in sudden anger or alarm, but vicious and brutal violence systematically inflicted deliberately and cold-bloodedly and with utter ruthlessness'.

Charlie Richardson was sentenced to a jail term of twenty five years, the longest ever handed down for grievous bodily harm. Charlie was released in 1984. Eddie was convicted again in 1990 and sentenced to thirty five years for his involvement in a massive drug heist. The brothers fell out whilst Eddie was serving his sentence, accusing his brother of fraud. It was almost bound to end this way. Honour amongst thieves evaporates where big money is concerned. The brothers continued to be involved in crime, but any pretence to control the London underworld had long since passed. Charlie Richardson died of peritonitis in 2012. There were other criminals around at the same time as the Krays and Richardsons. They were clever and devoted months to careful and minute planning. But were they any more successful or did this group also end up behind bars?

Chapter 24

Swinging into the Sixties

Lack of planning cannot be levelled at the serial criminal Bruce Reynolds. At least not at the logistics he applied to one of the greatest robberies of the twentieth century. His failing came in his choice of associates. There were too many and why choose mostly old London lags with strings of convictions? Surely it would not take long for the police to be on their tails. Reynolds was by nature a flamboyant character, drawing attention to himself by driving a flashy Aston Martin. He had extensive contacts within the criminal underworld and presumably took great care in who were going to join him on this daring and dangerous mission.

The conception of the 'great train robbery' is shrouded in mystery. There was talk of an Ulsterman who gave Reynolds details of huge cash shipments being made by train. Making a detailed investigation over months, Reynolds devised a workable blueprint for success. Now all he needed was a team he could trust and someone with an intimate knowledge of railway procedures and importantly the working of signals. He chose Roger Cordrey who had that expertise and appointed his friend Gordon Goody as his second in command. Gradually the team was assembled, including Jimmy White, a tough ex-paratrooper who had worked with Reynolds previously. Another hard man was Charlie Wilson, who had in the past been involved in protection rackets, but was currently concentrating on his bookmaking business. Bob Welch and Tommy Wisbey already had experience in previous (albeit much smaller) train robberies on the Brighton line. Others included club owner Buster Edwards and Jimmy Hussey, a violent criminal with a string of convictions. An important member of the crew was the getaway driver. Roy James was their man, someone with pretentions to becoming a full time racing car driver. Also engaged was Ronnie Biggs, a small time crook known and trusted by Reynolds. John Wheater, a solicitor and Brian Field were also recruited as it was felt their expertise may well be needed at some stage. It is also thought that there were others involved but who were never caught.

On August 8th the gang lay in wait for the train travelling from Euston to Glasgow at Sears Crossing in Buckinghamshire, a deserted spot but within easy reach of London. A signal was changed to bring the train to an unexpected stop. It had been decided in advance that only minimum violence would be used, but in the excitement of the moment the driver James Mills was coshed and seriously hurt. The mail van was uncoupled and separated from the rest of the train. In an effort to save money there was no radio provided on the train. The assistant driver, twenty six year old David Whitby, rushed to report the hold-up but the cables connecting to the nearest signal box had been cut.

The robbers now formed a human chain gang, off-loading one hundred and twenty mailbags stuffed with money onto a waiting truck. They had chosen the deserted Leatherslade Farm for the distribution of the loot. It was a forty-five minute drive down minor roads. As they tuned into the police radio they were worried that the police were going to concentrate their search within a thirty mile radius, which was roughly the distance that the farm was located from the robbery site. They needed to hurry. It is easy to imagine the cries of disbelief as endless bundles of notes were distributed to each member of the gang.

How on earth were they going to spend it all? Most of the cash was in either one pound or five pound notes, together with quantities of ten bob notes. The robbery had taken place on a Thursday and their plan had been to lie low for two or three days, but they were spooked by a light aircraft flying overhead. With the money amicably shared out, they did set out to thoroughly clean the building and then they planned to return to torch it. Despite their best efforts some tell tale finger prints were left. With no sense of irony they had apparently sat down to play a game of monopoly to pass the time, leaving some vital prints that led to their downfall. Other clues were left on a sauce bottle and a saucer where they had fed a stray cat. By the time the police discovered the farm on

August 13th the gang had disappeared, struggling as they staggered off carrying suitcases stuffed with bank notes.

Enter Tommy Butler, head of the Flying Squad. The gang had left enough evidence for him to swoop. Train expert Roger Cordrey and another gang member were arrested in Bournemouth. It was unlucky for them that they had chosen to lodge with the wife of a police officer who noted the weight of the suitcases they were carrying. There was also a huge amount of money found in their car. In another breakthrough, bags containing one hundred thousand pounds were found in a wood outside Dorking. A receipt for a hotel in the name of Field was also discovered. Brian Field, the solicitor's clerk, was duly arrested. Not far away in Box Hill Jimmy White's caravan was raided, revealing another thirty thousand pounds. Numerous arrests followed as many of the gang were rounded up.

The trial began on January 20th 1964. There was a fair amount of admiration shown by the public for the audacity of the raid. Discussions in pubs and at dinner parties centred on how honest we all would be if we really thought we could get away with such an outrageous attempt to get rich. The jury of public opinion was out, but in court there were no such doubts. These men were guilty. Goody, James Hussey, Welch, Wisbey, Wilson and Biggs were all put away for thirty years. Field and Lennie got thirty five years, whilst Cordrey who pleaded guilty was given a sentence of twenty years. Bruce Reynolds remained at large for some time before being caught, and surprisingly as the organiser only received a twenty five year term. Estimates of the amounts stolen vary from six hundred thousand pounds to in excess of two million. Only four hundred thousand was ever recovered.

Charlie Wilson was known as the quiet man, never answering any questions put to him by detectives and remaining silent at his trial. Perhaps he already knew that his stay in prison was not going to be a long one. Presumably his escape from Winson Green jail in Birmingham was pre-planned. Certainly it was mired in mystery and surely involved prison staff. He was sprung just four months after his sentencing as three masked men forced their way into the prison and Wilson was spirited away. With so much cash still undiscovered, presumably huge incentives were on offer.

The story did not end there. Like Bruce Reynolds, Buster Edwards managed to avoid the police. He also flew to Mexico on a forged passport to join Reynolds with his family. Although it is estimated that Edwards managed to take as much as one hundred and fifty thousand pounds with him, life on the run as a wanted man was expensive. The money soon dried up and Edwards was homesick. He returned to Britain, serving nine years in prison. On release he went on to run a flower stall in Waterloo station.

Wilson eventually resurfaced in the French speaking region of Canada. By 1964 we find him and his family living with him in Mexico where he enjoyed a brief reunion with Bruce Reynolds and Buster Edwards. Returning again to Canada, he avoided capture for four years. An intercepted phone call by his wife to her parents in London led to his downfall and arrest. Returning to England, he served a further ten years behind bars and was the last of the robbers to be released.

Like so many criminals he moved to Marbella in Spain. He became involved with money laundering for a powerful drugs cartel. He was swimming in a dangerous pool and he had obviously seriously upset some ruthless enemies. On a bright warm sunny morning Charlie was preparing a barbecue for lunch. A young man with brightly dyed yellow hair sauntered over towards him. He had arrived on a motorbike and was reported to have a London accent. Sensing no danger, Charlie continued preparing the lunch. Did he know the young man or was he a stranger? Coolly he approached Wilson and shot him dead at point blank range before calmly getting on his motorbike and roaring away. Here was another case of a career criminal who spent a large chunk of his life in prison before being murdered. A high price to pay for a few years of comfort and luxury.

Ronald Biggs was a small time crook who following the time honoured tradition of deserting from his national service and was subsequently dishonourably discharged. He stumbled into a life of thieving before being recruited by Bruce Reynolds to take part in the robbery of the century. It was Biggs's fingerprints that were found on a tomato sauce bottle found at Leatherslade Farm. In 1964 he was jailed for thirty years. After serving just over a year in Wandsworth prison he escaped, scaling the prison wall using a rope, and dropped onto a furniture van parked handily alongside the prison wall and he lowered himself onto its roof. He arrived in Paris to have some plastic surgery before travelling on to Australia. A newspaper article suggested that Biggs was living in Melbourne. Time to make a hasty exit. He arrived in Brazil in 1970, a country that did not have an extradition agreement with Britain. He was hit with a personal bereavement when his ten year old son was killed in a motor accident. He was later contacted by the British press and was happy to give interviews, knowing he was safe.

In 1981 Biggs was kidnapped by a team of ex-British soldiers and transported in a boat that broke down off Barbados. Now the plot thickens. Thinking they could claim a reward, they were horrified to find that Barbados also had no extradition treaty with Britain and Biggs was returned to Brazil. By 1997 an extradition agreement had been settled between Britain and Brazil and Ronnie Biggs was back in London to serve the rest of his prison term. Despite many requests based on health grounds he was denied early release until finally, having a series of heart problems, he was allowed home a couple of days before his eightieth birthday. Miraculously his health improved and his autobiography was published in 2012 and a TV series based on his wife's life was commissioned. The following year Ronnie attended the funeral of his old friend Bruce Reynolds, the mastermind behind the Great Train Robbery. Biggs died months later at a nursing home in Barnet. So ended another true story stranger than fiction.

Too much murder and violence. Time for a little light relief. Britons' relationship with sex has always been difficult or possibly even repressed. This was not a failing that could be attributed to Margaret Campbell, the Duchess of Argyll. If she had been issued with a badge for each of her conquests they would have covered one of her longest haute couture winter coats. But was she really any worse than many of her contemporaries from upper society, most of whom appeared to be involved in a bewildering game of musical beds. Her problem was her lack of discretion that led to one of the most scandalous court cases of the twentieth century, allowing all us hoi polloi a full view of her colourful life.

Margaret was born in December 1912. The family had strong financial and social connections both in Britain and America. As such, Margaret was privately educated in New York. It was her good fortune or possibly a curse that even as a child she was considered to be beautiful. Sometimes childish good looks migrate into a spotty pudding face and puppy fat. Not Margaret, her beauty continued to blossom, attracting the attention of men whilst only in her early teens. This cut little ice with her domineering mother, although compensated by a doting father. Each day she was collected from school in a chauffeur driven Rolls Royce, surely an early example of a 'poor little rich girl'. She developed a slight stutter that men found irresistible.

Her father was slightly less doting when he learnt that she was pregnant after a fling whilst on holiday on the Isle of Wight. Uproar in the household as an abortion was hastily arranged. Her ardour was far from being dimmed and she quickly moved on to an affair with the eighteen year old David Niven. They remained lifelong friends and many years later she attended his memorial service. By the time she was presented at Court in 1930 she had notched up several other notable victims on her romantic belt. Claiming she had damaged her traditional virgin white dress, she turned up to be presented in a fetching off-white tulle number. This did not stop her from being voted 'Deb of the year'. Her coming-out ball was reputed to have cost her father forty thousand pounds. They all drank champagne and danced to the music of Bert Ambrose and his orchestra with vocal refrains from Al Bowlly.

The expense appeared well spent when Margaret's engagement was announced to Charles Greville, the seventh Earl of Warwick. True to form she decided she fancied someone else, Charles Sweeney, a hugely rich American businessman. No problem, one engagement cancelled and a new one announced. 'Whatever Margaret wants, Margaret gets'.

Was it Margaret's upbringing that produced such a complex character? A feeling of entitlement, yet an underlying vulnerability resulting in her constant affairs. A dominant mother and a besotted father produced a young woman often described as being aloof and distant. Photographs of Margaret at the time of her marriage to Charles Sweeney show her to be dark haired with a rather prissy look, other than her eyes that gave a hint of the fire and passion waiting to be unleashed. Before getting married to Sweeney she converted to the Catholic faith. Previously her father had intervened when it seemed likely that she might marry Prince Aly Khan. He objected to her marrying a Muslim, although there still remained prejudice aimed at Roman Catholics in Britain. A year after the marriage her father purchased a fine London house in Upper Grosvenor Street for her.

The outbreak of war and a near fatal fall down a lift shaft saw Margaret move into a suite at the Dorchester Hotel. With anti-aircraft guns positioned in Hyde Park, the Dorchester, because of its steel structure, was reckoned to be one of the safest buildings in London. The war meant the couple were often apart and Margaret continued to collect a string of lovers taken from the ranks of the great and good, including Max Aitken and Prince George the Duke of Kent. Her marriage to Sweeney did produce two children, but the marriage was increasingly fragile. It staggered on for fourteen years, finally ending in their divorce in 1947.

Her love affairs continued to escalate and she was not without powerful men wanting to marry her. These included Joseph Thomas, the boss of Lehman Brothers. She really fell for Theodore Rousseau, the Curator of the Metropolitan Museum of Art in New York. Regretfully she decided that he was not suitable stepfather material.

It was time for Margaret to find another husband. She had very extravagant tastes and children were expensive. Her choice was not a good one and proved disastrous for both of them. Ian Douglas Campbell was a hunting, shooting and fishing man. From Margaret's standpoint that was not very encouraging as she loved the high life in London, Paris and New York. Very much on the plus side was that Campbell was the eleventh Duke of Argyll. What lady would not want to be a Duchess? Later Margaret said: 'I had wealth and good looks. As a young woman I had been constantly photographed, written about, flattered, admired, included in the ten best dressed women in the world list....I had become a Duchess and mistress of a historic castle.'

Perhaps the Duke having already had two failed marriages ending in divorce should have been a warning to her. It soon became obvious that the Duke was a very heavy drinker with a violent temper. He also gambled and swallowed quantities of prescription drugs. Worse, he insisted he needed money for the restoration of his crumbling Inveraray castle and this had been partly instrumental in the breakdown of his previous two marriages.

It did not take long for the marriage to fall apart. She resented his constant call on her money whilst he was convinced that from early on in their marriage she was being unfaithful. Whilst she was on a trip to New York he employed a locksmith to force open a cupboard in the bedroom of their house at Upper Grosvenor Street. He got rather more than he had bargained for. Incriminating letters are one thing but many explicit photographs of his wife totally naked except for her favourite pearl necklace, in the arms of another man. Worse, another polaroid shot of her fellating a naked man whose face was hidden. Cue to employ top lawyers as their sordid (but somehow hilarious) story was paraded before an astounded and fascinated public. Who was the hidden man and why had she kept the photographs? Speculation went into overdrive, with crazy theories being bandied about, whilst newspaper circulations boomed with lurid headlines and maiden ladies reaching for the smelling salts as the case got underway.

The Duchess counter-petitioned, bizarrely citing her husband's adultery with her stepmother. She withdrew the case for lack of evidence on the day of the hearing. It was a costly mistake as her stepmother sued her for libel and was awarded twenty five thousand pounds at a later hearing. The Duke listed over eighty men he believed had enjoyed a sexual relationship with his wife. Sensationally these were said to include a couple of government ministers, but out-ranked by three members of the Royal Family. This from a titled lady now in her fifties. The judge could not contain himself, stating that: 'The Duchess had taken part in disgusting sexual activities'. The presiding judge Lord Wheatley concluded that the Duchess 'was a completely promiscuous woman whose sexual appetite could only be satisfied with a number of men'. But who were these well connected men? The judge continued: 'Her attitude of the sanctity of marriage was what might be called enlightened, but which in plain language was wholly immoral'.

Lord Denning was called on by the government to try to identify the headless man. He was asked to check the handwriting of the leading suspects, who included Duncan Sandys and Douglas Fairbanks Jr. For a time Sandys was favourite as polaroid cameras had only just come onto the market and it was known that one was used within his government department. Jokes abounded and identifying features of the offending penis caused much speculation but it was never identified. Privately the government concluded the headless man was Fairbanks and there were reports that he did accept that it was him. Even so Sandys offered to resign, but this was not accepted. Despite the finding the rumours continued and the Duchess remained tight lipped (sorry, pun intended!).

The rest of Margaret's life saw a gradual decline as her funds began to run out. She wrote a non-controversial autobiography, also writing articles for the Tatler. She was forced to sell Upper Grosvenor Street and decamped to a suite in the Grosvenor House Hotel until she was evicted for not paying her account, and she was largely shunned by society. Her children provided a place in a nursing home for her where she died in 1993. A television film 'A Very British Scandal' was shown to good reviews in 2021. She famously described herself as 'a poodle, only a poodle and three strands of pearls'. From poor little rich girl read poor sad old lady, but what a life she led making numerous men happy along the way.

Chapter 25

Changes and Reflections

Every decade produces massive changes which only become obvious in retrospect and none more so than the 1960s and 1970s. The sixties particularly saw the country lurch from war-time austerity to a period of creativity not seen since the 1920s. Suddenly everyone from around the world wanted to visit London. Gone was the cloth cap and bowler hat. Society as a new liberal spirit swept the country, led by the young. Music and fashion were at the forefront, together with films and theatre challenging previous norms. Deference was firmly placed on the back burner as shows like 'Beyond The Fringe' and the weekly television show 'That Was The Week That Was' lampooned politicians and the establishment.

New fashion designers like Mary Quant led the way, although it was an era hated by girls with heavy legs as the mini skirt swept all before it. Meanwhile young men headed to the boutiques of Carnaby Street as they started dressing like turkey cocks. The coffee bar became the place where the young met, generally scorning the pub and leaving the old grumbling into their beer and thinking that the world had gone mad. The availability of the contraceptive pill added to the general sense that the world had changed forever. Previously getting pregnant out of wedlock was perhaps the greatest shame that could befall a respectable family. Now it was the age of free love with few risks attached. Even the jukebox had been replaced by discos, all noise and flashing lights. It was not just the Beatles and the Rolling Stones, but a seemingly endless stream of popular hits from artists with unlikely names. Some were one-hit wonders, but the atmosphere for the young was heady and exciting.

Heady perhaps due to another major influence, which was the availability of drugs, with criminal gangs waking up to the huge possibilities that this offered them. Drugs had been around for many years, but generally only available to the wealthy in the 1920s and 1930s. The politician and diplomat Duff Cooper often confided in his diary his worry about his wife Diana's use of drugs. As far back as the nineteenth century opium and laudanum were openly available. By the twenties it was assumed that most of the drugs being sold came from the Chinese community in Limehouse. The best known dealer was an attractive Chinese man known as 'Brilliant Chang'. He ran a fashionable restaurant in Regent Street, where he supplied his well heeled clients with cocaine and heroin. He was eventually deported and during the war and the 1950s the use of drugs was mostly confined to jazz and blues musicians. Now it was time for the pop stars to take up the mantle. Young people hate to be left out of the latest trends, whether it be music or dress, and many were drawn into a drug culture. This would normally start by taking cannabis before moving on to LSD and hard drugs. This trend accelerated in the club scene of the seventies where youngsters wearing flares and awful hairstyles danced and smooched in a haze.

Members of the Metropolitan Police were already taking money from pornographers for turning a blind eye, and now the drug dealers were going to provide a new source of income for dishonest officers. One of the most interesting policemen at the time was a Detective Sergeant originally making a name for himself by being the scourge of criminals in Soho. Harold Challenor had served with distinction in the Special Air Service in the war before joining the police. Although outwardly zealous in his pursuit of criminals, he was also known to be corrupt and violent. He planted incriminating evidence on suspects, knowing that the courts would generally believe a decorated war hero over some small time crook, and so his reputation soared.

He stepped out of his comfort zone in July 1963 when a political demonstration took place outside Claridge's Hotel to protest against the visit of Queen Frederica of Greece. One of the demonstrators who was carrying a banner was Ronald Rooum, an influential member of the National Council for Civil Liberties. He was arrested and back at West Central police station was pushed upstairs to a detention room by Challenor. There he was repeatedly hit by the Sergeant, who reprimanded him for booing the Queen. Rooum denied this stating he was making a silent protest. The denial was rewarded with another blow to the ear. He was then accused of carrying an offensive weapon. The Sergeant then produced a piece of brick wrapped in paper from his own pocket. 'You can get two years for that', he told the rather bemused prisoner. Despite his denial Rooum was left alone to consider his fate. Later that evening another six demonstrators were brought into West Central police station. All including Rooum refused to sign a statement indicating they had been carrying bricks. Annoyed, Challenor refused Rooum bail, allowing him to call on the well known criminal solicitor Stanley Clinton-Davis.

The fact that Rooum had been kept in custody worked in his favour, as he had been unable to change his clothes, which were handed to his solicitor after the remand hearing. A forensic scientist reported that there was no sign of brick dust in any of Rooum's pockets and there was no scuffing of the pockets' lining. The magistrate that day at Marlborough Street Court was Edward Robey. Handling the brick, he observed how readily it broke off, leaving clouds of dust. Rooum was promptly acquitted but was probably annoyed at not being awarded costs. Another defendant was found guilty despite having the same legal and forensic team, and fined ten pounds. Others attending the demonstration had also been fined, but there was increasing unease about the convictions. Challenor had been showing increasing signs of being mentally unwell and was on sick leave. At this point the prosecution relating to all the defendants offered no evidence and suddenly Challenor was under pressure.

In June 1964 Challenor was due to appear at the Old Bailey charged with corruption. His solicitors claimed that he was unfit to plead and had been committed to a mental hospital. However, three of his colleagues on that night were found guilty and sent down for either three or four years. Lord Justice Lawton called on Challenor's boss, Chief Superintendent Rose, to appear before him. He said he wanted the Commissioner to be made aware of his grave disturbance about the case. He suggested that Challenor's irrational behaviour should have been picked up much earlier. A full enquiry was ordered, which resulted in a whitewash. The fact was that planting false evidence and threatening violence to those accused was commonplace at the time in the Met. We are therefore left with the impression of collusion between criminals and the police. This was particularly prevalent in Soho where the porn barons even went on holiday with Kenneth Drury, the Head of the Flying Squad, before he too was brought to book.

The 1970s proved to be a golden age for the drug smugglers, dealers and also some bent coppers. Many involved were hardened criminals, but Howard Marks was different in every aspect. He started dealing in cannabis whilst still at Oxford, where his charm and good looks were noted by MI6, and was assigned the agreeable task of trying to seduce women at the Czechoslovakian Embassy to pass on state secrets. Moving on, he was arrested in America when drugs were found and he was extradited back to Britain where bailed for two thousand pounds. From a secret hideout on the Isle of Dogs in east London he planned what was to become a huge operation worldwide. By now he rarely tried to adopt a low profile. In 1997 he was back in London for the birth of his second daughter and could be seen performing rock 'n' roll numbers in a Hammersmith pub. This at a time when he was smuggling tons of cannabis to the States. It took the combined efforts from police forces from Europe and the States to bring to an end the most successful independent drug dealer in the world. It was estimated that despite the size of his operation he had only made a couple of million dollars by the time he was arrested again in Florida and sentenced to thirty years in jail. Good behaviour saw him released in 1995. He was just another larger than life character to join our eccentric cast.

It would be a shame not to end on two more celebrated sexual scandals. They really mark a shift in power and influence from the entitled establishment to the power of money. The cases of War Minister John Profumo and Jeremy Thorpe a decade later illustrate the point. Both have been endlessly covered in the press, books and film, but it is the presumed sense of entitlement exhibited by both men that jars today. These were people who other than those within their gilded circle were given little thought or appreciation. This becomes obvious when reading the diaries of the likes of Duff Cooper or 'Chips' Channon. As they glide from dinner parties or five star hotels there is almost no mention of those who serve and support them. It is almost as if these outsiders scarcely exist or impede on their privileged lives.

Both Profumo and Thorpe belonged to that political and social elite who imagined that others of their choosing were there to do their bidding sexually, and they did not anticipate any unpleasant repercussions. They were both wrong. Both cases a decade apart would have stretched the imagination of fiction writers. Profumo had just enjoyed a civilised supper in the grand Berkshire surroundings of Cliveden House, the home of Lord Astor. Sauntering in the gardens, the guests, which included Prufumo's wife, the actress Valerie Hobson. Approaching the swimming pool, they were surprised and amused to be confronted by a beautiful nude Christine Keeler. She had been the guest of Stephen Ward, a society osteopath who rented a cottage on the estate and was allowed access to the pool. Keeler demurely covered herself and the host and his guests moved on laughing. Ward had a reputation for producing a succession of lovely girls at Clivedon and Profumo made enquiries about the girl he had seen that night and was given Christine's contact number. Profumo was a Minister of War who was in his mid-forties. It was his affair with the teenage Keeler that eventually led to his disgrace and indirectly the fall of the Conservative government. What he was not to know was that Keeler had already had a brief fling with Captain Ivanov, a Russian naval attaché and a spy.

It did not take long for the Secret Service to become aware of the affair and he was given a gentle warning. Rotten luck for Profumo, who broke off the relationship and this should have drawn a line under the affair. Things started going seriously wrong when Johnny Edgecombe, a jealous former lover of Keeler's, turned up at Ward's Wimpole mews flat. Being refused entry, he started firing randomly with a pistol. Cue for the press to take an interest in Stephen Ward and his collection of young girls including Keeler, particularly when it became clear she had been sleeping with a government minister and a Soviet naval attaché.

At this stage Profumo made his fatal mistake by denying in Parliament the rumours circulating. He stated that there had never been any impropriety and threatened to sue anyone repeating the allegations. The police investigation now started piling pressure on Ward, who felt he was being set up in some way as the fall guy. The Lord Chancellor instigated an investigation at the end of May 1963. Before returning to Parliament

Profumo made a full confession to his wife. It must have been an awful moment but she decided to stand by her man. He then issued a statement admitting that he had lied to Parliament, and resigned. Stephen Ward was charged with living off immoral earnings and appeared at the Old Bailey. That July, feeling betrayed and abandoned, he committed suicide before a verdict was returned. A sorry story that ruined several lives, that but for ill fortune would have gone unnoticed, because well connected men were usually able to pick up young women and drop them with impunity, and this sense of entitlement for this cosseted group had some time to run yet until they gave the floor to the Saudi princes, Russian oligarchs, pop stars and celebrities. But there was still one leading politician to be put through the public wringer. Enter the flamboyant and talented Jeremy Thorpe.

Thank goodness for wayward politicians as they certainly add to the sense of the ridiculous enjoyed by the country, and give us something to talk about rather than the weather. Where the scandal of Profumo involved spies, suicide, call girls and a minister of state, a decade later the debacle involving Jeremy Thorpe, the leader of the Liberal party, stretched the sense of incredulity even further. Like fellow MPs Tom Driberg and Bob Boothby, it was always suspected that Thorpe had homosexual tendencies and it was 1967 before the Act between consenting adults became legal (it was the year Thorpe became leader of the Liberal party).

It was seven years earlier that he met a highly strung young man called Norman Scott and they started an affair in Thorpe's mother's house whilst she slept in the bedroom next door. Scott became totally infatuated with the older man, who was charming, witty and charismatic. Thorpe arranged for Scott to have a flat conveniently close to the House of Commons. He took him to fashionable restaurants and they attended parties together (hardly discreet). After some three years Thorpe's interest was starting to falter and according to Scott tried to give him the brush-off. As far as Thorpe was concerned he had taken what he wanted and it was time to move on. Scott felt betrayed and appeared to suffer some sort of mental meltdown. Like a man scorned he told anyone who was prepared to listen all about his involvement with the politician. Later it was alleged that Thorpe on a number of occasions discussed having Scott murdered, as his career and reputation were being put in danger. Most assumed he was joking. Apparently he was not.

Supposedly offering a fee of twenty thousand pounds, his choice of a hit-man was as flawed as the whole crazy idea. Andrew Norton was somehow chosen to do the dirty deed. In 1975 he drove Scott to the wilds of Exmoor. Scott, a great dog lover, insisted on taking his Great Dane on the jaunt onto the moor. Norton was frightened of dogs and the Great Dane must surely have unnerved him because he shot it dead. Next he aimed the gun at Scott. Panic stations, it jammed. Norton put the car in gear and roared off, leaving Norman Scott weeping over the body of his dead Great Dane. Scott, not unsurprisingly, wanted to tell everyone about his frightening experience. Before long the press were onto what was a sensational story. The pressure grew on Thorpe and eventually in 1978 he was charged with conspiracy to murder. The national press could scarcely contain their excitement. Could all these revelations possibly be true?

The trial in 1979 was delayed by the calling of a general election. Finally in the May of that year all eyes were on the Old Bailey. Thorpe was represented by George Carman, a young barrister who became the 'go to' man for celebrities in the future. Thorpe and his associates in the supposed plot were all advised not to give evidence, and thus it was up to the prosecution to make their case. The witnesses, some of whom had sold their stories to the press, did not impress. The judge was critical of them in his rather stilted summing up. He pointed out the defendant's previous good character, whilst referring to Scott as a fraud. It was no surprise that Thorpe was found not guilty, but despite his continued claims of innocence the British public was sceptical. Members of the church raised concerns about the morals of public servants, the mud stuck and Thorpe's reputation was ruined and he gradually faded from public view, having lost his north Devon constituency to his Tory opponent. Like Profumo, Thorpe's wife remained loyal to him.

1979, the year of the Jeremy Thorpe trial, represented a turning point in Britain's history. This was the year that Margaret Thatcher became Prime Minister. Suddenly money rather than aristocratic or influential background was key. It no longer mattered so much about where you came from, but rather where you were going. The old school tie and privilege making way for the get rich quick society, characterised by Harry Enfield's ghastly character in his hit song 'Loadsamoney'.

The history of London gets swallowed up in the mists of time, but we do know that human settlements date back some fifteen thousand years, with flint tools found as widely as Southwark and Hampstead in north London. It is a history that continues to evolve and yet never ends. The emphasis on money was welcomed by London's criminals. Corners being cut and financial scandals offered many lucrative opportunities for the savvy 'Jack the lad'. Violence, murder and sexual scandal would continue for the years to come, but that is another story.

Bibliography

Ackroyd, Peter. London. Vintage Books 2012
Burford, E. J. London, The Synfulle City. Robert Hale 1990
Burford E. J. The Horrible Synne. Calder and Boyars 1973
Gilbert R. D. West End Chronicles. Penguin Books 2007
Glinert Ed. London Compendium. Penguin Books 2003
Grovier, Kelly. The Gaol. John Murray 2009
Hickman, Kate. Courtesans. Harper Collins 2003
Huggett, Richard. Binkie Beaumont. Hodder and Stoughton 1973
Inglis, Lucy. Georgian London. Penguin Books 2014
Inwood, Stephen. City Of Cities. Macmillan 2005
Linnanne, Fergus. London The Wicked City. Robson Books 2003
Linnanne, Fergus. London's Underworld. Robson Books 2004
Morton, James. Gangland. Warner Books 2003
Morton, James. Gangland Soho. Piatkus Books 2008
Morton, H. V. In Search Of London. Methuen 1951
Porter, Roy. London, A Social History. Hamish Hamilton 1994
Priestley, J. B. The Edwardians. Heinemann 1970
Roud, Steve. London Lore. Arrow Books 2008
Thomas, Donald. An Underworld At War. John Murray 2004
Sandbrook, Dominic. Never Had It So Good. Little Brown 2015
Summers, Judith. Soho. Bloomsbury 1989
Yass, Marion. Britain Between The Wars. Wayland 1975
Ziegler, Philip. London At War. Pimlico 2002

Index

Abbott, George 77, 78
Aberline, Frederick 97
Acton, Harold 120
Albert, Prince 98
Alexandria, Queen 134, 129
Alsatia 4
Amery, Leo 155, 156
Andrew Sisters 119
Anery, John 145, 146, 156, 157, 158
Argyll, Margaret Duchess 185, 186, 187, 188, 189
Argyll, Duke of 187, 188
Arkell-Smith, Harold 138
Astoria Dance Hall 45
Atlee, Clement 157
Austin, John 61, 110
Ave Maria Alley 87
Avery, Donald 169

Bacchus, Reginald 80
Baddeley, Sophia 112, 113, 114, 115
Baddeley, Robert 112
Bankside 1
Bankside Bear Garden 52, 53
Barker, Leslie 137, 138
Bartlett, Adelaide 28, 29, 30
Batten, Elsie 24
Battersea 22, 35, 67
Beak Street 7
Beaton, Cecil 149
Beaumont, Binkie 101, 102
Bedford Square 22
Bedlam 49, 50
Beer Street 2
Beresford, Lady 128
Beresford, Lord 127, 128
Bethnal Green 54, 70, 176
Biggs, Ronnie 181, 184, 185, 190
Billings, Thomas 25, 26

Billingsgate 87
Birdcage Walk 52
Bishopsgate 94
'Black', Harriet 90
Blackburne, Lancelot 79, 80
Blantyre, Lady 30
Blind Beggar pub 177
Boar's Head 1
Boleyn, Anne 43
Bond Street 145
Boothby, Robert 195
Boswell, James 90
Bottomley, Horatio 121
Bradwell 72
Bridewell 1
Brilliant Chang 191
British Union of Fascists 74
Brixton Prison 39
Brownrigg, Elizabeth 26, 27, 28
Buckingham Palace 101
Bull baiting 54
Burns, William 55
Bush, Edwin 24
Butler, Tommy 182
Bywaters, Frederick 33, 34

Cable Street 74
Cafe de Paris 143
Calico Act 70
Careleton, Billie 133
Carmen, George 196
Catford 177, 178
Challenor, Harold 191, 192
Chancery Lane 10
Channon, Chips 99
Charing Cross Road 4, 6
Cheapside 67
Chelsea 33, 45
Chesterfield, Earl of 79

Clarke, Anna 7
Clarkson, Thomas 58, 59
Clerkenwell 8, 46, 54, 70, 73
Cleveland Street 96, 97
Clifford, Harriet 7
Clifford, Margaret 17
Clifford, Mary 27
Clink (prison) 42
Cock Lane 87
Collett, Jack 103
Collins Music Hall 65
Cooper, Diana 193
Cooper, Duff 193
Courtneidge, Cicely, 94
Covent Garden 3, 5, 6, 81, 107
Coward, Noel 100
Cresswell, Elizabeth 90
Crisp, Quentin 99, 100
Cromwell, Oliver 44
Cromwell, Thomas 44
Cubitt, Sir William 38
Cummins, Gordon 147, 148
Curzon Street 163

Dangerous Drug Act of 1920 133
Davey, Ron 170
Davidson, Harold 82, 83, 84, 85
Davies, Lady Eleanor 50
Davison, George 29, 30
Davy, Margaret 36
Decker, Thomas 55
Defour, Judith 63
Dell, William 12
Denman Street 144
Deptford 20
Derry and Toms 151
de Veil, Sir Thomas 64
Dickens, Charles 3, 48
Docker, Lady 172
Dodgson, Rev. Charles 80
Dorchester Hotel 187
Douglas, Ella 84
Douglas, Lord Alfred 98, 99
Drake, Sir Francis 56
Draper, Doctor Nick 61
Driberg, Tom 195
Drury Lane 2, 4, 5,
Dudley Street 57
Dugdale, William 168, 169

Duval, Claude 107
Duval, Jack 178-179

Eastwood, Marguerite 139, 140
Edward VII, King 122, 124, 125, 126, 127, 128, 129
Eglinton, Earl of 109
Ellis, Judith 23, 34
Ellis, Rose 83, 84
Ellis, Ruth 35
Evans, D.H. 148
Evans, Timothy 35
Evening Standard 100, 145

Fairbanks, Douglas jnr. 188, 189
Fahmy, Marguerite 139
Fahmy, Prince Ali Kamel Bey 139
Farringdon Road 7
Fielding, Henry 64
Fitzroy, Henry 97, 98
Fitzroy Square 2
Fraser, Frankie 175, 177
Frederica, Queen 191
Frith Street 64
Frith, William 107
Frizer, Ingram 21

Gage, George 13
George III, King 78
George V, King 98
Gielgud, John 100, 101
Gin shops 63, 64, 65
Glencarn, Earl of 105
Golden Square 7
Gonson, Katherine 56
Goodby, Roger 81
Goody, Gordon 181, 183
Gordon, Lord George 73
Gracechurch Street 87
Great Fire of London 6, 46
Great Marlborough Street 92
Green, Pamela 170
Greville, Charles 186
Grewes, Jean 161

Hackman, Rev. James 81
Hackney South 121
Hammond, Charles 97, 98
Hanger, John 113

Index   201

Hanover Square 78
Harris, Jack 5
Hart, Richard 177
Hawkins, John 56, 57
Hayes, Catherine 25
Hayes, Charlotte 90, 91
Hayes, John 26
Hayward, Greta 146
Hazlitt, William 7
Henry II, King 6, 43, 44
Hickey, William 19
Highgate 105
Hill, Billy 161
Hockley in the Hole 54
Hogarth, William 15, 50, 54, 64
Holborn 10
Holland, Elizabeth 88
Holloway Prison 34, 138
Holywell Street 168
Hooke, Robert 50
Hoxton 69
Hulbert, Jack 94
Hunter, John 7
Hyde Park 108, 109

Jack the Ripper 14
Jakobs, Josef 44
Jews 43, 66, 151
Johnson, John 17
Jones, Mary 27
Jouannet, Doris 146
Joyce, Margaret 154
Joyce, William 151, 153, 154, 155, 156, 157

Keeler, Christine 194
Kent, Tyler 152
Keppel, Alice 129, 130, 131
Khan, Aly, Prince 187
Kings Cross 32
Kirkland, Doctor 18
Knight, Maxwell 152
Knightsbridge 144
Kray, Reggie 175, 176, 178
Kray, Ronnie 175, 176, 177

Langtry, Lillie 126-127
Leighton, Alexander 77
Lewis, William 89
London Bridge 48

Lynn, Vera 142
Lyons Corner House 145
Landsdowne, Lord 63

MacDonell, George 122, 123
MacLaine, James 107, 108, 109, 110
Marble Arch 83
Marks, George Harrison 170
Marks, Howard 193
Marlborough, Duke of 42
Marshalsea Jail 65
Marshalsea Prison 48
Martin, Richard 54
Martin, Samuel 71
May Day riots 67
Mayfair 116
Maynard, Lady Daisy 127, 128
Maynard, Viscount Charles 127
Melbourne, Lord 113
Melville, Alan 94
Messina brothers 158, 159, 160, 161, 162, 163, 164, 165, 166
Messina, Alfredo 159, 165
Messina, Attilio 159, 165
Messina, Carmelo 165
Messina, Enrico 159
Metropolitan Music Hall 65
Miller, Joan 152, 153
Mills, James 182
Molly houses 94
Molyneux, Lord 113
Moorfields 50, 51
Moorgate 90
Mordaunt, Lord 125
Mordaunt, Lady Margaret 125
Mosley, Sir Oswald 73, 74, 80, 150, 172

Newgate 46, 47, 48, 94, 107, 109
Newlove, Henry 97
New Palace Yard 64
News of the World 82
Niven, David 186
Northumberland, Duke of 115
Norton, Andrew 196
Norton, Eliza 119
Notting Hill 75
Novello, Ivor 94, 48, 49
Nyberg, Simon 135

Oates, Titus 44
Oatley, Evelyn 146
Old Bailey 45, 47, 115, 161, 162
Old Compton Street 100, 135
O'Kelly, Dennis 90, 92, 94
O'Neil, Joseph 136
Orwell, Dorothy 69
Orwell, George 69
O'Sullivan, Joseph 136
Oxford Street 83

Paddington 147
Page, William 105, 106
Payne, Leslie 117-118
Pentonville jail 34
Pepys, Samuel 167
Piccadilly 93
Pierrepoint, Albert 150, 157
Pillory 38, 51
Pitt, William 59
Plunkett, William 108, 109
Powell, Harriet 114
Pratt, James 95
Price, Charlie 119, 120
Punch Magazine 169

Quant, Mary 190

Rainbow Club 46
Ramsay, James 58
Ray, Martha 82
Raymond's Revue Bar 170
Reynolds, Bruce 182, 183, 184
River Thames 82
Richardson gang 197
Right Club 152,
Rochester, Earl of 52, 53
Rooum, Ronald, 191
Rothchilds Bank 122
Rupert Street 164

Sabini, Darby 134, 135, 136
Sabini, Fred 134
Sabini, George 134
Sabini, Harry Boy 134
Sabini, Joseph 134, 135
Sacheverell, Henry 68
Salisbury, Lord 97

Sandys, Duncan 188, 189
Saville Theatre 94
Scott, Norman 195, 196
Sharp, Granville 58
Simpson, Wallis 152
Smith, John 95
Smithfield 95
Soho 84-99
Somerset, Lord Arthur 97
Spilsbury Sir Bernard 33
Spitalfields 54, 70
Spot, Jack 172, 173, 174
St. George's Fields 72
St. Giles 63
St. Martins Lane 73
St. Paul's Cathedral 69
St. Paul's School 58
Swan and Edgar 148
Sweeney, Charles 186
Swinscow, Charles 96

The People Newspaper 162
Thomas, Joseph 181
Thompson, Edith 35
Thorndike, Sybil 101
Thorpe, Jeremy 193, 194, 195, 196
Tothill Fields Prison 119
Tottenham Court Road 54
Tower of London 42, 71
Trafalgar Square 73
Transportation Act of 1717 39
Tyburn 10, 46, 79

Upper Grosvenor Street 188

Vassallo, Carmelo 160, 161
Veck, George 97

Wakefield Tower 43
Wandsworth 148
Ward, Stephen 195
Wardour Street 46
Warwick, Lady 128
Watts, Martha 159
Webb, Duncan 161-162-163-164-165, 166 173, 175
Wellington, Duke of 73
Westminster Hall 60

Whicker, Captain Alan 157
White, Alf 173
White City Estate 75
White, Jimmy 181
White Tower 42
Whittington, Richard 45
Wilberforce, William 57, 59
Wilde, Oscar 99
Wilford, James 16
Wilkes, John 71, 72, 73
Williams, Sarah 16

Wilson, Harriette 116, 117
Wilson, Mary 92
Wilson, Sir Henry 136
Winchester, Bishop of 103
Winchester geese 87
Wolkoff, Anna 151, 152, 153
Woolworths 148
Wright, Charlie 156
Wright, Doctor Maurice 156

Young, Sir Allen 126

Dear Reader,

We hope you have enjoyed this book, but why not share your views on social media? You can also follow our pages to see more about our other products: facebook.com/penandswordbooks or follow us on X @penswordbooks

You can also view our products at www.pen-and-sword.co.uk (UK and ROW) or www.penandswordbooks.com (North America).

To keep up to date with our latest releases and online catalogues, please sign up to our newsletter at: www.pen-and-sword.co.uk/newsletter

If you would like a printed catalogue with our latest books, then please email: enquiries@pen-and-sword.co.uk or telephone: 01226 734555 (UK and ROW) or email: uspen-and-sword@casematepublishers.com or telephone: (610) 853-9131 (North America).

We respect your privacy and we will only use personal information to send you information about our products.

Thank you!